GOOD IS NEVER LOST

The Teachings of Mother Mary Mae Maier of Mt. Shasta

By Jeff Whittier

GOOD IS NEVER LOST
June 2014

ISBN 978-0-696-24255-1
Eastern Gate Press
Palo Alto, California

Contents

PREFACE 5

INTRODUCTION 9

1. MARY MAE MAIER'S YEARS IN LOS ANGELES 18

2. THE ORDER OF DIRECTIVE BIBLICAL PHILOSOPHY 33

3. ATLANTIS SPEAKS AGAIN 55

4. JAGADBANDHU 67

5. MOTHER MARY'S FIRST TRIP TO INDIA, 1950-1 75

6. THE GREAT WHITE CHIEF 83

7. THE MEETING AT SAND FLAT IN JULY, 1962 91

8. MOTHER MARY'S SECOND TRIP TO INDIA, 1966 102

9. THE LAST YEARS AT THE INN 111

APPENDIX 1 - Writings of The Order of Directive Biblical Philosophy 118

APPENDIX 2 - Numerology of The Order of Directive Biblical Philosophy 148

Notes and References 169

PREFACE

In 1951 Mother Mary Mae Maier walked barefoot from India into Tibet and was taken to a hidden city of 5,000 saints, sadhus, and yogis. She lectured them on the need to serve humanity. She said only a few understood her message, but those few asked her, upon her return to America, to move permanently to Mt. Shasta and to open what was to be called "The Inn." These few Great Ones told her they would use their spiritual powers to send to her those who she could help on the Path. She said, "10,000 came." I was one of them.

I saw the same thing happen in one way or another many times. Someone might be driving up Hwy. I-5 on a Sunday night and simply get hungry, turn off into town and find that her restaurant was the only place open. Although she was alone upstairs in her room, she would know that a seeker had arrived, and would come downstairs unbidden, sit at the next table and strike up a conversation. Within a few minutes, she would be giving this person the knowledge or teachings they were meant to receive, in the most humble and informal way.

She did not believe in "guruism," did not take disciples, did not put on "holy" airs, and very few indeed understood who and what she really was. She valued anonymity. Despite what has been variously reported, she did not start any "Shree Shree Provo" sect, and was fond of saying, "Don't join anything." She truly believed that each person is individually responsible for their own path through many lives, and that each person should and will find their own way to God. God, after all, is within us. One time, as if reading my mind, she said to me, "If you really want to help me in my spiritual work, be sincere. That will help me the most of all. If you make 100 million mistakes, sincerity will bring you through."

The title of this book, "Good Is Never Lost," was an aphorism of hers. It is found in a phrase from Phylos the Tibetan, "Nothing good can ever perish." It is also a teaching from the Bhagavad Gita, "In this path, no effort is ever lost and no obstacle prevails; even a little of this righteousness (dharma) saves from great fear." For me it has a special meaning, which I will present here. In the 1980's and 90's I attended an Alice A. Bailey study group in Berkeley, California. One night, our discussion turned to "The Divine Plan of Evolution." I suggested to our group that two favorite sayings of Mother Mary were relevant to this subject, and illustrated how we ourselves could make a contribution to human evolution. The first is "Nothing for the good is ever lost," and the second is, "There is no great or small." One of the members of our group couldn't understand what I was saying, and asked me several times to repeat it. So I gave him her alternate, "No good is ever lost." At this, my friend proceeded to de-construct these statements into, "You never lose any good thing," and "Nothing is good and it's lost," and a couple of other such permutations as well. I was actually very irritated, but being a reasonably civilized man I held my tongue with an expenditure of will-power and went on. I thought of Mother Mary, and said to her deep in my heart, at least I tried.

Several months later, I contacted everyone I could think of who had known Mother Mary, and invited all to meet up at Sand Flat on Mt. Shasta on July 4, 1992. When I called Henry Fuller, one of Mother Mary's closest friends for many years, he immediately agreed to come and told me how much he was looking forward to being there. A few days later he called me back, and told me, "I have a telepathic message for you from Mother Mary." I thought to myself, "Sure, you do." But, being a reasonably civilized man, I held my tongue once again.

Despite the fact this book is about Great Ones, Astrology, Brothers and Space Brothers, I really do consider myself highly skeptical about spiritual claims. For instance, in this book there is information about a numerological system which Mother Mary said is derived from the base-12 system used in Atlantis by the Sons of Solitude. But in a true base-12 system, there are no double-digits until the number 13, so the numbers 10, 11, and 12, cannot be reduced to 1, 2, and 3, respectively. Also, there are teachings about music and keynotes which were written about a century ago, when the values of these notes were different. Most Americans today believe the tone A equals 440 Hertz, however, this is historically not the case. I have seen tuning-forks from 1900 marked A=426. My math book from 1960 gives the value of A as 436 Hertz. I myself make musical instruments for sale in Europe, and the order I am working on right now, as of this writing, is a batch of bamboo flutes for the Malmo production of "Miss Saigon," where they use the value of A=442 Hertz. So, comments made in this book about the Key of F major, for instance, could actually be something around the Key of E today, particularly in Europe.

When Henry told me he had a message for me from Mother Mary, I really didn't believe him. I asked him what it was. He said, "I don't want to tell you over the phone. I'll tell you at Mt. Shasta." When we met at Mt. Shasta, I asked him again, and he said, "She told me to tell you that when you speak with people, tell them 'Good is never lost.' She told me that she didn't figure out how to put this phrase until she left the body. She used to say, 'No good is ever lost' and 'Nothing for the good is ever lost' but after she left the body she realized that starting the sentence with a negative deflects the understanding of the listener. If you want people to understand, it's much better to say 'Good is never lost.'" I was very surprised by this message. Taught me a lesson.

In the summer of 1969 I happened to tell Mother Mary at The Inn about a newspaper article I had read earlier that day in the SF Chronicle regarding a Vatican committee who had decided that 200 or so "saints" actually never existed, and so these saints, like St. Christopher, were to be erased from the Catholic heavens and the doctrine of intercession of the saints. When I read this article, I thought to myself it was a victory for rationalism over blind faith, and I expected a similar response from Mother Mary when I told her about the piece. To my surprise she said, "It's a dark day on the inner planes. People have prayed to these 'saints.' Now these people don't know where to turn. It's a blow to their sincere belief in God." This comment taught me a special respect for the inner lives of other people and I have never forgotten it.

In the same vein, I would recommend to the reader to contrast the section called by Henry Fuller "Rainbow Gems" with the similar section of teachings taken from *Atlantis Speaks Again.* These two lists of aphorisms were written many years apart, and Mother Mary's own evolution during that period is apparent in them. Between the two, she reached *nirbkalpa samadhi*, which she called "The union of Soul and Spirit." If you use your discernment, you will feel the energy of that light emanating from her later work, yet the promise of it is in the earlier material as well.

This book is not intended as a comprehensive biography of Mother Mary's life. I do not believe that she wished such a book to be written, as she did not desire to have followers and did not want any emphasis put upon her personality. Instead, I am trying to present enough biographical and historical information for the reader to have a sense of where and how Mother Mary's teachings originated, and to present the teachings themselves in such a way as to facilitate reflection and study. She herself wanted people to follow their own understanding and live responsible lives with concern for others. Although her writings contain many Biblical references, I do not remember her ever quoting the Bible. She did not promote any one philosophy over any other, and often stressed that we must live what we know, only then will we find more.

Atlantis Speaks Again is full of information on numerology and astrology, but I myself do not remember her ever mentioning these subjects, except once. It was not part of my experience with her, and I am not a numerologist or astrologer, though I am familiar with the basic ideas of both systems. Mother Mary did discuss these subjects with a few other people, such as when she sat down on one occasion with Saul Barodofsky and explained to him the meanings of each letter in the English alphabet. As far as I know, the only person to whom she taught anything about the numerology of the Order of Directive Biblical Philosophy was a young Canadian man, Stuart Allistone, and she gave written lessons in "Enoch's Throne Block" to Saundra Boone, the daughter of George Van Tassel and the wife of Daniel Boone. I have included the system in this book not because I am a numerologist, but because I am the archivist of the material. However, I do know that the numerological system of which rudiments are published in her book was actually practiced by her privately, silently. The only time she ever mentioned its existence to me was to express disappointment that the person to whom she had taught it had chosen a different path in life. It greatly influenced her thought, and was of immense importance to her. For that reason, it has been included in this book.

Lady Mae declined to give people much advice, saying she did not wish to be responsible for the actions of others. Usually she would tell stories of her experiences, and these experiences would illustrate truths. She had certain ideas which she loved to present and most of the teachings in this book could be condensed into just a few pages of these basic truths. It would read something like this, all phrases I heard her use at one time or another -

Good is never lost.

There is no great or small.

Sincerity will bring you through, even if you make 100,000,000 mistakes.

Service should be for all, not just for my group or your group.

The Saints and true Sadhus are the light of the world.

Control the mind by counting.

Pay attention to your daydreams, you might get ideas that way.

Have compassion for all, and treat all with equanimity.

You are self-responsible for your life.

You cannot walk the path for someone else - a guru who tries to do this interferes with his disciple's evolution.

Love will take you places nothing else can.

Let it be natural.

Each nation has karma, and every nation will sometime suffer from its karma.

The higher consciousness of the New Age will first emerge in children.

Women will have a special place in the New Age.

Every human being has both male and female characteristics within them, and these qualities may be in perfect balance.

The woman holds the energy - the man gives it direction.

Joy moves us forward.

Curiosity ain't enough.

Some animals are more highly evolved spiritually than some human beings.

There are seven kinds of people, the seven-rayed race. You can learn to discern each one.

Speech has great power. Be kind in word and deed.

Live the real, and be silent.

Live what you know, and you will find more.

Your conscience will tell you what to do.

Pray for the welfare of those who abuse you, but have a sense of justice.

When you speak to a person, speak to the Spirit.

INTRODUCTION

Mary Mae Hoffman was born in Philadelphia on Dec. 29th, 1894. Her father was John Jacob William Hoffman, a wealthy and successful German immigrant from Hamburg. At the age of 21, she moved to Los Angeles, California. After a very unsatisfactory first marriage which ended in divorce, she married Max Maier, who worked as a piano tuner. She herself worked in the film industry, designing and making costumes for various films under the professional names "Peggy Hamilton" and "Mae Hamilton." The couple had one son, John.

In 1923, she was reading the book *A Dweller on Two Planets* written by Frederick Spencer Oliver, amanuensis to the adept Phylos the Tibetan, when she opened it to a page that said only, "Go to Mt. Shasta." It startled her, and she put the book down. She opened it the next day to another page, which also said only, "Go to Mt. Shasta." The third day, she opened it once again, and this time it said, "Go to Mt. Shasta in three days." She didn't have the money for a train ticket, and she and Max had some difficulty raising it. When she did get on the train by herself three days later, two men walked up to her and said, "When you get to Mt. Shasta, look up Mack Olberman." Then they left her. She had no idea who Mack was. He is remembered today as the man who built the Sierra Club lodge at Horse Camp on Mt. Shasta, and Olberman's Causeway, a path of stones leading up the mountain from Horse Camp. James M. Olberman was born in Kentucky in 1862, and was 60 years old when he became caretaker of the Sierra Club facility.

When she reached the train station at Mt. Shasta, she made inquiries as to where she could find Mr. Olberman. She eventually walked up Hwy. 99 to his cottages-for-rent north of town, and he put her up in a cottage which curiously had a picture of a woman who looked just like her on the wall. He said to her, "Oh, how long I have waited for you to come." He didn't say much else. They were very close friends for the next 23 years until his death. During those years she found that he knew much about Mt. Shasta, and she considered him the wisest person she ever knew. He would sometimes give her information about the spiritual work, but anytime she asked him a direct question with some spiritual angle to it, he would cut her off in mid-sentence, reach in his shirt pocket and pull out a Bull Durham bag of small gold nuggets. He would pour them out on the table and say, "I never used one of these for myself." She said, "I hated those nuggets." It was a test for her. He used the nuggets to support widows, widowers, and children, and sent some through college with the money from the gold. Many years later, when Mary Mae Maier lived in The Inn, one of the people who had been sent to college by Mack Olberman came to The Inn and told her the story of how it had taken place.

In the late 1930's, only a few years before his death in 1946, he started to answer her questions. He was losing his eyesight, but he took her up on the mountain and showed her from a distance the entrance to a Temple built in Atlantean times, described in *A Dweller on Two Planets.* On that day Mack and Lady Mae, as she liked to be called, talked with each other about what that Temple had been in Atlantis, and shared with each other their memories of that time and place. This entrance is exactly southwest of the summit of the mountain above the tree line, and in Atlantean times a road or path led up the mountain toward it. Mack also told her that in the 1800's she had been a Native American woman in Siskiyou County, and that a photograph of her in that life is in the

County Museum in Yreka. Mary Mae Maier was the first person Mack Olberman allowed to walk on the stones of his causeway, which she called "The Cosmo-Way."

She rarely spoke of her past lives, but sometimes she would mention that she had been at Mt. Shasta in Atlantean times when events went very badly at the Temple, and that karma from that time still affected her own life and the work of the adepts at Mt. Shasta. This is the origin of the title of her book, *Atlantis Speaks Again.* One of the worst of those events was the extinguishing of the un-fed "Maxin Light" described in *A Dweller on Two Planets*, and found on the cover of *Atlantis Speaks Again.*

Mother Mary also stated that she was the re-incarnation of a Hopi holy woman whose room is still kept today by two elderly women on the First Mesa, because there is a prophecy that she would someday return to that room. She went with her friend Henry Fuller up to the door of the room, but would not enter, because she did not believe that she should fulfill the prophecy at that time. She did much work with the Native Americans, who called her "Rainbow." Part of this work was to publish the book, *The Great White Chief,* and most of the copies of this book were given to Native Americans.

During her years in Los Angeles, Mary Maier created several venues for lectures and presentations, including the Rainbow Auditorium at 3210 West Pico Boulevard in Los Angeles. She made these venues available to many speakers from a myriad of viewpoints, including scientists, at a nominal fee. Ralph Elmer, who traveled to a hidden valley in Tibet, Baird Spalding, who wrote the books, *Life and Teachings of the Masters of the Far East*, and Guy and Edna Ballard, who started the "I Am" movement, also called "The Saint Germain Foundation," were among the many who gave presentations at her lecture-halls. One of her great disappointments in life was the counsel she gave to the Ballards after they had their spiritual experience at Mt. Shasta. They came to her in Los Angeles for advice, and she suggested that they should start an organization. She bitterly regretted this later on, when this very organization became, in the words of Alice A. Bailey, "a travesty of the real." The plagiarism by Guy Ballard of *A Dweller on Two Planets,* as well as works by Baird Spalding, William Pelley, Marie Correlli, Annie Besant, David Anrias and many others has been well documented in the 1940 book *Psychic Dictatorship in America* by Gerald Barbee Bryan. This plagiarism was even adjudicated in 1941 when Borden Publishing and Leslie Oliver, the son of Fred Oliver, sued the Ballards for lifting passages from *A Dweller on Two Planets.* Curiously, when the Ballards first advertised their organization, they did so in ads printed in bold red and black. For some reason, Mother Mary carefully preserved one of these ads. Years later, the "I Am" movement would become very intolerant of these same colors, and today members of the organization are easily spotted on the streets of Mt. Shasta City wearing only pastel hues.

A friend of Mary Mae Maier named Dr. Minor called her in 1933 and invited her to hear a lecture of the World Fellowship tour given by a young Bengali graduate student named Mahanam, who spoke about the Bengali avatar Jagadbandhu of Faridpur, East Bengal. This was the first time she ever heard the name, "Jagadbandhu," which means, "Friend of the World." Around the turn of the century, the avatar lived alone in a small hut in his ashram, which he never left. His disciples would pass food to him through a screen, and he would sometimes communicate with people by little notes left at the screen. However, people in many parts of India would see him, and from time to time he was seen abroad as well. He could apparently appear at will whenever, wherever, while his physical body was alone in his room at Faridpur. Many years after his death in 1921, he was sometimes seen in her meditation room at the Rainbow Auditorium, and one person who saw him there, Henry Fuller, said that he seemed entirely physical, not at all like an apparition or a vision. Henry said Jagadbandhu smiled at him.

Mother Mary was in telepathic contact with the avatar after he left the body, and she said that in 1944 he appeared to her and told her, with his usual sense of humor, that, "You must come to India. I will give you no rest. I will bother you every day until you come." In 1950, she did visit India, and spent months with Jagadbandhu's disciples in Calcutta and Faridpur. Henry Fuller published and re-published several books about Jagadbandhu, and maintained contact with disciples of the Jagadbandhu ashram until his death in 1997. Jagadbandhu was somewhat infamous in India for having made the statement "Initiation by a guru in the modern world is superfluous." When Mother Mary made statements such as "the saints are the Light of the World," Jagadbandhu was one of the ones she had in mind.

In 1938 Mary Mae Maier became involved in "The Order of Directive Biblical Philosophy," which was founded in 1928 by Lillian Bense. Mrs. Bense was in contact with the adept Phylos the Tibetan, who in the 1880's had dictated *A Dweller on Two Planets* to Fred Oliver in Yreka, California. The account of how Mrs. Bense met Phylos in 1913 and then was directed to meet the mother of Fred Oliver, Mary Elizabeth Manley Oliver, is presented in *Atlantis Speaks Again,* excerpted from an essay by Lillian Bense. In 1921 Mrs. Bense received from Mary Manley Oliver the archive of material, both published and unpublished manuscripts, which was left behind at the death of her son. Mrs. Oliver informed Mrs. Bense that her son Fred had been told by Phylos in the fall of 1899 that sometime in the future a woman would come who would establish her identity by revealing her knowledge of the formula 26:17::25.8+30:24, originally meant to be included in *A Dweller on Two Planets* but left out of the published edition at the insistence of the publisher, who said it couldn't be solved. This woman was to be given all the materials which Fred Oliver had produced.

Lillian Bense had been active in the Women's Christian Temperance Union, and the only known photograph of her is from the February, 1901 edition of an Omaha magazine called *Woman's Weekly.* Most of the source materials of *Atlantis Speaks Again* are from this study group known as The Order of Directive Biblical Philosophy, which Mother Mary always referred to as "Phylos' inner group." Under the direction of Phylos the group practiced a system of numerology, said to be derived from the ancient Atlantean numerology of the Sons of Solitude mentioned in *A Dweller on Two Planets*, which is base-12 in origin, with direct correspondences to astrology. This system is sometimes called "Enoch's Throne Block" and is based on a philosophy which Phylos referred to as "The Ethical Vibration of Numbers." The formula which Phylos intended to be published in *A Dweller on Two Planets* was said to be a key to this ancient numerology.

The book *An Earth Dweller's Return* was compiled by Lillian Bense, under the nom-de-plume Beth Nimrai, from the archive of material given to her by Mary Manley Oliver, and from a first-generation type-written copy of the manuscript of *A Dweller on Two Planets* given to her by the woman who had typed it up for Fred Oliver in the 1890's prior to certain changes which were introduced into the published version in order to make in more marketable. Mrs. Bense considered *An Earth Dweller's Return* to be more or less a corrected version of *A Dweller on Two Planets.* It was edited in 1939 and published in

1940 by Dr. Howard John Zitko, who had his own group called "The Lemurian Fellowship" based on written lessons in esoteric Theo-Christic philosophy first prepared by Dr. Zitko in 1936. Dr. Zitko believed that the teachings of his Theo-Christic philosophy had been inspired by Phylos, but he had never heard of Lillian Bense until he received her manuscript unsolicited in Wisconsin in 1939. It was accompanied by a letter which explained that Phylos had told Lillian Bense to send the manuscript to Dr. Zitko, and asked him to edit it and publish the final text. Dr. Zitko edited it under the name "the Lemurian Scribe," which was the name he had previously used when writing his lessons in 1936. The Lemurian Fellowship, of which Dr. Zitko was the vice-president, raised the money to publish the finished book. In 1946, Dr. Zitko was forced out of the Lemurian Fellowship by the president of the group, and went on to found "The World University" now located in Benson, Arizona.

The successor to Mrs. Bense as leader of The Order of Directive Biblical Philosophy was Maud Meserne Falconer, who was a piano teacher by profession. Maud Falconer and Lillian Bense composed much material on such subjects as "Spiritual Keynotes" and "The Power of the Word," some of which can be found in *Atlantis Speaks Again.* In 1939 Mother Mary revealed her knowledge of the formula left out of *A Dweller on Two Planets* to Mrs. Falconer and Mrs. Bense. The formula was first printed in *An Earth Dweller's Return* in 1940 and had not yet been released to the public. Maud Falconer understood the significance of Mother Mary's knowledge in the light of Phylos' prediction, and in 1941 copies of most of the materials of the group were turned over to Mother Mary, with the rest willed to her upon Mrs. Falconer's death. Lillian Bense had to convinced by Maud Falconer that Mother Mary should be given the materials, but eventually she came to accept the transfer of the materials as the fulfillment of Phylos' instructions. She prepared some essays to help Mother Mary present the material in the future to those for whom she believed it was destined - children of the New Age. Later in life, Mother Mary sometimes called herself "the last Director of The Order of Directive Biblical Philosophy." This term may not have referred to a legal office which she occupied in the incorporated non-profit group, but to her position as the custodian of the materials which were passed to her in the fulfillment of Phylos' instructions to Fred Oliver in his last days.

During the 1940's the Maiers moved for a time to Ojai, and she started "The Creative Hobby Clubs," a small chain of clubs to encourage handicrafts. She was very proud of this endeavor, and considered it part of her spiritual work to encourage people to make handicrafts and to sell their products. She considered hobbies to be a kind of meditation which would help an individual align with his or her own soul. Many people involved in the Creative Hobby Clubs were of a spiritual bent and participated in events at the Rainbow Auditorium, and they held many meetings on various spiritual subjects as well. Over the next ten years some of the clubs evolved into "The Esoteric Hobby Clubs" and "The Creative Research Clubs" but she soon dropped these names and the spiritual activities divorced from the Hobby Clubs became known as "The Eastern Research Society" in the 1950's.

While living in Ojai she was a neighbor of J. Krishnamurti, and on a few occasions took it upon herself to scold him for wasting his time lecturing elderly ex-Theosophists, who she called "deadwood," and implored him to work instead with children and youth. Another anecdote of those years told by friends of Mae Maier from this period, is that the song *Nature Boy* was composed by Eden Ahbez late at night in the kitchen of her Ojai home in the early forties.

When Jagadbandhu appeared to Mother Mary at Ojai in 1944 and implored her to come to India, she told him she didn't want to go. She told him that she thought her work with the Hobby Clubs was more important, as so many people from young to old were benefiting from the activities, and it was helping to prepare for the future work. He said, "No, you have nothing. Blow a balloon up and prick it, that's what you have. You must come to India." She asked him why. He replied, "To walk barefoot on the ground." When she recounted this exchange many years later, she said at the time she had no idea what he was talking about, but it came to pass.

In the late 1940's, the family moved back to Los Angeles. Max Maier was taken ill and could not work. Lady Mae's son John got scarlet fever and almost died. She herself got sick and could not run the Hobby Clubs. The family went $9000 in debt, which at that time was a lot of money. Jagadbandhu again asked her to come to India, and she told him that she simply couldn't afford to. He suggested that she should sell their second house in Ojai. She did this, but the family and the Hobby Clubs owed so much money that all the money from the sale of the house went to pay bills. During this difficult time, she told Jagadbandhu that she would indeed come to India, if she could raise the money. Soon after that, there were two deaths in her family and she used $1400 of the inheritance to buy a plane ticket.

In 1950 while Mother Mary was making preparations for this first trip to India, she received a phone call from a member of the Hobby Clubs, Dr. George Ferguson, telling her of a dream he had about her upcoming trip in which Jagadbandhu appeared to him. The doctor invited her to visit him, and she gladly accepted the invitation. On the first night she slept at his home, she awakened in the middle of the night to see the Sufi Hazrat Inayat Khan standing over her. Inayat Khan had left the body many years before. Inayat Khan told her of her future trip, and told her that she would be transformed by Jagadbandhu in India. He also told her that during her journey she would make contact with the ancient Sufis, who have been with humanity through all the ages since the very beginning, embodying the ways of the Creator.

Several weeks later, while sitting in the passport office in Los Angeles waiting for her visa appointment, she met Paramahansa Yogananda, author of *Autobiography of a Yogi*, who was accompanied by Daniel Boone and other disciples. Yogananda and Mother Mary took a glance at each other, and immediately recognized one another. Yogananda sat next to her and said that he was going to leave the body soon, and told her further that he had several disciples who would need help after he died. He asked her if she would take them as her own disciples. She explained to him that she did not take disciples. He told her that they needed her, and implored her to help them. He said that he had the knowledge to guide them to her after his death. She told him, "I will not take them as disciples, but I will walk with them." He delighted in this answer, and it was so. Two of these disciples were Daniel Boone and his brother-in-law Norm Paulsen.

It is said by his disciples that Yogananda took birth on earth after the Master Jesus came to Babaji, a Himalayan ascetic, and guru of Yogananda's lineage, and told him, "My followers in the West have forgotten how to meditate. Will you help me re-establish this knowledge in the Western world?" Yogananda then took incarnation to do this very work, the re-awakening of the knowledge of meditation in the West. When Mother Mary spoke of "the Light of the World," she had Babaji and his line of Lahiri Mahasaya, Sri Yukteshwar, and Paramahansa Yogananda in mind as well.

When she reached India she spent two months in Calcutta and visited the Jagadbandhu ashram in Faridpur several times, in what was then East Pakistan and is now Bangladesh. Jagadbandhu appeared to her around daybreak after her first night at this ashram. He told her of a forest glen in the Himalayas which she would eventually find, and gave her much confidential information about his mission and his ashram. After returning to Calcutta from Faridpur, she went first to Hardhwar and then to Rishikesh, staying at the ashram of Swami Sivananda, the Divine Life Society at Laxmanjula, across the Ganges from Swarg Ashram. At this time, Jagadbandhu appeared to her again and gave her a meditation technique by which she could reach *nirbkalpa samadhi*, the highest state of yogic meditation, described by Mother Mary herself as "the union of Soul and Spirit." After returning to America, she kept in touch with Sivananda's ashram, and Swami Satchidananda later came to visit her several times in Mt. Shasta, including the last time a week before she died.

When she left Rishikesh, she went to the Tibetan border along the same road Lowell Thomas had taken before her. At the border, she had difficulty getting her visa to enter Tibet, and took a room in the Government Rest House. In this room, she practiced for 14 days, from Dec. 24, 1950 to Jan. 6, 1951, the meditation technique given to her at Sivananda's ashram by Jagadbandhu and spent several days in *nirbkalpa samadhi*. Her body turned black - as if she had died. Her guide, Benu Ghosh, stood over her and called her back into her body, saying, "Come back. Come back. You must come back, your work is not finished." She did return to her body, and it took some time to recover. Her visa came through after this, because no one in the visa office wanted to deny a visa to a "Great Yogini" as they now called her. She was taken into Tibet to a hidden city of saints and yogis, and lectured them on "Service to Humanity." She said few understood her. She implored them to have a world convocation of spiritual adepts to further the Divine Plan, which eventually took place a few years later.

After leaving the sacred city, she found the glen in the Himalayas which Jagadbandhu had told her about in Faridpur. In this glen, she was blessed with the powers, or *siddhis,* which the Great Ones manifest. In this state of Divine Empowerment, she danced barefoot. She said, "The trees danced with me. Especially a little pine tree, who danced very fast. He wanted me to see him." Jagadbandhu spoke to her at this moment and said, "This is the power that created the universe. It must never be misused." From this glen she traveled across Tibet to Lhasa and met the Dalai Lama, who was then a boy. The journey through Tibet and back to India took three and a half months, and she later said this was the most important time of her life.

Several years after her return to America she journeyed to Mexico, and this trip was the beginning of a chain of events which resulted in the publishing of the books *The Great White Chief* and *Atlantis Speaks Again.* The name of the first book is the title of the leader of a tribe called by Mother Mary the White Indians in Southern Mexico, who is called Eachita Eachina. The book was not written by her, but by a Mormon adventurer of Native American background who traveled in Latin America looking for lost cities and Inca gold. He wound up with the White Indians in Southern Mexico in the area near Mitla. This tribe has an unbroken spiritual lineage going back thousands of years and also has a tradition that Jesus visited them centuries ago, before the Spanish, much as the

Mormons believe. The book was printed as a favor to Eachita Eachina, who Mother Mary visited in Oaxaca. Some information about him and his tribe can be found in the book *The Coming of the Great White Chief* by Dorothy Thomas. When Lady Mae was given the manuscript of the book by Eachita Eachina's granddaughter, she knew nothing about the craft of bookbinding, and took classes to enable her to typeset, print, and bind the book herself with her own hands, which she did in Henry Fuller's printshop. That's why both books are so full of misprints. It is of interest to note that both organized agriculture and writing developed independently in the New World at about the same time they developed in the Near East, in this very area of Southern Mexico at the dawn of the civilization now called Zapotec.

In 1960, while she was producing the last few copies of the book, Henry Fuller wanted to give her a break from the 16 hour days she was working, and took her to a movie about Native Americans which he had seen advertised in the paper. At the end of the movie, there was a scene with a Native American medicine man who both Mother Mary and Henry immediately recognized as a man of true knowledge. When the movie was finished, they said to each other, we have to find this man. When they left their seats, to their amazement this very medicine man was sitting in the lobby of the theater. She struck up a conversation with him and found that he had been touring with the movie, but this would be his last day. He told her that his spirit guide had told him to sit and wait in the lobby. He'd been there all day. As she talked with him for a few minutes, he told her he was going to a gathering of the tribes in Canada the next day. She told him the story of how she had been to see the Great White Chief, and published the book for him, and that he had specifically asked that copies be given to the council members of the Six Nations. The medicine man told her that these were the very people he was going to see in Canada, so she asked him to take six copies of it with him to give to those who should have it, and keep one more for himself. He was very happy to do this. She apologized to him about all the misprints and told him how she had typeset it herself, and that despite her best efforts, the typos kept appearing. He said to her, "Don't worry about the misprints. That's how we get our directions."

Having learned every step in the production of a book, she soon put her skills to use again to publish *Atlantis Speaks Again*. This book is based primarily on materials from the group of Mrs. Bense given to Mary Mae Maier by Maud Falconer in 1941 and presents the provenance of those teachings. Mother Mary hoped that those who study this book would find help on their own path, and she used her spiritual abilities to charge each copy with a spiritual energy. She also intended to correct certain errors which crept into the original edition of *A Dweller on Two Planets*, and to present the rudiments of the numerological system used by The Order of Directive Biblical Philosophy.

In November 1961 Mother Mary was working on the last 50 copies of *Atlantis Speaks Again* when she was inspired to write a letter to the owner of the property in Mt. Shasta called "The Black Butte Inn," asking if it was for sale. She leased it with an option to buy, and took possession on Dec. 15th, eventually buying it a few months later after some title issues were ironed out with the previous owner. She changed the name to "The Inn." During the years Mary Maier visited Mack Olberman and Mt. Shasta while she lived in Los Angeles, she had often stayed in this very hotel, then called the Park Hotel, and she said that she had her first inner contact with the adepts of the mountain while staying in Room 16 of the hotel in 1930. On the very first day she went to Mt. Shasta and met

Mack Olberman, she had an intuition that later in life she would live in this hotel, but at the time she thought it would be as a guest, not as the owner. When she told Mack of this premonition, he said, "You are a dreamer, but it is a reality." Very soon after moving into The Inn, Mother Mary left for Mexico and delivered the first copy printed of *The Great White Chief* to Eachita Eachina, which she had set aside for this purpose when the book was produced.

When Lady Mae moved to Mt. Shasta City, also living there at that time was Nola Van Valer, who on March 21, 1922 had met the Master Jesus in Richmond, California as recounted in her book, *The Tramp at My Door*. Jesus in this meeting promised to send her and her husband Jerry to "A Master Teacher," and that later turned out to be Phylos. Nola along with her husband and others were taught directly in the physical body by Phylos while camping in the area of Widow Springs for 10 summers during the 20's and 30's and were taken physically inside the Temple at Mt. Shasta on June 17, 1930 through an entrance which is exactly southeast of the mountaintop just above the tree line. Nola and Mother Mary often worked in co-operation with each other, though they sometimes had their differences as well.

In 1962, Maxine McMullen and Mother Mary called for a gathering of seekers and servers to be held at Mt. Shasta in the first week of July. They sent out invitations to everyone who they thought might be interested in coming and many people did heed this call, including Nola and many of the students of her group. It resulted in a truly remarkable and unique meeting at Sand Flat on July 5th and the following days, during which one of the adepts of the mountain emerged from the retreat inside dressed in his spiritual robes, and mixed with the group. There was also another adept incognito in the group. The existence of the Spiritual Brotherhood inside Mt. Shasta was first revealed to the general public by Fred Oliver at the end of the Nineteenth Century, and since that time so many have sought to contact it. Those people who answered the call to seekers and servers were very fortunate among all those who both Lady Mae and Nola had sought to help on the path during many years of service, as they had their confirmation of the existence of this Brotherhood at Sand Flat. This was a moment of great significance.

Mother Mary took a second trip to India for four and a half months in 1966. She stayed with Benu Ghosh again, visited the devotees of the Jagadbandhu ashram in Calcutta, attended the *Kumba Mela* in Allahabad, traveled to see the Dalai Lama who was now living in exile in Dharmasala, and again stayed at the ashram of Swami Sivananda in Rishikesh. During this trip to India, she met an adept who appeared to her three times and gave her information about the future spiritual work, after the time "when the real will be separated from the unreal."

She became ill in India, and never fully recovered. She cut her trip short, and after returning to the U.S. she regularly took therapeutic touch healing treatments from Joe Jessel in Ashland, Oregon, and these probably prolonged her life. Joe Jessel's waiting room had a sign on the wall which read, "I felt sad when I had no shoes, until I met a man who had no feet."

In the late 1960's Mother Mary worked with an entirely different group of people at The Inn who had not been part of her work during the many years she had lived in Los Angeles. Many of the people who had known her at the Rainbow Auditorium, the Hobby Clubs and the Creative Research Clubs or Eastern Research Society had passed on, and the meeting at Sand Flat brought much of that era to a close. Some of the people who sought her out in her last years were quite young and with them she sought to plant seeds for the future work, speaking less and less about Atlantis and more about the New Age. Numerous people helped her run The Inn, giving of their time and lives to further the spiritual work. Some of these were Daniel Boone, Elaine Pratt Bragg, Clark Coffee, Jack Darrow, Jan Darrow, Henry Fuller, Al Jennings, Helen Ruth, Stuart Allistone, Andy Anderson, Linden Carlton, Robert Williamson, and Maxine McMullen, who later owned "The Golden Mean" bookstore in Ashland, Oregon.

Lady Mae died on January 4, 1970 at The Inn.

1. MARY MAE MAIER'S YEARS IN LOS ANGELES

Mary Mae Hoffman moved to Los Angeles in her early twenties. She established herself in the Hollywood film industry as a costume designer under the professional names of "Peggy Hamilton" and later, "Mae Hamilton." She worked on costumes for the 1923 Cecil B. DeMille silent epic, *The Ten Commandments.* She was especially well known as a costumer for the silent film actress Pola Negri, and also made skimpy outfits for Theda Bara. She was a confidant to Mae West as well, who she said was much misunderstood by the public. Somewhat later, she had a shop called "Long Beach Costumer" at 1077 American Ave. in Long Beach under her married name, Mae Maier. She was commissioned by the city of Long Beach to design floats for the city as entrants to the Rose Bowl Parades, and her entries won the Theme Prize in 1933, 1934, 1935. They were called, respectively, "Queen of Beaches," "The White Swan," and "Venus." Each of them featured a swan made of flowers.

This professional career spanned several decades, and she later said that she made and spent a fortune, twice. Much of her money was spent on winter relief supplies for the Hopi Indians, who were profoundly grateful for her help, and who kept a little adobe dwelling for her on the Third Mesa which she visited for the last time in 1967. Unfortunately, much of the relief material bought by her and sent to the Indians was stolen by the various truck drivers who were to deliver the goods. They would drive to another city and sell the supplies. This continued even after she put the project in the hands of a Native American relief organization. The newsman Chet Huntley helped to publicize the Hopi's plight with live broadcasts from the Hobby Clubs. Eventually, she and her own friends, including Henry Fuller, rented trucks, loaded them, and drove them to the Hopi reservation in order to assure safe delivery.

During her years in Los Angeles, she organized a number of spiritual endeavors, including the Rainbow Auditorium at 3210 West Pico Blvd. in Los Angeles, the Creative Hobby Clubs in Ojai, and the Eastern Research Society from her home at 1812 North Ivar St. in Hollywood. At the Rainbow Auditorium a large variety of speakers from many scientific disciplines as well as spiritual traditions gave presentations, and during those years Mother Mary must have met at one time or another almost every person in the Los Angeles area who was interested in spiritual subjects. In addition to the many lectures by the wide range of speakers, her groups were fond of banquets and good fellowship. It was mostly members of the Hobby Clubs who assisted her in her efforts to help the Hopis.

In 1958, three years before she purchased The Inn and left the Los Angeles area, she wrote an article for the first edition of the Eastern Research Society quarterly which gives an overview of her work in the previous decades and reflects her vision of the future. This edition of the quarterly was disseminated at the Giant Rock UFO convention.

BEFORE OUR FIRST CLUB WAS FORMED
By Mother Mary

It was in 1921 that I first visualized that which Creative Hobby Clubs are now undertaking. At that time, experiences had rushed across my path, taking with them many tens of thousands of dollars which were earned in businesses which I had built and operated.

It would not interest you, dear reader, to know all that happened. For me, oh! It was an experience, not without pleasure. I had caused hundreds to find food, raiment and warm beds and in that, I had great satisfaction. As for the money, it fed and clothed, so why should I regret its loss?

My regret, or my sad experience, came from the great charities. But that is another story which is not to be told. The lesson learned in this experience has impressed upon me the ideal of honesty, integrity, and sincerity in purpose.

At that time I wondered how and when my work could be re-organized under another banner, and with power and personnel to push it to a success. I waited, always hopeful, always sincere, always prayerful. During the interval, I purchased property in Ojai, and there made friends unto myself and my plan.

We, my friends and I, got together and had great times under the guise of a Club, but without any real formation. My property was destined to serve as headquarters for all comers - Club members and friends, of course.

Many have been the joyful gatherings of friends and neighbors. And, dear reader, many of those who came were doctors, lawyers, scientists and educators. They joined in the fun and the deeper spirit of the work. Today those same good people, great and small, are supporters deeply and financially, and in spirit, of the Creative Researcher. May the work roll on to bless every life, and every town or city through Creative Research Groups.

The Master of all has given to men two great, constructive principles which interest us here, i.e., "Man, Know Thyself," and his statement to Adam, to who for himself, his wife and their posterity, was given the earth and all that is immediately in and around it, upon which they were to make their eternal home. They were to take dominion, to subdue and control the earth and the elements thereof, that they might enjoy all which was prepared for them, "even before the foundations of the earth were laid."

The stupidity of man has him walking in large circles on the crust of our planet, eating and drinking and fighting, and yet finding in the great plan that his race was to persist throughout the ages. All through time, man might have enjoyed a well-understood and cultivated earth. Man knew not himself. He was given five senses with which to feel his way, but no, he permitted his senses to master him. The result was fights, quarrels and pain. He has made himself a yoked beast, always hunting food, clothing, shelter, and seeing little beyond these things.

Here and there among man a few have had visions of possibilities. These few translated the Bible, secured freedom of thought and speech, wrote and installed the great Constitution of the United States, instituted schools and universities into which they led men to educational paths, and through their effort you and I have the good, free lives possible for us to enjoy today.

Let us follow these men further - they discovered electricity, its control and many of its uses. They introduced irrigation by which millions of acres of barren lands have been converted into farms and homes of the first order; they have fought diseases, stagnation, and poverty. They have gone to great lengths to make the human family comfortable and the earth a pleasant and agreeable home for all, that we can but thank them and show our appreciation by carrying on to ever greater progress.

In 1886, the United States Commissioner of Patents reported that few new inventions could be expected in the future as practically everything had now been invented. Television, radar, automation, etc., were all creations overlooked as possibilities in 1886. About that time Jules Verne wrote of a world advanced years ahead of even our generation. Edward Bellamy saw down through our time when one could sit at home and there see and hear his minister preach, and hear the choirboys sing in a church far away. He envisioned paper towels, fireless cookers, and clothing of a quality which could be cast aside for new, clean articles when the need was manifested.

Today a few men of vision lead out. Many others want to have some part in the advancement of society, but they stand wondering, because of their lack of opportunity, and hide their desires under a bushel. The world shall now know what it might have had, had society made the way open for men who wanted expression of their creative vision.

The Urge today is to make possible the means of expression and extend to all a welcome to a shop, a studio, an office, a laboratory, a research program - anything to help bring out of man that which will advance society. Creative Research Clubs are in the formative state now. The program is clearly planned and many advances have been made. The work is to be world-wide. Men of all nations shall contribute to the building and administration of the great Research City, plans for which are even now taking definite form.

Thinking, forward-looking men and women are stepping over to investigate. They want to affiliate with, and live in the atmosphere of builders: creative, alive, active, unselfish noble men and women who are reaching for and are willing to obey Universal Law. They may be accepted, even though they be only one from a city, two from a nation, who knows? They will come and bring with them all that is necessary for the realization of the great work and plan. There shall be men with genius and exceptional powers to do research work. There will be men and women who shall give freely of the things of the world which must be had to make the program possible.

Meantime, Creative Research Groups will continue forming and gathering in the chestnuts for the happy time ahead. It is gratifying to know that Creative Groups are widening their work and interests, covering greater and ever greater activities. More power to them and may the year ahead see their work spread across the many waters.

America became the Arsenal of the World, then helped in the action necessary to bring the war to an end. How was this land capable of the part which it carried? Because its people are many times above the average in productivity among peoples of the world. Leaders today agree that it is necessary for this nation to hold the leading position among nations. This can be done only if the people of the nation are given expression. There are truths hidden in the minds of common, fine Souls who strive to make themselves heard. It is our first duty to give them utterance.

Again the World has a great need and this need must and shall be met through our young visionary scientists. The time is now, to assist these young scientists and let expressions come forth for the good of all mankind.

I am holding meetings every other Friday evening to act as coordinator to bring these ideals and thoughts forth. The meetings are held as a clearing-house for advanced thinking and planning. Please call Mother Mary, at Hollywood 5-3572, for a personal invitation to attend these Friday meetings.

When Mother Mary established the Hobby Clubs, she sought to empower others to use the same format to pursue their own endeavors. The 1946 first edition of the "Creative Researcher" magazine was subtitled "Suggestions for Creative Hobby Club Organization" and the magazine contained such articles as "Photography as a Creative Hobby" and "The Shut-Ins Hobby Page." Mother Mary had already delegated the actual operation of the Hobby Clubs to others by this time, and only provided a little material for this edition. She was simply referred to as "our founder" by the officers of the corporation and the editors of the magazine, and the publication presents a multitude of viewpoints, most of them dissimilar to her own.

The one article with which she was associated is an account of the travels of Ralph Elmer in Tibet, first published on September 2 and 3, 1945 in the San Diego Union, written by his friend, Edmund Rucker. At the end of this article was a picture of Elmer, and Mary Mae Maier asked him two questions. This article is an interesting prequel of her own trip to Tibet five years later.

THE WALLED VALLEY OF TIBET
by Edmund Rucker

Shangri-La is no Asiatic pipe dream to Ralph Elmer, who once penetrated mysterious and almost inaccessible Tibet, and who yesterday made public a report of researches he was privileged to observe there 40 years ago on the career of Jesus of Nazareth.

Elmer claims to have solved the historic mystery concerning Jesus' whereabouts during the years between His appearance in the temple at the age of 12 and the beginning of His ministry - 18 years on which the scriptures have been strangely silent.

Shangri-La tripped into modern man's vocabulary through James Hilton's novel, *Lost Horizon,* generally regarded as pure fiction, but Elmer declares the yarn is built around a solid core of facts, and he insists that Hilton borrowed much of his descriptive detail, if not the entire inspiration of the book, from lectures by a San Francisco physician, E. W. Clark, who used to spend his summers in San Diego.

Invited To Orient

It was by invitation of this physician that Elmer made his journey to the Orient. Their acquaintance began here through Methodist church work. Elmer, then 19, was a student at the State Normal School - now State College.

Dr. Clark, who was 81, was deeply religious. Besides being a student of the Bible, he possessed a flair for the occult. Already he had made three trips around the world, on one of which he contrived to enter Tibet, and he thrilled the youth with tales of a unique Christian School he had discovered there in what he called "the walled valley of Tibet," an institution of vast antiquity. When he announced his intention to return there, and offered to take Elmer with him, Elmer eagerly accepted.

Sail New Year's Eve

They sailed from San Francisco on New Year's Eve, 1905. Although Dr. Clark had a considerable income from gold mine investments in Northern California, he preferred to travel in slow steamers, preferably tramp freighters. He said he "wanted ample leisure to study the Oriental mind in its methods of expressing religion."

"You will witness strange and baffling things in Tibet," Clark kept murmuring as their ship labored across the Pacific.

After tarrying two weeks in Japan for sightseeing, they crossed the China Sea to Shanghai, where Clark chartered a Chinese sampan for a voyage up the Yangtze River. The sampan was owned and operated by Leng Po, who had been born and reared aboard it, his father before him, and all of Leng Po's children. He boasted that his son, 18, had never set foot on shore. The sampan was sailed and poled 1500 miles up the Yangtze in about three months. Then Clark engaged native coolies and guides and they rode horses 1000 miles across China. Finally, there came a day when they noticed signs of nervousness in their guides, who presently informed them they were approaching the border of Tibet.

One morning the Americans awoke from sleeping on the ground to find themselves by half a hundred armed men who revealed themselves as the Tibetan border patrol. The white men quickly discovered that their coolie guides had vanished during the night. The Chinese had deserted, as they afterward learned, in a panic of fear. For some reason it was never made clear why the dreaded the Tibetans.

Carry Strange Arms

The border patrol was armed with a strange assortment of weapons, including old firearms and bows and arrows. Their small shaggy horses were tethered nearby. Clark, who was a student of Oriental languages, was able to communicate to the guard his desire to enter Tibet. But he told them he would have to await permission from Lhassa, the capital. The Yanks were kept under guard for three weeks, and although they were treated with courtesy and provided with excellent food and comfortable tents against the biting winds, they never were allowed out of sight of the patrol.

Word finally came from Lhassa; admission to Tibet was refused. They were compelled to retrace their journey to Shanghai. As they trotted east, Clark kept assuring Elmer that he would find a way to enter Tibet. He said he would have no difficulty in crossing the western border. From Shanghai they sailed to Manila and from there to Calcutta, and there the real adventure began.

Three Meet Vessel

As their steamer warped into the sun-drenched dock at Calcutta, Clark and Elmer stood at the rail of the upper deck watching the motley crowd waiting on shore. Suddenly Clark exclaimed, "They are here!"

"Who" asked the astonished youth.

"See those three men at the edge of the crowd at this end of the dock?" Clark said excitedly, and added, "They received my message." The three men were clad in what Elmer afterward learned was the garb of Tibetan highlanders. He noted that they had the bronzed skin of Asiatics, but their features were Caucasian. They greeted Clark affectionately and shook hands with Elmer. He saw that they and Clark were old acquaintances. He decided at once that they were men of intelligence and education, and he noted that they spoke flawless English.

Travel Through India

Traveling by elephant, camel and donkey, they pushed their way north through India and finally turned east. After two months of steady plodding, Elmer became aware of a marked change in climate and terrain and in the appearance of the natives who passed them on the roads. The temperature had fallen to the freezing point and it kept falling. From his companions, the San Diegan learned that they were in Tibet. The border crossing had been accomplished without his being aware of it.

They plodded on through a pass in the Himalayas. A pass 16.000 feet above sea level. Once through it, they found themselves in a sparsely populated region devoted to pasture and agriculture. Grazing animals were chiefly the yak. A fortnight later they came in view of a panorama of harsh and rugged scenery. "There," Clark murmured, "is the famous walled valley of Tibet, and in the valley nestles the most remarkable institution of learning on this planet."

When Ralph Elmer of San Diego and Dr. E. W. Clark gazed at the famous walled valley of Tibet, it appeared as a giant crack in the mountains with towering, almost perpendicular sides, the craggy tops of which jutted outward as though trying to lean toward each other. In the valley's center, a towering shaft of granite pierced the blue casque of heaven like a colossal needle. Young Elmer learned that inside this granite shaft was hewn the legendary school which Clark had described.

Mountain Shaft

As they drew nearer, Elmer saw from an elevation that the ends of the valley were walled up with solid masonry rising as high as an old-fashioned three-story residence. Entrance was through an immense wooden gate. The walls were at least 25 feet thick, he estimated. The entire valley appeared to have been created by some prehistoric cosmic

24

upheaval which split a mountain apart, leaving a splintered shaft standing in the center. The valley he estimated to be more than three miles long and to vary from 150 feet to a mile in width. A hewn passageway led into a vast circular high-domed room 250 feet in diameter "like an orange cut in half with the flat side down," Elmer described it. This huge chamber, he learned, was the school's assembly room. It opened into 4 smaller rooms, each about 100 feet in diameter, which he learned were classrooms.

No Heating Problem

From the great hall, a corridor led to a dining room. Other corridors gave access to many small bedrooms, one of which was assigned to Clark and Elmer. The lad was interested to find that despite the severe winters of Tibet, the school had no heating problem. All rooms were cut so deep in the granite that none was closer than 200 feet to the outside. Each room was provided with a ventilation shaft similar to those which the ancient Egyptians connected with the King's burial chamber in the heart of the pyramids. Temperature throughout the school remained at 68 degrees Fahrenheit the year around.

Hidden Lighting

The institution had its own electrical generating equipment, Elmer said. Illumination was by hidden, indirect lights which cast no shadow. There were no control switches. The lights were controlled by beams of "black light" so that a man's entry into or exit from a room caused the lights to go on or off.

Visitors were coming and going constantly, but what business they were engaged in or what communications they bore, Elmer said he never learned. He found that although the natives of Tibet were either Buddhists or Confucians, the school of the walled valley was a purely co-operative, spiritual Christian community whose members referred to one another as "disciples." And although there was a head to the community, known to his associates only as "Otto," all appeared to have the same rank. Every disciple performed menial labor.

Christmas Observed

The teaching faculty numbered between 30 and 40, but the colony appeared to comprise between 250 and 300 disciples. All were vegetarians who ate only fruits, berries, roots and herbs, but at Christmas they offered to make an exception for their California visitors by serving roast turkey, and Elmer observed on the dining table what appeared to be the largest stuffed turkey he had ever seen. But when he started to eat he discovered it was composed of nuts and grains. His disappointment was attenuated by its delicious taste which he declared differed but slightly from that of honest-to-goodness roast gobbler.

Subjects taught at the school covered everything that affects a moral being spiritually or economically, Elmer reported. But the chief interest of Clark and himself was in the school's ancient archives. Aging records on sheepskins and papyrus which they were permitted to inspect, had been handed down from the apostolic age and even before, they were told. Some records showed the school to have been in existence more than 1000 years B.C. Besides being familiar with modern languages, Clark was a student of the dead languages, and he spent days pouring over the ancient documents of the school. He told Elmer they revealed important facts hitherto unknown about the early life of Jesus.

Concerning this phase of their visit to Tibet, Elmer said, "Bible students long have been puzzled over the silence of the scriptures about the 18 years of Jesus' life before the beginning of his ministry. There has been much speculation as to His whereabouts after He was lost in the Temple at the age of 12. Where did He spend those 18 years and what was He doing?"

Secrets Revealed

"Clark said the ancient sheepskins cleared up this mystery. He told me they recorded that the Jewish priesthood of Jesus' day required a priest to give but 20 years of his life to that profession, and no one was permitted to speak from the temple until he was 30." The New Testaments record that Jesus spoke first in the synagogue at Capernaum on the shores of Galilee. He was then just turned 30. "But the most important revelation that Clark found in the walled valley records was that those 18 years of the Master's life were spent at the school in Tibet - spent in study and contemplation. They showed also that it was from this school that the three wise men set out upon their journey to pay homage to the infant Jesus, taking with them gold, frankincense, and myrrh."

Power of Healing

Members of the faculty of the school have the power of healing, Elmer declared. There is no sickness in the valley and any person not in good health when he arrives from the outside world was quickly healed. The San Diegan recalled the case of a young Tibetan - not a member of the colony - who was rushed before the disciples from a nearby village after he had been bitten by a venomous reptile. Already shaken by convulsions, the stricken youth stared through glassy eyes that protruded from a livid face, Elmer reported. He was laid on a couch in the center of the assembly hall and the disciples took positions around the wall, then began a slow march around the circumference of the room. In a little while, the reptile victim's paroxysms subsided perceptibly until they finally ceased entirely. The man's features became relaxed and presently he arose and strode across the room, apparently in normal health.

Leave For Palestine

After 3 ½ months at the school, Clark decided to leave for Palestine, and they traveled there by way of Bombay, Teheran and old Baghdad. After a year in the Holy Land they went to Egypt and lived for months in the shadow of the pyramids. But the high spot of his world-girdling travels Elmer declared remains the stay at the school of the walled valley in Tibet.

Manuscript Lost

On his return to America, Clark toured the principal cities of the United States and Canada, lecturing on Tibet and writing a book about his experiences there. The manuscript was completed when he was 97, but soon after it was set into type, and before the galley proofs were read, the print shop in San Francisco where the job was being done, was burned to the ground. Clark had not the enterprise to start the work over, Elmer declared. Dr. Clark spent his last years in Los Angeles, where he died at 103. He was never married until nine months before his death, when he took as his wife the 60-year-old woman who had been his nurse.

May Write Book

While Clark lived, Elmer felt that since he had made the journey as a traveling companion, he had no right to publish any report on the adventure. Since Clark's death he has hoped to find the leisure to do a book on Tibet himself, and he still looks forward to writing it, he said yesterday. Meanwhile his days are occupied with the operation of a stamp collecting agency and with church work.

NOTES

Notes on the above article by Mr. Elmer:

The story above is a word for word reprint of the articles as written by my friend Edmund Rucker. There are however some statements which he did not get clear and these I want to call attention to and will cover at a later date, as on page four, mention is made of "the King's burial chamber in the heart of the pyramids." The pyramid here referred to is the "Great Pyramid of Gizeh" and I shall give you an article on this marvelous structure in another time.

We are now in the closing days of a cycle in the history of this world and are about to enter into a new era in which vast changes in the modes of living and thinking by the peoples of the world will take place. The school referred to in the article above is a forerunner of the things to come. Do you want to learn more about them or take part in the things about to happen? If you are interested in my work and desire to know more about it and the part you may play in coming events, I shall be happy to keep you posted. Send me your name and address - Ralph Elmer

An Interview With Ralph Elmer
By Mary Mae Maier

Q. Was there a purpose in printing the article above?

A. After 38 years of study in and with the school, permission was granted by the school to let the story be given to the press and it was printed in the San Diego Union, Sept. 2nd and 3rd, 1945.

Q. What is the plan which the school has in mind?

A. The Great School has at times in the past instituted schools in different parts of the world with different purposes in view. All have had to be withdrawn from the world because of various reasons. The school now knows that the time is at hand to bring to the people of America, the teachings of the school and are planning a model community in which the teachings of Brotherly Love as exemplified by Jesus, and a co-operative way of life as lived by His disciples and the early church, shall be lived and demonstrated.

"RAINBOW GEMS"

The following is advice to all, written on the stationary of the Rainbow Auditorium, 3210 West Pico Blvd, Los Angeles, and called by Henry Fuller, her friend of that time, "Rainbow Gems." It is easy for the reader to get a sense of her spiritual activities in Los Angeles from studying this material. Some of this reads like James Joyce - "book," bookkeeping," "boomerang," and "affairs," affectionate," "affirm," for instance. In the book Atlantis Speaks Again, *Mother Mary wrote, "A thought is a creation. It is more; it is a power more or less potent for good or evil." These aphorisms should be regarded as thoughts which Mother Mary during her years with the Rainbow Auditorium wished to send out as a power for good. The order is sometimes curious, but it should be regarded as having something to do with the way the mind indexes information, as does James Joyce as well. These sentences represent mostly the "A, B & C's" of her spiritual vocabulary, and were probably influenced in the format by the numerological system of The Order of Directive Biblical Philosophy. There is one sentence here which recalls her life as a Hopi, "Don't break or destroy anything good."*

Read a good book.

It is good to know bookkeeping.

Look out for a boomerang for your bad deeds.

Be sure your will is in good order.

Your affairs should be looked after. Arrange proper papers.

Are you affectionate? It is all right to be in your case.

To affirm, when at the right time, brings your wish.

Are you afraid? You need not be.

Alchemy is a good future for the young.

Make allowance for your loved ones.

All your life your wish was to act. Why not?

Be an ambassador of good will.

Go among flowers and beauty and you will overcome.

Analyze what you are doing.

Ancient books will give you what you are looking for.

Do not get angry - change to some other words.

An animal is good for children - he must have a yard to play in.

You are anxious about something. It should come the way you see it.

Do apologize and your troubles will let up.

Take better care of your appearance.

Appreciate what may come - it could make a turn not so good.

To accent, sing your wish.

Accept what is for you. To accept, reason it out.

Be happy now.

You are beside yourself at times - take it easy and things will get better.

Who wants to be the best man, just smile.

Your enemy cannot betray you if you watch.

Improvement can always be made.

Give your body a chance - stay away from billiousness.

Take your blessings where they come.

Do not be blind to the good you see, and forget the other.

Let them boast of themselves - it does no harm.

Yes, they still can blush.

Let your word be your bond.

A trip to the beach is helpful - even to have a bonfire.

You should go to a place where a large audience will be and have a good time.

You could be an author.

Go to the top head who has the authority - things will automatically take place.

Act when the thought comes, going over your plans first.

Do not advance in business too fast.

It is advisable to wait and think things over.

Alter your habits a little.

Ablaze your desire as if on fire.

You are able-bodied to do the right - go on.

To abstain from the unreal is to find happiness for oneself and others.

Have abundance - plan it right.

You are very artistic.

Stay with your first idea - you have nothing to be ashamed of.

Your happiness will come. Look for happiness - don't stay as you are.

Happiness is not as soon as you expect.

You will be doing it soon.

Give it time for your own good. Other things to come first. What a difference a week or months - just so the right thing happens.

Leave your troubles behind and start new.

Make a picture in the mind's eye and believe.

Don't dislike - love a little more.

You should have the property that belongs to you.

You are beloved by your friends.

Yes, he does love you.

Yes, she does love you.

You will benefit by your kindness - keep it up.

If you feel you as if you could go berserk from your nerves - you need a change.

A broken life can be built new again - go to new places.

Bruises can injure - also takes time to heal. The right quality of love can overcome any brutality.

On the day everything is wrong, time makes a bright light, and darkness goes like a broken bubble.

Stay busy only with the beautiful.

A mind busy with the real will leave the other alone.

Busy-body meddling…an officious person. Try not to help by keeping your own mouth closed.

Go to the mountains, even if the cabin is small.

Calling a friend on the phone may help.

Capital for the future does not always have to be money - put your mind to it.

Capitalize on your own doings to make a future, and be free and happy.

You will meet a new friend - go out often.

Watch your associations.

Help to vote the right judges to the bench.

Be more athletic - your health needs it, but not too much.

Attune yourself to your feelings, you are right many times.

To criticize or censure any person brings heartaches.

Centralize all your thoughts as if you were building your home.

Get happy - hold as if you would have a century to live.

Don't make a cesspool of the matter you will take up - if angry, think it over first.

Don't be chained or chain anyone either. Say "No" to both sides.

Pertaining to magic or occultism - look out for the charlatan. Challenge, the real is wise.

Chamber - a private room to think things out will save you many mistakes.

Seek to enjoy the hero.

Take a chance - it may be a risk, a possibility, or an opportunity.

Do you wish to change? Sleep over it.

A channel may be open - the water also deep. Always look into the depth.

You are completely in need of sleep and rest and change.

You have much charm.

Chase, capture, and drive after the business.

Be morally pure, modest and refined.

You made your mind to be obedient - that is why your home is clear.

Don't listen to the chatter - they will not know if you close your ears.

The person who cheapens himself pays a high price in time.

Cheating, deception and defrauding will always show up and come out in the open.

Be cheerful at all times, and love will find a way.

To cherish is wonderful, but do you believe that you can keep always?

Would you like to meet a childhood friend?

Make a choice - you should.

Discount as circumstantial what you see or hear - if possible give the person help.

Have they any claim on you? If not, stop every act.

You could be clairvoyant.

Ceremonially pure thought can change your whole life.

Sometimes the comedian is the one who has the most heart. Try to understand.

If you are comfortable, why move?

If you have any comment, listen first.

Find a woman or man for the right companionship.

Have compassion for them now.

Capture a home, trip, love, invest in a car - anything that comes to mind. It is within your own mind to get what you want just by going after it.

Building castles in the mind even to put the pieces of the life together helps to make a path to try wonders that can be done.

A cataclysm is hard to take, but it may make better human beings.

Is your vision impaired? Get glasses, the need may be great.

Suddenly you want to catch hold of what you are after. Why not try just at the moment before it leaves your thought.

What category do you belong to - find out.

Cat-o-Nine-Tails lashes hurt. Are we not glad they're out of date? Hope when feelings are hurt, they can also forget.

Causation of harsh words - what a difference between kind and loving words.

Always be cautious of your acts.

Are your thoughts of building sanctuary for safety?

Could you make a chapel of worship within yourself?

A chaperon should not be needed.

Character of the other person is better than you think - find out for yourself.

Direction can be had.

The one you love is charitable.

Good should come like an avalanche.

Awakening to what you should do is timely.

You think at time you are awkward - that isn't right.

You should approve - it will make you happier.

The architecture of your planning is good.

Make an archive and keep a record.

Keep away from argument as much as you can now, to help all.

Arise in the morning and take a walk in the fresh air to think things over.

Make a change like an arrow.

Your wants will be there. According to what you think, you can have.

Take an account of what is to be.

Have you an ache in your heart? Wait a little longer. The suffering and ache you feel will soon leave.

Your background is very good.

Never go backward - go on now.

Balance and power are what you need.

Stand as if on a balcony looking down and see what you can do.

To acknowledge the wrong is to find things will come for the betterment of all.

A person who will call a child a brat gives you an insight into them - always be on guard.

Be brave. When trouble comes you will overcome hurts.

Don't break or destroy anything that is good, even a heart, and watch how good comes back.

A breakdown of anything can be built up again.

Bring yourself to do a little bit of what you want to do every day.

Broaden yourself and visit broad-minded people.

To beautify will give life and you can do more.

Try and comprehend what is being done.

Don't condemn now - it may come on slowly.

Confession does not always bring happiness, but the way you are now living does.

A confidential friend is wonderful to have.

Do not confine yourself to your home - get out.

Do not be confused. It cannot always stay the same.

Congratulations can be a happy event for both parties.

If your conscience is clear, go ahead.

Get consent before you do anything.

Consider action for others before you claim any part.

To contest, get all details.

Take it to your lawyer before signing a contract. If you have an idea, copyright it.

Contribute to the real and the good, always looking to all parts.

Cooperation with your fellow men brings friendship.

To be too crystallized is not the best way out.

Be captain of your world. You can make it beautiful and real.

Captivity can be in your own being - get free.

You may be at the bottom now but you need not stay there.

Use your brain - you have a good one!

Catalog what you are doing - pick the best from your list and try to do it.

2. THE ORDER OF DIRECTIVE BIBLICAL PHILOSOPHY

A few months before he died at the age of 33 on November 15th, 1899, Frederick Spencer Oliver, amanuensis of *A Dweller on Two Planets,* told his mother Mary Elizabeth Manley Oliver that the adept Phylos had given him instructions on what was to be done with the manuscripts and materials which would be left behind after him. She was to hold the material for the future, and sometime later a woman would come to whom all the materials should be given. According to Phylos, this woman would establish her identity by demonstrating her knowledge that a mathematical formula had been left out of the original published edition of *A Dweller on Two Planets.* This formula is **26:17::25.8+30:24**, or "As twenty six is to seventeen, so is twenty five point eight plus thirty to twenty four" or "As twenty six is to seventeen, so is twenty five and eight tenths plus thirty to twenty four." The publisher demanded that this formula be deleted from the book, as no one could solve it. In addition, Phylos made some comments to Oliver about the clothes and hair style of this "woman who would come later" which he relayed to his mother. He also told his amanuensis that in 1941 the material would be transferred again.

In Mother Mary's book *Atlantis Speaks Again* the story is told of how Phylos appeared to Lillian Venona Thornton Bense in 1913 at her home at 1931 Castillo St. in Santa Barbara and directed her to find the mother of Fred Oliver. As with the amanuensis, Lillian Bense sometimes could see Phylos, but more often simply heard his voice. Following the direction of Phylos, Lillian Bense was able to locate Mary Manley Oliver. Mrs. Oliver immediately recognized Lillian Bense as the "woman who would come later" by her inquiries about missing material from the published version of the book, and by her hair and clothes. Mrs. Oliver spent her later life promoting her son's work, and realized that Lillian Bense was the person who would carry this on after her. At some point, Phylos gave the two women the solution to the mathematical problem which was placed in a sealed envelope, meant to be opened sometime in the future and incorporated into a later edition of *A Dweller on Two Planets.* This envelope was in the possession of Mrs. Oliver who later passed it to Mrs. Bense.

Lillian Bense was a tutor who had been active in the Women's Christian Temperance Union. In the February, 1901 edition of the Omaha, Nebraska magazine *Women's Weekly*, Mrs. Bense is described as "State Superintendent of the Department of Purity in Literature and Art" for the Nebraska W.C.T.U. In an article about her work, she is quoted as saying that the purpose of this department was "the study of the Bible as the highest form of literature." This statement is important as an expression of her own inner bias, or the attitudes which shaped her mind as she approached the teachings of Phylos. In the 1920 U.S. census, she gave her employment status as chaperone, "employed by studio to travel with actors."

In 1921, Lillian Bense received the archive of Fred Oliver's unpublished writings from Mrs. Oliver. Some years after the death of Mrs. Oliver, Lillian Bense began to refer to her 1913 encounter with Phylos and the subsequent meeting with Mrs. Oliver as her "appointment as the messenger of Phylos." She did not use this appellation while Mrs. Oliver was still alive. Mary Manley Oliver told Mrs. Bense about the Phylos prophecy regarding the "woman who would come later." When Mrs. Bense had first read *A*

Dweller on Two Planets, she instinctively realized that the text had been altered. At her very first meeting with Mrs. Oliver in 1913, she asked her if the text had been changed in any way, and Mrs. Oliver confirmed the suspicion. This was an affirmation to Mrs. Oliver that Lillian Bense was in fact the "woman who would come later." However, it does not appear that Mrs. Bense specifically realized that it was the numerical formula which was missing, but was able to sense that certain other parts of the text had been altered and did not represent Phylos' original intention.

In addition to the materials given to her by Mary Manley Oliver, Lillian Bense was given a copy of the original manuscript of *A Dweller on Two Planets* by the woman who had typed it up years before for Fred Oliver in the 1890's, and had retained a copy. This copy was different from the published edition of the book, as it did not contain certain changes written into the manuscript at the insistence of one "Mrs. A. E. P.," a friend of Mrs. Oliver's who wielded undue influence over the young man, and who convinced Fred Oliver to make changes in the text, especially regarding "soul-mates." These changes were suggested in order to make the book more marketable and similar to some popular spiritual fiction of the time, such as Marie Correlli's *Romance of Two Worlds.* Perhaps the title of Fred Oliver's book was meant to echo Correlli's work, though of course the content is completely different. This first-generation copy of the manuscript was to become an important source material for Mrs. Bense's future work, and it confirmed her intuition that the published text had been altered significantly.

Mrs. Bense began her earnest study of Fred Oliver's materials in 1921, and after assimilating the system of numerology said to be given by Phylos, she began to teach the system and the philosophy it is based on to a small group of students, including Maud Meserne Falconer. The numerological system was known to them as "Enoch's Throne Block" and the practice of it was said to help in the unfolding of the latent spiritual senses of those who used it. In Mrs. Bense's teachings, the numerological system and the philosophy behind it are so intertwined that they cannot be considered separately, and Mother Mary followed in this path as well. Throughout Mae Maier's writings and public addresses are hidden references to the numerology of The Order, which would be noticed only by those who are familiar with the system.

The study group called The Order of Directive Biblical Philosophy was formally begun by Lillian Bense in 1928 and incorporated as a non-profit in October of 1930, based on all the materials from Fred Oliver. Along with her co-worker Maud Falconer and other members of the group, Mrs. Bense believed that she was in regular telepathic contact with Phylos and other masters from inside Mt Shasta, whose spiritual philosophy was said to be derived from the teachings of the Sons of Solitude, a term for the adepts of Atlantean times found in *A Dweller on Two Planets.* In ancient times, there were many different versions of numerology based on calculations of the numerical values of letters, such as the Cabbalistic *"gematria,"* a Greek system called *"isopsephy,"* and an Islamic system referred to as *"khisah al jamal."* "Enoch's Throne Block" was considered by The Order to be a remnant of the numerological teachings of Atlantis, and the basis for an ancient Hebrew or Biblical numerology now lost. Another name for the philosophy behind the numerological system of Phylos is "The Ethical Vibration of Numbers." A brief tutorial in the basic functions of this numerological system is found in Appendix 2 below. In due course, Lillian Bense informed Maud Falconer of the prediction by Phylos to Fred Oliver of a "woman who would come later." She probably told this story from the point of view that she herself had already fulfilled the prophecy, but Maud Falconer took note of the date 1941.

Mother Mary, who knew Mrs. Bense and Mrs. Falconer well, said that Mrs. Falconer was born, or rather re-born, with the knowledge of the power of the word and was a reincarnated Atlantean. She lived at 1337 Valencia St. in Los Angeles. The themes of "power of the word" and "Atlantis" are found throughout Mrs. Falconer's writings, and she was the author of some material first published in *Atlantis Speaks Again*. Mother Mary considered her own book to be an extension of the work of The Order of Directive Biblical Philosophy and most of it is derived from the teachings of that group. Some of the original texts of her source materials are reprinted here in Appendix 1. Maud Falconer was to become Lillian Bense's successor as leader and teacher of the group, and maintained a close relationship with Mother Mary. She addressed her letters to Mary Mae Maier with, "My dear little sister."

Many other members of the group contributed to the study materials of The Order as well, and they seem to have had the laudable ethic that anyone may express the truth, not just the leaders of the group, and the expression of truth or sincere aspiration made by anyone was held in high regard by them. The poem *Warning!* by Addie M. Squires included on page 44 of *An Earth Dweller's Return* is an example of this. Facing this poem on the 45th page of that book is the original frontispiece of *A Dweller on Two Planets* containing the missing formula.

The early editions of *A Dweller on Two Planets* contain a reproduction of Fred Oliver's drawing of Phylos, sketched while Phylos posed in a chair in the Yreka home of the Oliver family. The chair in which Phylos sat when the picture was drawn was eventually kept in a room in The Inn which Mother Mary called "the spiritual room." This room contained many artifacts which Mother Mary collected from her travels to India, and some furniture from the Oliver family, such as the desk upon which *A Dweller on Two Planets* was written. Mother Mary republished the original frontispiece with the formula yet again on page 176 of *Atlantis Speaks Again,* and reproduced the drawing of Phylos.

Many writings of The Order of Directive Biblical Philosophy are essentially commentaries on the published and unpublished manuscripts of Fred Oliver, which Lillian Bense and Maud Falconer studied in detail and shared with their students. Concepts like "Spirituality of Thought" belong to this category. This term is found in Fred Oliver's writings, and many permutations or interpretations of this idea were explored by the group, with varying degrees of success.

In *An Earth Dweller's Return* the concept "Spiritual Telepathy of Thought" is defined in passages 486-7 and 491-3. These teachings are attributed to Phylos –

> "Knowledge is power. Within well defined limits, this is verity. If behind the knowledge lies the requisite energy to realize its benefits, then only is it a true saying. In order to exercise command over Nature and her forces, the would-be operator must have perfect comprehension of the natural laws involved. It is the degree in attainment in this knowledge which marks the lesser or greater ability of the performer, and those who have acquired the profoundest understanding of the law (Lex Magnum) are Masters whose powers seems so marvelous as to be magical. Uninitiated minds are absolutely awed by their incomprehensible manifestations. (Mention of the above law is made with respect to Spiritual Telepathy of thought, one of the primary Unseen Powers.).....

"When one's will is attuned to God's will, a veritable psychic spirit of scientific knowledge enters the mind through the channel of receptivity. Thou must know that scientific knowledge is one view of knowledge: that psychic knowledge is a different view: and that scientific psychic knowledge is still another view, all of which is well to understand, thus differentiating as to the place and operation of each. Then thou canst obtain psychically, through the channel of receptivity, what is really scientific knowledge.

"When one has attuned to the will of the Heavenly Father, then He, the Creator of all things, wills this spirit of knowledge to enter the mind, and the recipient can do likewise, the door being open to all who observe the law. Know this, that if thou dost not comprehend my meaning upon the receipt of these words, the channels of thy receptivity are obstructed and thou shouldst hasten to clear them, for this is the key to all wisdom. "When you comprehend, then shall the Heavenly Father, Creator of all things whatever, enter into thee: and thy spirit, which is a ray of His spirit, shall reunite with Him. And because he creates by constant Logos all things and states of being, and is immanent in all - knowing it all - so when He entereth thy soul, thou shalt know all things likewise, and in less measure, create also."

The Order believed that their search for truth was guided by Phylos, but unlike Nola Van Valer, who also had contact with Phylos and was taught by him, they did not try to "channel" Phylos' teachings. Instead, they formed in their own minds the truths which they believed were inspired by Phylos and other masters of thought from inside Mt. Shasta. The laws of this process of thought-transference or "spiritual telepathy of thought," in contrast to "channeling," are discussed in the material presented here, and are found throughout the writings of The Order, such as the section "Memory," found in Appendix 1 below of teachings from The Order. This was a favorite subject of both Lillian Bense and Maud Falconer.

A related term for this telepathic process, the "Philosophy of Intensification," is found in *An Earth Dweller's Return,* and signifies a telepathic rapport between the masters of thought and those who they try to reach on the plane of souls. This second book attributed to Phylos was compiled by Lillian Bense over a period of many years, from the Phylos-related material left by Fred Oliver. She used the name "Beth Nimrai" for this compilation, one of several nom-de-plumes that she employed. The same material was also the basis for lessons she composed for her students, but those lessons were more specifically intended to teach the numerical system, which Lillian Bense believed was in itself a conduit for spiritual knowledge from the masters. She was fond of saying that if one were to practice the system, it would unfold one's consciousness, and suggests this as another meaning for "Intensification." In addition to telepathy, "Philosophy of Intensification" refers to a kind of force-transference by which Phylos and other adepts reach those who are receptive to them. As well as the section "Memory," this term is also related to the teachings on "Space" in the section of the same name in the Appendix. The term "Space" in The Order's writings is identical to the Sanskrit word *Akasha* and the Sanskrit word shows up in the material in the phrase "Akashic records."

All of the members of The Order of Directive Biblical Philosophy had read and re-read *A Dweller on Two Planets* many times, and a familiarity with this text is necessary to understand their writings. The group itself, including Mary Mae Maier, reviewed Lillian

Bense's text of *An Earth Dweller's Return* before its publication, and the members studied every word of the printed edition like a textbook. The writings of The Order can only be understood in the context of these other two works. For instance, one of Phylos' teachings regarding physics is that there are not discreet elements, but that those elements classified in the periodic table are all specific speeds of one universal element. This concept of "speed" is frequently found in The Order's manuscripts, and was one of the first bits of information given by the adepts to Fred Oliver, when he was still a teenager, and was used by him in a high school chemistry class paper. This hypothesis is presented in the first pages of Chapter IV in *A Dweller on Two Planets,* "Ante Incal, Axtuce Mun." Some of this section reads as if Fred Oliver lifted a block of text from his class paper.

The same teaching appears in *An Earth Dweller's Return* in the very next paragraph following the passages cited above, namely paragraph or Section 494.

> "Only one element exists, and this is operated upon by varying degrees of the one force. Light, heat, sound, and all solid, liquid and gaseous substances, therefore will be seen to be different, not in material but in speed. This fact underlies all life, physics, chromatics, electrics, calorics, and every other manifestation of Nature. Such is the supreme law of the Heavenly Father. He is Nature, though Nature is not conversely, in Posied phraseology, God."

In poor health and knowing her life was drawing to a close, in 1939 Mrs. Bense sent the compilation of *An Earth Dweller's Return* to the scholar Dr. Howard John Zitko, who edited the text under the name "The Lemurian Scribe," the name he had used when writing his work *The Lemurian Theo-Christic Conception* in 1936. During the writing of his 1936 work, Dr. Zitko himself had felt that he was under the impression of Phylos, although he had no knowledge of or contact with Lillian Bense. Dr. Zitko received the manuscript while he was living in his parents' home in Wauwatosa, Wisconsin. It arrived out of the blue, unsolicited, with a letter explaining that Phylos had told Lillian Bense that if she sent the book to Dr. Zitko, he would publish it.

Dr. Zitko found that the manuscript consisted of a single enormous paragraph. Due to Frederick Spencer Oliver's unschooled writing skills, and Lillian Bense's style of compilation, the editing was a daunting task. Some time later, he received a second letter from Lillian Bense asking him what he had done with the manuscript, and he wrote her back explaining the difficulty of editing it, and lamented that he had no secretary to help him with it. A short time later a woman knocked on his parents' door, and asked, "Do you have work for me?" This of course was how people found work during the Depression. Dr. Zitko asked her, "Can you type?" and she became his first secretary. He read Mrs. Bense's text aloud, making the necessary corrections as he went, and his secretary typed it up with numbered paragraphs. Again, he received another letter from Mrs. Bense inquiring about the progress of the work, and this time he told her that there wasn't any money yet to publish it. Soon therafter his group, "The Lemurian Fellowship," was able to assemble $5,000 to produce 3000 copies and it was published in 1940.

After leaving the University of Wisconsin in 1932, Howard John Zitko sought to develop a career in writing. While sending a manuscript around to various literary agents in the hope of finding someone who could place it with a publisher, he was introduced to Robert D. Stelle, who offered to read it and make suggestions. Stelle told him that what he had was not really a book, but a series of lessons, and offered to help market the work as a mail-order series. Stelle claimed to have experience in marketing the La Salle correspondence courses, although this was never confirmed. These Theo-Christic lessons became the basis of the formation of The Lemurian Fellowship, and for eighteen months R. D. Stelle and Howard John Zitko worked together in the Zitko family home promoting the newly formed spiritual organization.

The Lemurian Fellowship was founded on Sept 16th, 1936, as a collaboration between Dr. Zitko and R. D. Stelle. This date was taken from the calculations of the Great Pyramid-ologist David Davidson, who made measurements of the Pyramid and believed that humanity would "enter the King's Chamber" on this day.   The Order of Directive Biblical Philosophy was also aware of this calculation, and believed that the Aquarian Age began on this date.

By 1939, R. D. Stelle had moved from Wisconsin to Southern California and the headquarters of the Fellowship was established at the Gateway Estate in Ramona, which was purchased with funds supplied by Dr. Zitko's wife, Dorothea. Stelle at that time had no money and was recently divorced. Stelle soon married Hattie Falk, a member of the Milwaukee Lemurian Fellowship. In 1939, when the manuscript of *An Earth Dweller's Return* arrived at the Zitko family home in Wisconsin, Stelle occupied the Gateway Estate. Stelle expressed no opinion about the manuscript. In 1942 Dr. Zitko followed Stelle to California and founded the chapel of the Fellowship, which was called "The Temple of the Jeweled Cross," a term found in the Theo-Christic lessons representing virtues of the spiritual path.

Dr. Zitko had a particularly trying experience with the publication of *An Earth Dweller's Return* when due to success of the publication, differences in the direction of The Lemurian Fellowship emerged.   At the insistence of Dr. Zitko, the unwritten partnership between Zitko and Stelle was terminated in favor of a non-profit corporation chartered in the State of California, with Stelle named President and Zitko Vice-President. Dorothea Zitko was Treasurer, Hattie Falk Stelle held the office of Secretary, and Theresa Zeller, a senior minister of the Temple of the Jeweled Cross, was named the fifth member of the board.

On Sept. 16th, 1946, exactly ten years from the founding of the Fellowship, the whole thing started to unravel. The president and vice-president had a meeting, and Stelle told Dr. Zitko, "Now I'll do the writing, and you'll do the marketing." Zitko replied, "You're no writer, and I'm no salesman." During the previous four years, Stelle had not called a meeting of the board, and when he finally did, he announced that the purpose of the meeting was to expand the board to seven members. When others objected to this, he simply adjourned the meeting. A second meeting of the Board revealed that the minutes of the first meeting had been falsified by Hattie Falk Stelle to show that R. D. Stelle had a controlling vote on the Board and had ruled that the Temple of the Jeweled Cross was to be closed, with all the assets to be brought to his headquarters at Ramona. Stelle then revealed that his newly built headquarters was now owned by a member of his personal staff, converted into private property where Dr. Zitko was not welcome.   Dr. Zitko realized the situation was hopeless and decided to leave the outcome to Karma.

His wife Dorothea however was not so forgiving, and decided to take Stelle to court in San Diego in order to recover some of the money they had donated to the Fellowship. One of the members of the Fellowship, Charlotte Hoak, made inquiries to the district attorney in San Diego, but he declined to take action unless there was a civil suit showing criminal fraud. When the civil suit was tried, Stelle eventually took the stand and declined to answer the questions of Mrs. Zitko's attorney, who was named Bumpus. The judge directed him to answer the questions, but he would not. The judge then called Stelle a fraud, entered a summary judgement for the plaintiff, Mrs. Zitko, awarded her several thousand dollars, and walked off the bench in the presence of many members of the Fellowship and the Temple. The last time Dr. Zitko ever saw Stelle was in the courtroom in San Diego.

Howard John Zitko only met Lillian Bense once, after the publication of *An Earth Dweller's Return,* when Lillian Bense was very advanced in age. He also met Mother Mary only once, when they were both on the same stage in a Los Angeles presentation. On this occasion in 1952 Mother Mary showed the audience a small bowl which she had been given in Tibet, which had been filled with *vibhuti.* One of the Great Ones gave her this bowl to sustain her until she returned to India, and she had eaten a little every day. In 1962, Mother Mary, who seemed to know all about Dr. Zitko's difficulty with Stelle, told a group of people at The Inn that Dr. Zitko's experience had been a spiritual test. Being stabbed in the back by a close associate is typical of the trials experienced by seekers on the Path, and a very old story indeed. After the collapse of the Fellowship, Dr. Zitko re-located to Tucson and later Benson, Arizona where he established the Desert Sanctuary Campus of the World University. The World University continues today to distribute mail-order lessons in Theo-Christic philosophy, and is affiliated with progressive spiritual and educational groups all over the world. It espouses a philosophy dedicated to the formation of the next great world civilization, based on spiritual values, much as the book *An Earth Dweller's Return* has predicted.

Acting under telepathic direction given to her by Phylos, in 1938 Mother Mary first approached the members of The Order, but she got a cold reception. A year later, she demonstrated to them her knowledge of the missing mathematical formula, and the numerical system it is based on, which was left out of the original edition of *A Dweller on Two Planets.* She may have brought the numerological knowledge over from her previous life in Atlantis, or received the information telepathically from Phylos, or perhaps both. The details about the formula missing from Fred Oliver's book must have been supplied to her by Phylos. The existence of the formula had not yet been revealed to the public, as it was first published in the 1940 edition of *An Earth Dweller's Return.* Maud Falconer, not Lillian Bense, realized that Mary Mae Maier was connected to Phylos, and that Phylos intended all the materials of the Order, including the archive of Fred Oliver, to be passed to Mother Mary. In 1941 copies of all the materials in Mrs. Falconer's possession were given to Mother Mary, with some legal papers drawn up to certify the transition. Not all the members of the group were comfortable with this event. Lillian Bense had some reservations about giving the archive to Mother Mary, and sought to place restrictions on her use of the material. She did, however, oversee the transfer of the materials and specifically prepared some papers for Mother Mary's use, which indicates she consented to the transfer. Mother Mary studied the numerological system for several years with Maud Falconer in great detail, assimilating its most arcane nuances, and practiced it regularly for the rest of her life. According to Mother Mary, in 1944 Phylos stopped teaching The Order due to negative psychic conditions on the inner planes caused by the turmoil of World War Two, and the contact was never resumed.

A few manuscripts from The Order still exist, and Mother Mary used some of them, and other fragments, as source materials for *Atlantis Speaks Again*. The complete manuscripts include *The Development of the Senses* and *Promises and Stepping-Stones* penned by Lillian Bense under her own name. *A Conference and a Questing for the Soul of a Nation*, *In the Garden of Delight*, and *In the Garden of Life* were written by Mrs. Bense under the nom-de-plume Beth Nimrai, sometimes spelled Beth Nimrah. This was also the nom-de-plume she used for her compilation of *An Earth Dweller's Return* from the material given to her by Mary Manley Oliver. Excerpts from *In the Garden of Delight* regarding the meanings of each letter in the alphabet were published in *Atlantis Speaks Again* by Mother Mary. *At the Watergate of Jerusalem* was written under the nom-de-plume of Bek Nown, sometimes B.E.K. Nown, which Lillian Bense said was the name Phylos used to refer to her in ancient times. She claimed to have been one of the members of the party who accompanied Phylos to Suern in a scene from *A Dweller on Two Planets*, and said that she was known to Phylos in that life as "Thirtle." The reader may refer to the first article in Appendix 1, "Rules and Regime of Flow of Thought for the Study and Teaching of the Philosophy of Intensification," for Lillian Bense's explanation of these pen names and an overview of the founding of The Order.

Fred Oliver was referred to by the group as "Isschar," which appears in *An Earth Dweller's Return*, and all these nom-de-plumes were apparently based on the names of each individual in ancient lifetimes. "Issachar" also appears in *Atlantis Speaks Again* as the name of the ninth son of Jacob, associated with Gemini. It seems that only a short time before his death he realized that he was "the Mainin of the story," and *An Earth Dweller's Return* is told from this point of view. Like the section "Sons of Jacob," found in Appendix 1, numerous short essays, notebooks, and poems written by various people from The Order were used as source material for *Atlantis Speaks Again*. Some years after the first edition of *An Earth Dweller's Return*, Dr. Zitko asked Mother Mary, as the last director of The Order of Directive Biblical Philosophy, for access to these unpublished materials in order to put out a second edition, but she declined his request.

Whenever possible, the original papers have been used as the source for this book. However, there are discrepancies in the original handwritten notes, where in some cases more than one version of the same information or text exists. Each student carefully hand-wrote his own copy of the teaching when receiving it, and often an extra one or two as well. Many copies of unpublished lessons were promulgated in this fashion. For this reason, it is sometimes not possible to ascertain who is the original author of a certain passage, as there may be hand-written copies of the same passage in the hand of many different members of The Order. Sometimes, for the same reason, exactly which hand-written version is the final and authoritative one is also subject to debate.

To the chagrin of an archivist, Mother Mary used mostly the scrawled and messy notebooks for her source material in *Atlantis Speaks Again* and not the nicely typewritten manuscripts mentioned above. As examples of these discrepancies, one may see in the section "Let There Be Light" reprinted in Appendix 1 and also found in *Atlantis Speaks Again*, references to base-10 numerology, but some of the material is also base-12. In addition, in the notebooks of Mother Mary and Lillian Bense there is a letter-number chart in the form of a circle, which is base-8 numerology in character, a variation of the so-called "Chaldean" system with a few differences. Whether or not this chart can be attributed to Phylos is an open question, and it may be related to Kabbalistic numerology.

In Lillian Bense's possession, passed on to Mother Mary, was a 1912 edition of *The Kabbalah Unveiled* by S. L. MacGregor Mathers published by the Theosophical Publishing Company of New York. A single one of Mother Mary's notebooks contains a version of the Throne Block which is composed of 10 columns, while every other numerical worksheet has the Throne Block of 12 columns. In the writings of The Order, there are two separate listings of correspondences between musical keys and astrological signs, and each of them is different. All of this material must be sorted out by the reader's own discernment, and therein lies the enjoyment. In two subjects however, the information on "The Meaning of Numbers" and "The Meaning of Letters," the material is remarkably similar, even if different words are used by the three sources, Lillian Bense, Maud Falconer, and Mother Mary. The idea expressed for each letter or number is clearly the same, even though the vocabulary may be different in the three authors' writings. It is as if they have some unknown *Quella* from which each has derived the same material, and this source may be the unpublished manuscripts of Fred Oliver.

The question should then be asked, where did this numerological system come from? There are essentially two possibilities - either the unpublished writings of Fred Oliver, or Lillian Bense herself. Apart from the omitted formula, there is only one clear reference to the numerical system in *A Dweller on Two Planets,* and that is found in the very last section of the book written 13 years after the main part of the manuscript, and only a short time before Fred Oliver's untimely death on November 15th, 1899. This section is entitled "The Mighty Capstone" and contains the following sentences –

> "Beloved, remember these words which were spoken by the apostles of the Christ: that they said in the Last Time before the end of the Age, 'There will be mockers walking after their own impious lusts (10). These indeed blaspheme what things they do not understand: but that which they know naturally, as do the irrational animals, in these things they are corrupt (19). These are they who separate at the Dividing of the Way, going in the finite direction, not having the Spirit (7) and are placed as an example, to endure the retributive justice of an age-ending fire."

The passage taken above is from the 1905 Baumgardt edition. This edition was published by Mary Manley Oliver eight years before she met Lillian Bense. Mrs. Oliver was given $10,000 to publish this printing by strangers who remained anonymous, and supported herself in her old age by selling copies of this edition of the book for $5 each. Since this passage was written 13 years after the rest of the manuscript, it indicates that the numerical system was given to Fred Oliver in the intervening years. Curiously, in the 1940 Borden edition, the numbers appear as (6), (16) and (7), respectively. Borden had contact with Lillian Bense, and she refused them permission to use the picture of Phylos drawn by Fred Oliver in later editions. The numbers in the passage above refer to the negative aspect of the first two, and the positive aspect of 7, similar to the information found in the sections below on "The Meaning of Numbers." The second set of numbers more closely resembles the numerological system used by Lillian Bense and Mother Mary. Perhaps Lillian Bense had them corrected by Borden after comparing them with the original text.

Lillian Bense wrote an essay in the nom-de-plume Beth Nimrah which she titled, *As Twenty Six Is to Seventeen, So Is Twenty Five and Eight-Tenths Plus Thirty to Twenty Four* which is reprinted here in Appendix 1. Much of this essay, but not all, was reprinted in *Atlantis Speaks Again* as the section "Historical Background." This piece gives Mrs. Bense's account of her initial meetings with Phylos and Mary Manley Oliver in 1913. In this text, the numerological system is described in the following sentences –

"A hidden or obscure passage anywhere can be interpreted accurately by this method…That method was used many Great Cycles ago. Certain learned ones have tried to obtain it in the present cycle, Pythagoras among them, but even he failed to solve it. No one without being shown can understand it, and only those of the Aquarian Cycle, whose senses are developed to the necessary degree of receptiveness, will be able to comprehend its workings and interpret it correctly."

In this account, Lillian Bense then continues with this sentence –

"It is certainly something that I should like to study."

This sentence itself indicates that the method was in the Fred Oliver writings, and that Lillian Bense learned it from studying these unpublished manuscripts after 1921, and was not the originator of it. *An Earth Dweller's Return*, having been compiled by Mrs. Bense, contains many references to the numerical system. This passage is from the section "The Ruling Unseen Powers" –

"The figure five shows man as the five-pointed star ready for six which originates thought. Seven balances thought, as seven is the number of balance. In eight, man is ready to discriminate as to thought, and in nine he is prepared to materialize, demonstrate and defend it. In ten, he is desirous of promoting his thought into a new condition; in eleven he is ready to give it publicity; and in twelve he is making it subservient to material uses."

There is a reference in the essay of Mrs. Bense to a second passage in *A Dweller on Two Planets* which may contain a reference to the number system, and is certainly a puzzle. It is a footnote which appears near the end of Chapter 10, on Page 106 of the Baumgart edition. Mother Mary referred to the number 17 as symbolizing "The Tree of Life" and it is one of the numbers found in the formula which is the title of the essay.

"It hath ever been thus; the seed sown in the Acre whereof the corners are marked by posts of which the first hath but one side, the second five sides, the third six sides, but the fourth again only five – hath been scorned by man. That seed growth a tree seventeen-branched. So was Suern. In another day it would be watered by Posied: later it must be in Poseid. Yet again this would be after it was pruned by its Sower. Then it must grow until the day's end, and become great in the next day. But greatest at the end of that day. I have spoken a riddle that whoso unfoldeth it proveth him of the Tree I have spoken, and filled with **deathlessness**. Hear, O Israel! Seek, O Manasseh, and Ephraim, seek! Land of the Starry Flag, open thine eyes, and thou too, O Mother land!"

The earliest writings of Lillian Bense, some of them poems from her teenage years in the 1800's before she met Mary Manley Oliver, are found in the book *Promises and Stepping Stones,* some excerpts of which are reprinted below in Appendix 1. After seven years of study by Mrs. Bense of the materials given to her by Mary Manley Oliver, this book was put together from many carbon-paper typed fragments in 1928, the first year of The Order of Directive Biblical Philosophy, and was used as lessons by Mrs. Bense for her students.   It is highly devotional in character, as befits a Bible student.   The "Promises" of the title, are the promises of God to all mankind, and the subject of the book is the fulfillment of these promises.   In this book, many hidden references to the number system are made, such as the use of the terms "vibrational range," "the ongoing," "the lines of endeavor," "defended by" and other terms which actually refer to numerological analysis in this method.   It is clear that Mrs. Bense was already highly skilled in the numerological method when these passages were written.   Lillian Bense was obviously thinking in terms of the numerological system when she wrote the passage in Appendix 1 below titled "The Right Word" from *Promises and Stepping Stones* and was probably looking at a numerological analysis chart for this phrase like the one shown in Appendix 2 for the word "Heaven." This style of discourse, based on a numerological chart, is found in her earliest teachings. The numerology seems, therefore, to already be completely developed when Mrs. Bense started writing about it, which indicates that she learned it from the materials given to her by Mary Manley Oliver, written by Fred Oliver.

There are certain cyphers in the teachings of The Order.   The reader will notice specific phrases like "to make a new condition" which appear over and over.   In the numerology of The Order, this phrase of 19 letters adds up to 91, and was deliberately used by them to sound the vibration of the number 10.   This was one meaning termed by them "the vibrational range."   These connections become more apparent when the numerological information and the astrological information are compared side-by-side.   If a word or phrase seems curious, try a numerological analysis of it.   Also, try looking up such a word in a good dictionary, preferably an old one. The information on the numerical system is incomplete, but enough of it is there to give a general idea or outline of the teachings.   Anyone familiar with tropical astrology will immediately notice parallels.   For instance, the teachings on the number 8 are very similar to conventional wisdom on the sign Scorpio, the 8th sign in the Zodiac when numbered from Aries as 1 to Pisces as 12.

The writings of The Order were said to be inspired by Phylos if not actually dictated by him, and the members of The Order also believed that they were in contact with other members of the spiritual brotherhood living inside Mt. Shasta as well, especially an adept named Holtah.   The retreat inside Mt Shasta was referred to in *A Dweller on Two Planets* as "the sach" and in *An Earth Dweller's Return* as "the sachem," a Native American term from the Algonquian tongue, and this term was sometimes used by The Order.   The important section of *Atlantis Speaks Again* regarding how to pray according to the signs of the moon is attributed to Holtah, and is reprinted here in the Appendix.   Some aspects of the numerical system are also attributed to him. This group of adepts from the retreat inside Mt. Shasta was often referred to by members of the study group as "The Order of Azariah," but one should not infer from this name that the adepts themselves founded some formal organization of this name with membership cards and all the rest.   Indeed, the Third Chapter of Book II in *Dweller on Two Planets* specifically states that the masters confer no degrees.   In choosing which teachings from The Order to reprint in this book, I have taken the position that if she included something in *Atlantis Speaks Again,* Mother Mary must have believed it worthwhile and representative of Phylos and the adepts, and I have sought to publish related fragments here.

In 1922, the Master Jesus, dressed in shabby clothes, knocked on the door of Nola Van Valer's home in Richmond, California and asked her for some food.   This story is recounted in Nola's book, *The Tramp at My Door*.   Nola was a Christian Science Bible student, as were other members of her family. When she made breakfast for the tramp she recognized as Jesus, he gave her teachings and promised to send her to "a Master Teacher." Some time later, when her husband Jerry was travelling by train through Northern California, he was taken off the train at Mt. Shasta and made contact with the adepts from the mountain, including Mol Lang, who appears in the book *A Dweller on Two Planets.* The Master Teacher to whom the family was sent by Jesus turned out to be Phylos. This began a period of spiritual training which reached its zenith with their visit in 1930 to the Temple built in Atlantean times inside the slopes of Mt. Shasta, in the area of Mud Creek.

The first and nineteenth chapters of Nola's book, *My Meetings with the Masters on Mt. Shasta,* give the story of the family's experiences inside the Temple, as told to Eltra Gentry. The rest of the book is composed of "channelings" which were transcribed in 1961 from tapes of Nola speaking by Elaine Pratt Bragg, a close friend of Mother Mary who for some years acted as Mother Mary's private secretary. Unfortunately, the months of effort by Elaine came to naught when the manuscript was lost, and the entire project was repeated some years later by students of Nola's Radiant School. Elaine Bragg was privately skeptical of the origin of the channelings, having had her own contact with Phylos. Elaine suspected that much of the channelings were the product of Nola's imagination, yet still the imagination of someone who had actually known Phylos and might contain something worthwhile. Some of the material in the channelings is, at the very least, subject to serious questioning. For instance, Nola made numerous statements about "the white race," but Mother Mary used this phrase with two meanings very different from the common usage, and if Phylos might have used this phrase to Nola, he probably would have intended Mother Mary's meanings, and not the common one. One of the meanings of "the white race" in Mother Mary's usage was to refer to the White Indians of Southern Mexico, who she claimed were the descendants of people who came to earth from another planet in very ancient times with the aim of furthering the evolution of the human race. In addition, Mother Mary sometimes spoke of a group of adepts, one division of "the Brothers," as she liked to call them, who are born inside the spiritual retreats such as the ones within Mt. Shasta and live their entire lives there, not venturing into human society. She said that if you happened to see one of them, you would think he or she was a 15-year-old youth, as their skin is very pale and doesn't age. These were also ones who Mother Mary referred to as "the white race." Curiously, the alternate name given for Phylos the Tibetan in *A Dweller on Two Planets* is "Yol Gorro," and according to one source with whom Mother Mary was in contact, "gorro" is a Tibetan word which refers to those adepts who are born inside a retreat, and who are in their last life or lives on earth, before progressing to some higher form of existence.

Nola Van Valer and her family were taught in the physical body by Phylos in the vicinity of Widow Springs, on the eastern slope of Mt. Shasta, over a period of ten summers. Nola said that Phylos taught her how to read and study two books, the Bible and the dictionary. As he also did with the students of The Order of Directive Biblical Philosophy, Phylos called to Nola's attention many passages in the Bible which hold special meaning, and had her use the dictionary to find unexpected meanings hidden in the origins of many profound words. On one occasion, Phylos took Nola to a place on the mountain which she said resembled a gravel pit. In fact, it is full of gold, and was the source of Mack Olberman's nuggets. Phylos said to her, "Take all you want." She chose to take some flowers which grew among the rocks, then pressed and dried them in her Bible. The adepts choose their students well.

When Nola, her husband Jerry, his nephew Bill with his wife Leona and two children were taken inside the Temple on the afternoon of June 17th, 1930, they first sat at a table seemingly made of gold-flecked rock, but in which visions of their past lives would appear, wave after wave. Jerry and Bill were taken inside a second room, and had an experience so profound neither would ever speak of it. They both emerged from this room crying. Jerry was so shaken that he absent-mindedly left his family Bible behind when they went out of the temple and back down the mountain to Widow Springs. About 30 years later in the 1960's, one of the Brothers, the adepts of the mountain, gave this Bible to Daniel Boone with instructions to return it to Nola. When he did so, Nola burst into tears. She never expected to see it again and was profoundly grateful for its return.

Those who have studied the Theosophical works of H. P. Blavatsky and Alice A. Bailey will notice many parallel passages and ideas in the writings of The Order. For instance, the section titled "The Term Son of God" written probably by Mrs. Falconer, clearly refers to the First Root Race of *The Secret Doctrine*. The term "Egoic dweller" or "Egoic being" found in *Atlantis Speaks Again* is virtually identical to the teachings of Alice A. Bailey (or her Tibetan teacher, Dhwal Kul) found in passages regarding the "Solar Angel" and "the Ego." Similarly, the word "Devachan," which was used by Fred Oliver and the Order, is a word of Hindu origin, but it is not used in the Hindu meaning by them. Instead, it used after the manner of the early writers of the Theosophical Society such as H. P. Blavatsky and Annie Besant, to refer to the after-death state, explained in detail in *A Dweller on Two Planets.* This usage of the term in the Theosophical context indicates some familiarity with the teachings of the Society, which was founded in the U.S. in 1875. Although most students of esoteric teaching know the names of the founders of the Theosophical Society, H. P. Blavatsky and Henry Olcott, they are less likely to know that the vice-president of the Society was Abner Doubleday, the man often credited with inventing the modern form of baseball. Theosophy in the 1880's was often a hobby of the educated and wealthy classes in American and European intellectual life during what might be called the "Orientalist period." It is up to the judgement of history as to how much of "The Mikado" is present in the Liberal Catholic Church, C. W. Leadbetter's contribution to Theosophy.

In Chapter VII of Book II in *A Dweller on Two Planets,* the following teaching is attributed to Phyris –

> "When Man was born into the Earth from Mars, as he is eventually to be born from the Earth into Hesper, that was the basis for the allegory of Adam and Eve, but back of them came all their lesser brethren, the animals of land, sea, and air. And back of the race birth were the race lives on Mars, and ere then lives on two planets, neither of which are of matter which the Earthly eye can perceive. There is in them now no life process, for these world souls are resting, and so also is Mars. Thus have I spoken of four of the seven planets to which the human race makes cyclic visits, going from One to Two, to Three, to Four, (which is the Earth), to Five (Hesper), to the one which Man will go after his years on Hesper, and thence to the Seventh or Sabbatic world. These two last, like the two first, are imperceptible to the eyes of Man on Earth. Seven are the worlds, and seven times

the race of Man circles them; three times already hath Man circled the series and arrived en masse at the fourth of the number on this, his fourth Round."

Sections 899 through 902 of *An Earth Dweller's Return* contain the following text –

"The centuries which lapsed told of the Eocene period, and how it aged, became extinct and was followed by the Miocene period. By the middle of this latter period, the last of the Lemurians ceased to be. Cavemen outnumbered them with a Devachanic majority. Other lands emerged from the ocean's depths, and the remnant sank in equilibrium. Man, savage and animal like - the rear of the great human army - came into being, while the vanguard of these civilized Lemurians lingered in the lethal shades of the passive life. Thus was ushered in the Great Fourth Root Race of mankind - the Atlanteans. Far back in the night of time, almost three million years ago, the Third Race had been introduced to earth. The Second Race had perished by waters before. In the old Azoic rocks, we can still see the igneous remnants of the First Root Race of man in his Fourth Round on this earth."

These passages are obviously the expression of doctrines found in Theosophy, and some Theosophists like Geoffrey Hodson have made an entire career out of explaining the theories of the Root Races and the Rounds. Skeptical commentators have suggested that Fred Oliver took this information from some Theosophical work. However, there is another cogent explanation, that the Indo-Tibetan masters who inspired Theosophy were members of the same Brotherhood to which the adepts of Mt. Shasta belong, and they all espouse essentially the same philosophy. Mother Mary called them the "The Brothers." Alice A. Bailey suggested that the correct translation into English of one of the names for this Brotherhood is the phrase "The Society of Organized and Illumined Minds." Further information about the planets or states of consciousness to which humanity evolves can be found in Chapter 43 of *Autobiography of a Yogi* by Yogananda entitled "The Resurrection of Sri Yukteshwar." One may compare this text with the description of Hesper or Venus in *A Dweller on Two Planets.*

Members of The Order in the 1920's and 30's were mostly Bible students from the Santa Barbara area and may or may not have been familiar with Theosophical teachings or writers such as Blavatsky or A. A. Bailey, but they were certainly aware of Annie Besant, who lived for a time nearby in Ojai, as did several members of The Order. Lady Mae herself had a very well-thumbed copy of *Isis Unveiled* by H. P. Blavatsky which she left behind at the time of her death full of little bookmarks. Her public statements often contained references to the coming Seventh Root Race of mankind, the establishment of which she considered to be the goal of evolution to which the effort of the adepts is dedicated.

Chapter Three of Book II of *"Dweller on Two Planets"* contains the following paragraph, an excerpt from a longer presentation about Walter Pierson's visit to the retreat inside Mt. Shasta –

"Mendocus, Master, now perceived that the lurid glow of the atmosphere had been neutralized by the light of the blue sphere, which, full twelve inches through, rested motionless in completion, its glorious, radiant center of entrancing loveliness. He raised his hand slightly, as if giving an unspoken command. Upon this the sphere of light rose to perhaps eight feet from the floor, where it hung without visible means of support. Again the hand waved in command, and the sphere moved horizontally over our heads to a point about fifteen feet from the center of the chamber. Here it was permitted to remain. Although everyone present was intuitively aware of all that was about to occur, I will describe every incident for the benefit of my readers. Following the blue light came a sphere of intense indigo color upon the brazier, its process the same as that of its predecessor, and when complete it was assigned position thirteen feet from its neighbor, on the same eight-foot plane. Next came a sphere of violet, of equally intense brilliancy, differing only in color, not size. Then followed a globe of pure red, then one of orange, another of pure yellow, and lastly one of glorious green. Every one was at the same height from the floor, and equidistant, approximately, from its neighbors. Any attempt at describing the extreme beauty of these iris-hued spheres would indeed be futile, as they hung motionless, above our heads.

Anyone who is well versed in the subject of "The Seven Rays" from the works of Alice A. Bailey will immediately recognize these spheres of light as being the energy of the Seven Rays. It is instructive to note that when the Masters teach their initiates the reality of the Seven Rays, they do not require their students to read Alice A. Bailey's five volumes on the subject, but simply show them the energy itself, and leave it up to the initiate's own soul or consciousness to fit it all together. During my years of involvement in Bailey study groups, I was once asked, "What is the method by which we can learn to see the Seven Rays." I answered, "Love. If you study the written material on the Rays, you will see those qualities first in your loved ones. The Rays will reveal themselves to you in the character of those you love." The person to whom I gave this advice didn't really understand it, and I perceived that she had read too many books.

One belief which people connected to Phylos have in common with at least some of the Theosophical community, such as Alice A. Bailey, Cyril Scott and David Anrias, as well as the followers of Yogananda, is that they regard the Master Jesus, and his disciple Beloved John, to be alive and present in the world, incognito, today. Al Jennings, a student of the Edgar Cayce material who was interested in healing, was present at The Inn when Jesus came to the back door of the kitchen and asked Mother Mary for food, just as he had done with Nola Van Valer many years before. Mother Mary invited him in, sat him at a table with Al, and served them both dinner. In the 1960's Mother Mary said that Beloved John, a man of color, had spent many years in a cave in Hawaii, and had recently returned to the mainland to undertake a work to further the establishment of the New Age, and was working with a small Indian tribe in Nevada. According to Mother Mary, Beloved John has a close relationship with the White Indians, who have a special role to play in the founding of the New Age. She predicted that Beloved John will lead some of the White Indians from their hidden city to the United States, but they will not be welcomed by mainstream American society.

There is a saying in Buddhism, "If the Buddha had been born in China, he would have had a goatee." That is to say, the spiritual adepts accept the customs of the culture in which they live. Nola, her family, and the members of The Order of Directive Biblical Philosophy were all Bible students, and Phylos used the scripture most familiar to them to present the truths which he sought to impart. When such adepts teach Tibetans, they quote from the Buddhist scriptures and when they teach Hindus, they quote from the

Bhagavad Gita. Indeed, this is one of the lessons of *A Dweller on Two Planets*. Few people today know that in the time of Jesus, Samaritans were reviled by the Judeans as inferiors, and the Bible story of "The Good Samaritan" was a slap in the face to this prejudice. Similarly, in the days of *A Dweller on Two Planets* the Chinese were reviled by whites in California and American society in general, and to cast the character who led Walter Pierson inside Mt. Shasta as a Chinese railway worker, Quong, was a deliberate slap to the prejudices of that era. Although these teachings of The Order are presented in Christian terms, they should not be regarded as belonging only to a Christian point of view, but have a universal character which could be expressed in any religious tradition with a little bit of re-phrasing.

In 1962, Lady Mae said that the work of Fred Oliver was almost finished. Much of it had already come to pass. By this she meant in part that many of the scientific inventions predicted by Phylos had already been developed. For instance, in the 1880's, Phylos said that there would be a musical instrument created which would be played simply by passing the hands over it. This instrument is the theramin, used by the Beach Boys and the television show "Dr. Who." It was invented by the Russian scientist Lev Theramin, sometimes anglicized to Leon Theramin or Theremin, less than 30 years after the prophecy. Theramin was later taken from New York City by Stalinist agents, and was forced to serve the interests of the Soviet state, who gave him his own laboratory. Although in the West it has been assumed that Theramin was kidnapped, in a 1989 interview with the French musicologist Olivia Mattis, Theramin stated that he returned to the USSR voluntarily and referred to his years in the United States as "an assignment." Theramin invented the cavity microphone imbedded in the wooden Great Seal of the United States which was given to the American ambassador in Moscow by Russian schoolchildren and discovered to be a bugging device in 1952. In 1960 it was held up to the United Nations by the U.S. Ambassador Henry Cabot Lodge as an example of Soviet espionage and duplicity. The device was based on an harmonic electronic technology previously unknown to western academic science, but which is implied by Phylos' physics. Anyone interested in the science of Phylos would be well advised to investigate the work of both Theramin and Nikola Tesla, whose knowledge of gravity and electromagnetic harmonics was highly unusual and similar to the teachings of Phylos. Another invention predicted in Oliver's text more than a century ago was a mechanism which would produce a hard-copy print-out simply by speaking into a microphone. Thanks to modern speech-recognition programs, this device now exists. Mother Mary specifically stated that a hidden purpose of *A Dweller on Two Planets* and *Atlantis Speaks Again* was to re-awaken reincarnated Atlantean scientists to their ancient knowledge.

Mother Mary never resolved what was to be done with the numerological information given to her by Maud Falconer. She was told by Phylos to train only one person in this method, and did partially train one, but he went his own way. She referred to it as the numerological system of the Brothers of Solitude in Atlantis. It was very important to her, and she herself practiced the system privately, without revealing its existence to the public, except for a few cryptic references in *Atlantis Speaks Again*. As one by one the members of The Order of Directive Biblical Philosophy passed away, the method seems to have died with them. Enough is given here for an overview, but those who were proficient in this system practiced it with a level of detail and precision which is not possible for someone who has not been specifically trained in it by a competent user.

Lady Mae held the opinion that when mathematicians could solve the formula left out of *A Dweller on Two Planets* they would leave the maths of modern science behind and adopt this system left from the Brothers of Solitude. What she meant by such a statement is unclear, but this belief may have a simple explanation. Perhaps the number system of Atlantis was base-12. The current decimal form of arithmetic and the binary form of computer language are by no means the only possible number systems. Algebra, calculus and every other form of modern mathematics are not the only possible maths. Indeed, there are innumerable possible maths. Perhaps if the Atlantean math was founded on a base-12 arithmetic it led to certain discoveries which modern man has yet to achieve. The Antikythera mechanism and recently discovered texts from Archimedes demonstrate that the ancient Greeks, who gave us the word "Atlantis," were far more sophisticated both in mathematics and technology than has been commonly accepted. The technical achievement of the Antikythera mechanism was not duplicated in human society for another 2,000 years after it was lost, until Swiss clocks of the 19th century. Who knows what minds like Archimedes may have lived in ancient civilizations now lost?

Every few years, the scientific community issues a promissory note which assures us that the solution to the fundamental mysteries of nature will soon be found. In reality, many scientists are comfortable with the paychecks generated by the fossil fuel industry, or employment in creating some of the over 900 compounds which populate the California Proposition 65 list of toxic chemicals, or producing genetically modified organisms with unknown effect on the biosphere, privatizing the profits and socializing the consequences. Indeed, the standard scientific response to any charge of culpability for the extremely negative effect their toxic chemicals or radioactive contamination have had on Mother Earth is to sing a refrain of "I'm not responsible for the application, I just do the research." Richard Feynman was speaking for many scientists and engineers in the military/industrial complex when he remarked that "a powerful sense of social irresponsibility" had made him "a very happy man." Modern society is marked by much science, and little conscience. History will show that the ancient belief that animals, plants, rocks, and humans have souls is far less dangerous to our planet than the belief that they do not. Global warming is the legacy of the mechanistic paradigm.

Science at the present time has no model or theory of consciousness, despite the colorful MRI's produced by neurobiologists. The rule of scientific certainty (as opposed to the quantum rule of uncertainty) is that the results of scientific investigation will be determined by who's paying for the project. Einstein had a certain disdain for the field of quantum physics, which relies on a statistical analysis of random sub-atomic events. His famous dismissive comment was, "God does not play dice with the universe." The very assumption of randomness in quantum phenomena itself may be false. One of the current theories of sub-atomic phenomena, string theory, posits multiple material dimensions, and events which seem random in the dimension in which they are measured or observed may actually be orderly across all the dimensions in which they occur, unrecognized by today's quantum physicists. The mechanistic paradigm of modern science and its quantitative method are like an old joke. A drunk stumbles out of a bar after heavy drinking one night and loses his keys on the ground. As he's looking around under a streetlight for them, his friend comes out and offers help with the search. His friend asks, "Where did you lose your keys?" The drunk replies, "I lost them down the street." His friend says, "Then why are you looking under the streetlamp?" The drunk replies,

"There's more light here." Science has done well in fields which are easily quantified, but in areas where quantification is elusive, like the study of consciousness or intelligence, there have been few results.

Based on the information given by members of The Order of Directive Biblical Philosophy found below in the writings on "The Meanings of Numbers," my own suggestion for the interpretation of the Phylos formula, **26 : 17 :: 25.8 + 30 : 24,** is based on a teaching found in *An Earth Dweller's Return,* which is, "Will is the fiat of consciousness." The use of the term "Interpretation" does not necessarily mean "Solution," which is probably numerological. Some of the meanings of the numbers used in the formula are given by Mary Mae Maier and Lillian Bense as follows –

> 26 - Rule or Ruin, Rulership, Rule Yourself
> 17 - Spiritual Sources, "Look to the Highest," "The Tree of Life"
> 25 - A spiritual number under the Law of Motive
> 8 - Learn to choose, make a choice
> 30 - Finality, Completion, "Goodbye to the Old"
> 24 - "The Crown of Life," Comprehension of All Things

Based on these values, it is possible to see a certain pattern in the meanings represented or symbolized by the numbers, which is consistent with the teaching on Will. In her essay, "Let There Be Light" Lillian Bense gives the following significance for the number 25 - "Reciprocal dealings are to be made into new conditions by each individual from universal sources on the material and physical plane." In the formula, it is the ".8" which defies conventional logic, but I believe that it should be interpreted as indicating an eighth degree of the number 25 signifying choice. The number 25.8 would therefore denote, "choosing to live in the world with spiritual motives." It should be noted that the number 26 is an 8 as well, and that "Rule or Ruin" is an aspect of Will indicating choice. "Rule or Ruin," or "Triumph or Failure," indicates the consequences of one's choices in meeting opportunities. It could be rendered as "Overcoming Self." The number 17 is also an 8, and in this context it signifies that spiritual consciousness is the result of right choices. So, my interpretation of this formula is as follows –

"As following Divine Will (26) is to the attainment of Spiritual Consciousness (17), so is choosing to live ethically in the world with spiritual motives (25.8), and leaving the past behind (30), to Spiritual Realization (24)." A plain text statement of the same teaching would be, "Spiritual Consciousness is attained through overcoming self and following Divine Will. Spiritual Realization may be accomplished by living in the world with spiritual motives, making ethical choices, and leaving the conditioning of the past behind." Another version following the logic of the math formula would be "Will is to consciousness as ethical conduct and spontaneous awareness is to illumination." It is essentially a statement denoting the importance of ethical living as a significant factor in Spiritual Illumination.

The Sufis have a saying, "When a pickpocket looks at a saint, all he can see is his pockets." In other words, one's perceptions are determined by one's character. Indeed, character is the measure of one's place on the spiritual path. Life constantly presents us with ethical choices, and how we respond to them is the factor that unfolds character and consciousness itself. Individual conscience is a far more robust practice of meditation than any system of breathing practices or mantras, and it doesn't require adherence to any dogma. Conscience is the basis of the spiritual precepts right speech, right conduct and right livelihood, and spiritual practice without these qualities is adrift.

ENOCH'S THRONE BLOCK
Notes on the Number System by Mother Mary in Atlantis Speaks Again

In the days of Atlantis the Brothers of Solitude realized the system of numbers called Enoch's Throne Block, which was mentioned by Phylos in *A Dweller on Two Planets.* At that time they knew the System had to be taken away from the race of Atlantis because it was misused. They sought to preserve it for the future use of humanity, to give humanity a chance again. The returned Atlanteans and others will have the opportunity to use the system. The Number System for Atlantis is not as the use of numbers today. The page erroneously omitted from *A Dweller on Two Planets* is on page 176 of this book *(Atlantis Speaks Again.)* The mathematical system of numbers shown on the page omitted from *A Dweller on Two Planets* at the time it was first published, and never included in succeeding editions, is known as Enoch's Throne Block. This system is usable as a frame of reference in revealing the thought processes of mankind. The columns of the Throne Block are referred to as the Pillars of Enoch, for he is said to have walked with God. A pillar, in this sense, is a support for the columns of the Throne Block to commemorate Enoch's abiding faith in God. One should refer to Genesis 5:18 to learn that Enoch was in the line of generation from Adam, Seth, Enos, Cainan, Mahalaleel, Jared and Enoch. The Gospel of Luke, in 3:38, brings out that Enoch was seventh in the line of generation: also, in Hebrews 11:5, we learn that Enoch was translated from the earth plane and did not die like an ordinary man. Those known as the Sons of God who walked the earth during the last Aquarian Age were, from the present-day standpoint, giants in stature.

A vast change is expected to take place in world affairs and business procedure will be put on a reliable basis again in the matter of placing uses. However, that cannot be brought about unless the five physical senses are much better developed than they are at the present time, the interior senses adequately unfolded, and the word of action and its laws known and used. Motives under cosmic law will follow the same precepts that Jesus enunciated when he walked among us.

In years to come ethics, and not religion, will rule life in all its actions and phases, for ethics comprise the comprehension of uses in all things. Ethics are of the Fifth Degree, manifesting the word of power over uses throughout all interrelationships. That is the reason why it is necessary for discrimination to be exercised through ethical values and not through religion. Religion is manifested by the Ninth Degree word of power, with the power of the word over self, and not over human relationships. Under that condition, religion may move a nation to war, such as when an individual's makeup is so strong as to place the imprint of his beliefs upon a nation. This is exemplified by the creeds and doctrines of this age wherein the atmosphere of life causes dissention and war.

THE ETHICAL VIBRATION OF NUMBERS
from many different entries in Mother Mary's notebooks

0 - Creator of all things, Cosmic Law

1 - Direction, Loyalty, Attention, Order, Obedience to cosmic law, "The Leader," Overcoming

2 - Word of Power, Will Power, The Builder, Determination, One's Possessions

3 - Ongoing Fellowships, Interrelationships, Friends, Activities, Business, Religion, Science

4 - Man, Home, Country, Shelter, One's Interests, One's Character, Achievements, Earthly Environment, Desire

5 - Motive, Education, Intelligence, Faculties, Poise, Mercurial, Pivotal

6 - Uses, Work, Beauty, Health, Hygiene, Food, Labor, Commerce, Common Sense, Necessities, always the symbol of the Word of Action, Imagination, Thought of the highest order

7 - Inner senses leading to spiritual telepathy, Balance, Love, Finance, Harmony, Justice, Equity, Law, Contract, Covenant, Wedding, Divorce, Art, Music, Contact, Promise, Compromise

8 - Life and Death, Motive to Cooperate, Misery, Old age and death, Real Estate, Power of Discrimination, Duality of Thought under Unity, Reciprocity, a comfortable state of existence. Careful of throat and generative organs, Land

9 - Defense, Spiritual Energy, Religious Beliefs, Travel, Transportation, Wisdom, Construction or Destruction, Effort, Joy, Love, Hate, Warmth, War, Violence. Take care of feet.

10 - Ongoing new condition, Right Covenant, Honors

11 - Universal flow for everybody, the Way to the Heavenly Father, Elections, Public Life

12 - Material Plane, Man's interests in earthly things

13 - Summary

14 - the Symbol of the Movement of Life, God moves

15 - Scientific and mental activity, Work

16 - Power, great good if the use is right, otherwise not

17 - Spiritual Sources, Interest in man's spiritual motives, the source of spiritually directed thought and motivation, "Look to the Highest," the Tree of Life

18 - Eliminate evil by charming with the good. Civility. Man must keep his eye on 18.

19 - Mansion of the soul, Wisdom, Holding up the Light

20 - Past experiences

21 - Ongoing through past experiences

22 - Communication

23 - Opportunity for an individual

24 - The Crown of Life, Comprehension of All Things, Creative all-round progress

25 - Business number, also a spiritual number under the law of motive

26 - Rule or Ruin, Rulership

27 - Spiritual Recognition, Realization from on High

28 - Overcoming obstacles to make a new condition

29 - Building Mansion, Use your ingenuity

30 - Ongoing in the new, Finality, completion, "Goodbye to the Old"

31 - Personal Responsibility, Self-reliance

32 - Opportunity for the public

33 - Brilliance of thought and action, Division of thought and action, Soul Problems, Conscious thought, action, and uses, action in good uses

34 - Scientific, Material Science

35 - "Penetralia" - means the center of all

36 - Symbol of Joy

37 - The ethical value of obedience to Cosmic Law

38 -

39 - The Key of David

40 - Comes to an awakening, Awakening of Consciousness, the Voice of Conscience

41 - Strength, Courage

42 -

43

44

45 - 45 is its own word and law, symphonic

46 - Relativity of Thought, Teaches the word of new condition, new government

47 - Universal Values, Material Rules, Right Motives, Direction for Universal Good

48 - Comprehension

49 - Resource

50 -

51 - Common Sense

52

53

54 - Full and complete consciousness of what we are doing

55 - Creative

56

57

58

59 - Life and Movement

60 - A standard number, 60 will be the measurement of the New Age

61

62 - Discernment. 62 is a holy number.

63

64

65

66

67 -

68 - A number of the movement of life

69

70 - "Ye who follow Me"

71

72

73

74

75 - Word of Power

3. ATLANTIS SPEAKES AGAIN

Mother Mary, with some help from Henry Fuller, printed *Atlantis Speaks Again* in Henry's printshop with her own hands. There were exactly 333 copies bound and numbered by her. She intended these books to reach the ones who would or could respond to her note, and took out advertisements in *Fate* magazine to promote it. Most of the copies were given away and not sold, however. In a comment that revealed her own ideas about the book, she once said, "You don't even have to learn how to meditate. Just go to *Atlantis Speaks Again*, open it up, and you'll find what you need to know. I put a different 'jolt' into each copy. You should keep a pencil and paper with you when you read it. Some things will appear in it between the lines, and you'll never see it again. Write down what appears to you and you'll get direction in your Work."

Much of the material for *Atlantis Speaks Again* comes from The Order of Directive Biblical Philosophy, like the material for *An Earth Dweller's Return* published by Dr. Zitko, but some also comes from Mother Mary's own notebooks. She had a habit of buying a notebook, writing in a few pages of it, setting it aside and going on to the next one. She would write a thought down, but once it was written she seemed to just let it go. The formation of a thought was important to her, but she usually didn't organize the scattered ideas into any narrative or philosophy.

One of the motives behind the book was to correct certain mistakes in the published version of *A Dweller on Two Planets.* One of these was the omission of the mathematical formula from the first edition, and another was the teachings on "twin souls" and "the dividing of the way," both of which were said by Mother Mary to have been inaccurately re-written from the original version of Phylos' manuscript when Fred Oliver succumbed to pressure from friends, especially "Mrs. A. E. P.," who wanted these things presented in a different light. Mother Mary considered *Atlantis Speaks Again* to be the third and final book in the series begun by Fred Oliver under the impression of Phylos. She specifically stated that the book should not be reprinted in its entirety, but excerpts of it which show the essential teachings are presented here.

Some teachings presented in *Atlantis Speaks Again* are found in Mother Mary's notebooks, and most of the rest come from The Order of Directive Biblical Philosophy and perhaps the unpublished manuscripts of Fred Oliver. The members of The Order attributed most of the teachings of their study group to Phylos, Holtah, and the other adepts from the retreat inside Mt. Shasta who they referred to as "the Order of Azariah." It is left to the reader's own discernment to ascertain the measure of truth in this material, with no special claim for its origin. If it is true and worthwhile, it makes no difference where it came from.

56

RESPONSIBILITY

Every evil serves to bind us to matter so much the longer.

Death is only a laying aside of the gross materiality, but gross mentality endures for aeons.

It is mercy to exact the utmost tithe of expiation, in order that the sin may not be repeated.

Verily what evil we do here shall follow us as our Nemesis through many weary ages.

In retributive Justice there is nothing unjust. The penalty is not inflicted by any but ourselves. No job of evil ever dies of itself. It pursues us as a shadow.

Error is an active agent. Like a stone cast in a mirror-surfaced pond, it destroys the images reflected.

In every kind act or deed done we are atoning for sins committed here or long ago.

THOUGHT

All organized thoughts are actions and tend to build up a material counterpart of themselves.

To the Soul there is no hindrance in communion of Soul to Soul exercised by space.

The thoughts of one may be transmitted to another, provided a sympathy has been set up between them. High souls work in unison, and spatial distance is no bar. If one is in trouble, its call for help is heard. If a soul be high and pure, its psychic vibrations are higher, and its effects are seconded by all on its plane.

The first great Law is Order. The next is Harmony, while together the two are subservient to the great Nature which is good in all.

A thought is a creation. It is more; it is a power more or less potent for good or evil. Every thought has a definite shape, and is quite as material a body or substance as a bar of iron.

A thought affects not only man, but lower animals, and it is as much murder to kill a lower animal as to take a man's life.

A malignant thought can as truly wither the life of being as a knife, the only difference being that we cannot see the effect, not possessing that power.

It behooves us well to think no evil and then we shall not knowingly do any.

The Law tells us that Force travels in curves which return to themselves. Nothing is lost or wasted.

Energize material conditions with spirituality of thought. Thought, when directed aright, results in works, and there the Ego can take a step to advance.

EGO

The Ego is, in itself, equal to the whole of the universe.

The passive state of the free Ego is a union of all the conditions which it is possible to find in the Creation. The free Ego has no condition but All conditions.

Material conditions bind the ego to matter, and temporarily render it finite. All of the life that clings to the Ego is Magnetism. Life is hence finite.

Verily each Egoic One, conscious of being in harmony with the God-note, is a law unto itself.

The Egoic dweller of the body, being of the Celestial Plane of Being, and a Ray from God the All Knowing, knows all.

The Egoic Being is motivated by and from the Spiritual Plane of Being and its work is to transmute from lower to higher planes.

The Egoic Spirit Ray governs the Spiritual element and the Soul governs the physical element.

UNITS

All Nature is based upon the Law of Units.

The Unit of Color is Violet. The Unit of Sound occupies the same place to the Musical scale as Violet does to Color. Each Unit, of every class, is connected to the unit of Magnetism, which is the highest force in Nature.

The color of a plant is a sure indication as to its negative degree.

DIALOGUE

Every joy has its shadow and both joy and sorrow are something that you picture from Earth and in that State which is not Life.

Know that you Are. Trouble not whether you were, or will be, but be content with this "I Am." It is perfect.

Time is the law of the Creator, regulating the amount of energy to be devoted to any object whatever.

MAGNETISM

All vegetable life is of an opposite polarity to all animal life. During the day animals are positive, giving out that force, but receiving a negative flow. During the day plants are negative, parting with force of that polarity, and receiving positive magnetism discharged by the animal world.

"Being" is of the Ego purely, but Magnetism is one of the conditions of Being and Spirit, manifesting itself in an active state, as Life.

When we cut loose from Magnetism, we are free from condition, and have no "life" but only the Being which is, was, and shall be. Magnetism, then, is condition. Condition is force. Force is material.

Life embraces all things material, is all things material.

Life has various degrees of force imparted by the Spirit, and according to these differing degrees is more or less solid.

Things material are counterparts of things Spiritual. As is the Spirit, so is the life.

The highest degree of magnetism is intelligent Life, equal to all other degrees; being equal, it comprehends them.

All things in the Universe which are not incarnations of the Ego, are Magnetism.

Magnetism ranges from the highest degree, where it is so active that no sense can perceive it, to the lowest condition of activity. Magnetism manifests itself through vibration. Magnetism is light. It is heat. It is Life which is both heat and light. It is power, but it is bound by conditions.

The highest vibratory Speed is beyond the region of light, and heat, far out in the region of cold, so intense as to be immeasurable.

A stone is a low form of Magnetism, or life, a tree a higher form, dominated by an Ego, and so on through out this life.

The positive currents flow to the negative pole. That is the highest.

To produce heat from cold is to call into operation a law which makes the will master of nature.

Whenever hot things become cold, it is but in obedience to natural law which tends to keep things as they were created, i.e., in their natural order.

In nature nothing is ever lost. Magnetic unlikes attract, which is the law of Duality in operation. Equal quantities of opposites attract each other. Equal quantities of "likes" repel, destroy.

The negative pole is equal to the positive pole. Neither exceeds the other. Therefore, everything is provided with a natural affinity.

A perfect union is in accordance with Law. When the union is affected, action ceases.

Disease is a magnetic inharmony. When by our actions we disregard any law, we disregard Truth Order. The worse the disease, the greater the magnetic inharmony.

Insanity is not a trouble of the Spirit, but of the organ through which it manifests itself We can conquer all disease, by rigid observance of Law, through the non-observance of which the disturbance arose.

He who would perfectly see all there is in Magnetism would see the Universe in its whole.

THE DEEP THINGS OF LIFE

The most beautiful and the most wonderful thing there is in the whole world is the smile of a little child in its sweet innocence and play.

To enter the Kingdom of Heaven, that place where all things are balanced, we must become as little children. The only creed we need is the art of being kind. The only tenet should be our Accountability to God.

"Isms" are of the mentality, and are motivated by mentality, so they are illusions of the mind, and will pass away. "Believe" is of the Soul element and "a belief" is of the body element. That which is of the Spirit, Knows.

It is from the Spirit and through the Spirit that there is true motivation of action.

Seek for the Key that will open the door of the Citadel of Knowledge wherein you will find peace for your own soul.

We must learn that naught passes current but that which has a spiritual value. We must learn how to transmute physical, material, and mental values into spiritual values.

Fail not to help a brother or sister, whatever the call may be, else there will be a lack that will give spiritual nudity when we reach the Beyond. There is not a smile given, a kind deed done even to the least, but what is transmuted into spiritual coin for the giver and laid up for him when he reaches the Holy City.

We came from God, we are accountable to Him. We must go back to Him sometime, that is inevitable.

We must find the Way to reach the "Mountain Citadel" of our lives in order to understand just what He wants of us. The way to the Citadel is straight up the mountain side, the path is steep and rugged, few there are that find it. The Mountain Citadel contains all wonderful knowledge, where you can find out just What you want to Know.

The "Measure of a Man" means the capacity of understanding, or perception the man may have of the Truth.

It is to differentiate between enthusiasm and spiritual energy, that we must bend our steps toward the Mountain Citadel. There is no need of light in that Citadel for it is Light, it is you, your spirit.

We must know the laws of each part of our five-part being. The five parts of life on the earth plane are Ethical, Sexual, Mental, Physical, and Electrical.

One of the greatest problems of life is to be conscious of life on the four planes of Being, while in the Physical life.

The Citadel of Life is four square. It is where the Ego must live, move, and have being, clothed with Spirituality of Thought.

You cannot thirst in the physical when in the Citadel of your life.

THE DEEP THINGS OF GOD

The time has come for the people to find the Short Cut road to the Mountain Citadel of their lives. As you climb on the path to the Mountaintop you will find nothing but Truths that others have gleaned from communion with God.

Each time you stop to help another or show the Way it makes your own climbing easier.

All the time you are climbing, you are also building your Citadel with Spiritual material, and while still in the flesh.

We must return to purity of heart in order to reach the Mountain Citadel of our lives. Only upon the Mountaintop and in the real Citadel can we drink of the Water of Life or know how to sing the New Song.

The Father of All rules and we must accept His plans, His worlds, His Universe, and His Infiniverse.

The Kingdom of Heaven is the Celestial Plane of Life and Being. This is where the children belong.

Mountain means a place of thought where you can divide thought and discriminate as to thought.

MASTER THOUGHTS

Every thought, whatever its nature, is a creation of a definite shape.

Until you do a good deed to counterbalance an error, the mistake will continue to live, dogging your steps as a shadow.

It is only by individual effort to right a wrong, that this poor world will ever grow brighter.

The finite cannot describe the Infinite, nor can natural man comprehend the nature of Spirit. None can make a physical illustration serve to describe either Soul or Spirit.

One of the Laws of God is that every being, man or animal, is responsible for errors in the degree to which the intelligence reaches.

To that degree of sin and malice to which we can fall, to the same degree of truth and goodness can we rise. But no further till an atonement be made.

Life itself is a game and its purpose is the goal.

Little children must have a purpose to be happy.

Happiness is within the grasp of everyone.

All should improve every opportunity to learn what is necessary.

THE QUESTIONER

To "be natural" is constructive, and being natural is being normal. Observation will help one be natural.

Those who can reason will learn the Truth by the reasoning faculty, and the Truth will enable one to be free.

To reason is to exercise the natural faculty. "Be still that I may reason with you before the Lord."

The soul of a word is the use to which it is put.

Know ye that ye are the Temple of God and His Spirit dwelleth in you.

We are they who keep His Law. And His Words of truth when spoken are felt throughout the Universe.

The things of the material plane are but externalizations of archetypes of things on the Mental planes, which in turn has its prototypes on the Spiritual plane.

If there is a lack of aught, it is because something is amiss on the mental plane or the Spiritual prototype is not understood.

Ignorance is a sin common to many. Knowledge is the wing with which we can fly to Heaven. It is better to acknowledge your ignorance than to be a vain pretender to knowledge, an Ignoramus.

If you understand the fine distinction there is in words, you will know what spirituality of thought really is.

The power of words is beyond ordinary comprehension.

Patience is an Angel spirit sent from heaven to bless mankind. Blessed are those who win her merit for Peace and Happiness they find.

Patience is a mental and physical characteristic. It has nothing to do with spirituality of thought or the Spirit.

The physical plane of Being has four degrees - physical, mental, spiritual and Egoic.

The physical plane contains all that we physically sense of the Universe or Infiniverse. That is all that is manifested to us and in which we manifest.

You must, while in the flesh, differentiate between what is mental and what is physical, between what is mental and what is spiritual, and what is spiritual or what is Egoic or Celestial.

All things are of Spirit Substance. That which is of matter is but a varying of the Specific Speed of Substance.

Motivation by the Spirit not only gives us spiritual power but gives us mental power and physical health.

62

GARDEN STORIES

We have traveled far when we seek to know the scientific cause of all things. When we know the scientific cause of all things, it will help us remove the effects of all that is troubling the world today.

Remember, each of us is a Voice, and yet, that which we voice is a thought of God or of evil. Our voice simply expresses what comes through our thought channels.

The sins of Omission and Commission, the scarlet and crimson sins, are weeds in the Garden of Life. The sins of Omission are scarlet, and caused by a lack of determination, Will, courage, and indifference to the needs of humanity. The sins of Commission are crimson, and are caused by intrigue, greed, graft, miserliness, seclusiveness at the close of life, etc. The sins of Commission vary greatly in intensity, owing to the magnetic vibration in which they occur.

People who are under the God Power are but channels of thought and Doers of God's will. We are but thought channels to be used for good in God's service, by Him, His Son, and their ministering angels.

That which is of God is of spiritual motivation, and is of Egoic nature, possessing spirituality of thought. Mentality motivated by spirituality of thought is powerful against all evil.

Not by might, nor by power, but by Spirit says the Lord of Hosts.

We must recognize the power of His Spirit if we would succeed in battling with evil.

All things have a psychic encasement as well as a physical one.

Faith is love exemplified. If you have faith, you love deeply.

The Spirit may only suggest to the Soul. The Soul may or may not choose to do what the Spirit suggests.

When life is motivated by spirituality of thought it is fuller, freer, and more abundant.

Fatigue is a poison to the mechanism of the body.

Reciprocity and mutual cooperation should be the slogan of everyone in order to do constructive work.

The Hierarchies of Heaven are making ready for the seventh Day of Civilization.

The great work of the New Age is the training of young children to unfold their seven senses.

We are near the threshold of a New Age that is to exemplify spiritual values and the unfolding and development of the seven senses.

All knowledge is conveyed through thought channels by Intelligence from other planes of thought. The intelligence furnishing or sending the thought may be on this plane of thought or one beyond this in one or more degrees.

The plight in which we find civilization is caused by the wrong interpretation of God's laws of life.

It is up to us to find the nucleus to that which will give us a real civilization for the future, through developing the senses.

Civilization must be rescued through Spirituality of thought.

Intellectuality must receive its motivating power through the Spirit.

The Spirit knows All, is All and motivates All things when the Soul allows it to be done.

The Will must be subservient to the Spirit in order that the Soul be aligned with the spirit to receive thought through spiritual channels.

The motivation of thought through spiritual channels is the only method to receive thought that is basic.

Seek to differentiate between that which is Spiritual and that which is Mental.

Wisdom is the Father, Understanding is the Mother and Knowledge is the Child.

Everyone must sometime return to God in the at-one-ment of Soul with Spirit.

If each would "seek the ultimate" and make new conditions wherein labor, beauty, sex, law and commerce would be equitably balanced, civilization could be saved. Understand how to "Seek the Ultimate," which is the slogan for the Cycle of Capricorn.

The Mentalism and Materialism of the Piscean Age must be transmuted into Spirituality of thought of the Aquarian Age.

The Zidatic Force is used by the Hierarchies of Heaven to create certain vibrations among certain people on earth. The Zidatic Force is felt by the developed sense of touch. It comes to us through Sympathy and Intent. By using the Zidatic Force we are able to improve ourselves physically, mentally and spirituality.

There is nothing to fear. Create happiness and joy wherever you are.

We must come into Universal Love in order to understand the truths of the Deep of Life.

Love is the holy feeling of life. It is what makes life. It is life. It is the bondage which binds Ego to Ego.

Love is nearest its Divine prototype when it embraces all life, from weakest insect to the highest but troubled man.

Feed the Soul through Inspiration and revelation.

Many have Faith. Knowledge has been won by a few. There is a Way, and a High Way. No fool shall err therein.

Every child of the Seventh Day that has faith will surely come into knowledge.

All things, thoughts, and spiritual aspirations have the life of God, the Spiritual Sun, and rays come forth as spiritual, mental and material vibrations.

Except a creature is attuned to the keynote of a vibration, upon a given plane, it cannot produce precipitation of the God-note of that plane.

Discords, sins and evils are false notes.

Do with all your might whatever the inward God-attuned Spirit commands.

Individuality evolves by fealty to harmony and to its own keynote. Be attuned to your Divine Keynote.

In the realm of the highest or spiritual vibration is Finding the Kingdom of Heaven, which when found gives all lesser things of mind-matter.

Each of the Divine Trinity varies in rate of vibration, marking degrees, and height of wave, marking intensity. The Divine Trinity are intermingled, where one is, the other two are there also.

Spiritual success begets mental and material success.

Motivation through mentalism is of least avail.

A selfish prayer cannot arrest a spiritual action, nor can a prayer for mercy make manifest a divine answer sounding forth justice.

We must thrust ourselves into the Universal Sea of Life and become at-one with Universal Thought.

As the man is, so is his strength.

Follow the urge of your spirit, for it leads to safety.

The sense of physical sight is the first sense, holding in a potential state the six others.

One of the works of this Great Cycle is for the people in general to come into possession of the seven senses.

Symbols are but emblems to us of that which is more important.

There must be reciprocity in all the relations of life in order to have the best results.

Appreciation of truth draws from the heights of Spirituality of Thought more truths in which one may revel.

The mistakes of Life are as stepping-stones to higher things.

Life is a game and all the world should be playmates, playing zestfully and joyously. Then life would be fair.

There is no death or decay, for decay is but a simple resolving into new forms of life.

The Lord, His watch o'er Israel keeps; He never slumbers, never sleeps.

Use your will power with the lever of the knowledge of Truth and Justice.

Religion is the highest ethical instinct of which one is capable that helps the individual to attain a state of mind that is at one with his development.

When one fails in a worthy mission, despite his earnest efforts, he is entitled to a reward be it eve so small a token.

Life itself is a game and purpose is the goal.

To be happy have a purpose in life. Happiness is in the grasp of everyone.

When we recognize that we are all expressions of the Creator, then all that we do or say will be ongoing, as is His Word.

The most important study is to Know Thyself.

Give Justice and equity.

Virtue is its own reward.

Heed the Still Small Voice.

We must know the Truth even at the sacrifice of our lives.

Peace on earth to men of Good Will.

We are not poets, writers, sculptors, artists, but Doers of invisible forces.

There is a psychic law: Where there is a demand, a supply is available.

It is a psychic law that what is necessary to be done will be done. It is up to us to find the way.

The use of everything is the Soul of it.

Labor will never reach its completion until Justice and Equity rule.

"Discrimination" is the gold of character and the problem that is to be solved by all people of earth.

The Divine Nature is the gift of God to the spiritual Egoic-man.

Tree of Life - meaning the Ongoing Force - is the continuity of life.

The Solar Plexus of the human body with the pneumo-gastric plexus and its branches is the Tree of Life.

Man must recognize the Path of his Beginning, its superb sweep in the Cycle of Life, its morning, its meridian, its afternoon, its sunset.

Man will rejoin and be united in Spirit with Soul at the end of the Path of his Return.

Man came into physical life to develop one or more of his seven senses on the physical plane.

In Man's former spiritual state he had seven senses, and it is expected he will develop them again in One Great Cyclic Day. The Cyclic Day of this present Great Cycle is drawing to its close.

It is difficult to brush aside pre-misconceived ideas.

Hope on, hope ever.

When the physical development keeps pace with spiritual development, the Egoic Spirit truly has a Temple.

The Seventh Sub-race has all the seven senses developed up to a certain degree.

There is no need of physical suffering if the law of the physical senses is understood and applied.

As God is Spirit, the soul must be at one with its own Spirit to become at one with God.

That which is lacking in Soul must be restored by God through the Spirit.

Woman stands for the Power with the Will to do. Man stands for the Intelligence with the Will to do. True marriage gives the best opportunities for returning Egos to work out their problems.

A true marriage recognizes spiritual values as well as the value of the five-part being.

True marital life will bring happiness and peace in the sunset of life.

Happy the heart where graces reign, where Love inspires the breast.

Love shall strike our joyful strings, in the sweetest realms of bliss.

Be ready to go forward to a bright new condition with a loved one.

Enjoy nothing that is not good. Feel perfection while Enjoying.

Love is an ever fixed mark that looks on tempests and is never shaken. It is a star to every wandering barque

One way to receive transcendental powers is by the Grace of God; another way is through the unfoldment of the senses.

Those thoughts which were created in the Universal Mind we must fulfill some time. We will have a body until those Thoughts become real. If our thoughts are spoken in words, it gives the thoughts the power of action.

The Egoic Spirit is the Knower of All Things for the good of its own Soul, Mind and Body. It directs the Soul through Suggestion, not through commands. It is the still small voice one hears. Sometimes one receives what are called "hunches." It is good to take notice of them.

The Soul is that part of Egoic Man whose province is to sense the use of things and to direct their use to Mind and Body so Mind and Body may be able to do their part in making the foursquare, Spirit, Soul, Mind and Body-Man.

The Spirit directs the Soul to choose for USE or ABUSE of the Mind and Body those things that are worthwhile or otherwise. The Spirit connects through the Soul with the Mind channels of the body and hence with each body cell. This it can quickly do, as it is keen and all-penetrating in its vibration throughout.

4. JAGADBANDHU

There are very, very few writings available in the English language regarding the life of the Bengali Avatar, Sri Sri Prabhu Jagadbandhu Sundar. Mother Mary brought back from Calcutta in 1951 two books and a few other papers. Another book, *The Life and Teachings of Sri Sri Prabhu Jagadbandhu* by Navadip Chandra Ghosh, was given in 1974 to Henry Fuller by U. C. Chakraborti, who knew that Henry had seen Jagadbandhu in Mother Mary's meditation room a number of years after Jagadbandhu left his body. Henry misplaced it until 1992, when he re-published a facsimile copy of it. Linden Carlton and Robert Williamson found the two books brought back from India after the death of Mother Mary in the trash which was to be thrown out when her room was cleaned, along with other materials which they carefully preserved. These two are *A Message of Hope* and *The Life of Prabhu Jagadbandhu* written about 1920 by Prafulla Kumar Sarkar. A pamphlet containing aphorisms of the avatar was found after the death of Henry Fuller among some letters Mother Mary sent from India. These three books and the pamphlet are primarily the source of the following biographical information.

Jagadbandhu was born on April 28, 1871 to a brahmin family at Dahapara on the river Bhagirathi, in what is now Bangladesh. His father was Dyanath Chakravarty Nyayaratna, a scholar of the *Nyaya* philosophy, and his mother was Bamadev. There are several versions of his birth, including one that he simply appeared on the riverbank, and was found by his mother, who had lost previous children in childbirth. Bamadev died before Jagadbandhu was one year old, after which he was cared for by his uncle Bhairav Babu and his aunt Rahamani Devi. Rahamani died when he was three years old, and he was then taken care of by his cousin Digambari Devi in the family's ancestral home at the town of Govindapur in the district of Faridpur. After his father Dyanath died when he was seven, his cousins Tarini Babu and Gopal Babu moved into the family home with Digambari Devi and the boy, and cared for them. When this family home was carried away in a flood, Jagadbandhu eventually moved with his cousins to Brahmankanda, a village just west of the town Faridpur. He attended High School in Faridpur, and later in Ranchi, where he learned English as well as the usual studies like mathematics and science.

From childhood, he showed a devotional nature and especially liked to sing *Kirtan,* or religious songs. His family deity was Radha Govindaji. After his brahmin "sacred thread" ceremony, he began to practice *Brahmacharya*, or the self-discipline and self-sacrifice of a spiritual student, and started to cover himself with a sheet of cloth, or *chaddor*. He spent much time alone in his room, and would only allow Digambari Devi to enter it. Jagadbandhu revealed his divinity for the first time to Srijut Dukhiram, who had a shop in the Faridpur Bazaar, and was a devotee of the goddess Durga. Jagadbandhu and his high school friends would sometimes have tea and sweets in his shop. Srijut was a poor man and did spiritual practices with the hope of improving his material condition. Much to his surprise, Jagadbandhu seemed to be able to read his mind and see the practices which he was doing privately, and told him that these practices would take him no further on the Path, as true aspiration could not be based on material desire. Srijut asked him how he could know this, and Jagadbandhu took the form of the *Shada Bhuja Murti*, the six-handed divinity who is a combination of Ramachandra, Sri

Krishna, and Gauranga. In two hands are the bow and arrow of Rama, in two others the bamboo flute of Krishna, and the last two have the staff and jar of Gauranga. Srijut became his first disciple. *Shada Bhuja Murti* symbolizes the teaching that the same divinity manifested to humanity through Rama, Krishna, and Gauranga, and that they should each and all be regarded as manifestations or externalizations of Vishnu, Creator and Preserver of the universe.

At about the age of sixteen, he gave up his studies and devoted himself to the spiritual life, often mixing with *Kirtan* groups of any caste, sometimes playing the *mridang,* a two-headed drum. His bearing was stately, and many local people were attracted to him as the embodiment of spiritual ideals, especially young boys who joined his *Kirtan* parties, which earned him some resentment from their families who considered him some sort of Pied Piper. On one occasion, he was brutally beaten, and when his disciples wanted to exact revenge, he said, "No one is to blame. More miseries and torments are in store for me, but no one will be able to take my life. I have not come to punish, but for the salvation of the world."

There was a Dervish in the town of Pabna named Haran Kshepa. He was one of the Great Ones in the disguise of a dirty fakir. He had *siddhis,* or spiritual powers, and could see the past and future, and he was also known to heal the sick. He did not observe caste distinctions or prejudice, and taught Hindus as a Hindu and Muslims as a Muslim. Jagadbandhu would come to Pabna to see him. The avatar taught his monks to never touch others, or to wear the clothes of others, but whenever Jagadbandhu greeted Haran Kshepa, he would hug him dearly and they occasionally would give one another some garment. Whatever rules Jagadbandhu enunciated, did not seem to apply to Haran Kshepa. Jagadbandhu said that Haran Kshepa was the Advaitacharya of Chaitanya *Lila* and that he was 400 years old.

Jagadbandhu began to speak out against the practice of initiation, and hereditary spiritual offices. He taught that the only practice necessary to the path was to speak the name of God, *Harinam.* He did not intend for this to be done as *japa*, or mantra-like repetition, but with simple sincerity. He encouraged his followers to sing the name of God through *Kirtan,* or devotional songs, and sent them out in the early hours of the morning before sunrise to do this in the street. A Zemindar of Pabna, Banamali Roy, heard of Jagadbandhu's *Kirtan* practice and sought to honor him by sending one of his household with an elephant to bring him back to his palace. After staying there for some days, Jagadbandhu went on a pilgrimage to Vrindavan, the birthplace of Sri Krishna. It was on this pilgrimage that the famous picture of him sitting cross-legged on a rug was taken, at the age of nineteen. He traveled as far away as the Punjab before returning to Bengal.

After his return, his followers constructed a cottage for him at Brahmankanda next to a pond. He planted trees known as *Pancha-vati*, or *Tulsi, Bel, Tamal* and *Haritaki*, and also vines from Vrindavan. Jagadbandhu lived alone in this cottage with his food provided by a few disciples. He dressed in a plain *dhoti* and often wore *chaddor*, or the covering of a simple white cloth. On some occasions, people fell into *samadhi* when looking at his skin, and he tried to keep himself covered to prevent this from happening. Some disciples left offerings for him, and he used this money to support orphans and homeless children. Many of his followers were boys, and himself was childlike in his love and concern for everyone. He taught those who followed him to cultivate the virtues of humility, abstinence, and self-discipline, but while he was very strict with the monks who lived in his ashram, he was very tolerant toward the householders, who must live in the world.

While living at Brahmankanda, Jagadbandhu happened to meet on the road an argumentative man named Chandra Guha, who saluted the avatar without removing his shoes, as would be the normal etiquette in such a situation in the polite Indian society of the time. One of Jagadbandhu's followers named Kedar Shaha, who was from a Hindu caste low on the ladder, was upset by this failure to show what he believed was the proper respect to the avatar, and said loudly that it was improper for Chandra Guha to salute the brahmin Jagadbandhu with his shoes on. Chandra became very angry when he was spoken to in such a manner by someone from a lower caste than himself, and he began to design a plan for revenge. When Kedar Shaha and another disciple, Kunja, were out singing *Kirtan* on the street, they passed by Chandra Guha's home. Chandra called them in, and suddenly struck Kedar with a wooden sandal, causing a bleeding wound. Kedar and Kunja fled, and went back to the ashram immediately. Jagadbandhu seemed to be waiting for them. He said, "How fortunate Kedar is! How fortunate is he today. All his sins have been expunged. I am really very worried for Chandra. Oh, what will be his fate?" Kedar and Kunja wanted to lodge a complaint with the police, but Jagadbandhu talked them out of it, and told them they should leave Chandra's fate to Karma. A few days later, Chandra Guha was almost beaten to death by thugs, and he was saved by a follower of Jagadbandhu. He became a disciple of the avatar, and eventually became a wandering fakir, practicing *Harinam*.

In 1899, Jagadbandhu moved to the present location of his ashram Sri Angan, which Mother Mary visited, in the Faridpur district at a place called Goalchamat. His followers built a thatched cottage for him, and two other cottages. In this place he finished his short book called the *Harikatha* composed in a highly Sanskritized Bengali, with many unknown words whose meanings can only be inferred by a study of their roots, with some notes supplied by the avatar. The book deals with Sri Krishna *Lila* and Chaitanya *Lila*. When his followers complained to him that they could not understand the text, his advice was, "This is the book of great salvation. Read it every day by placing it with reverence on its own stand. As you read it constantly, you will be able to understand it and you will feel immense joy. Those who have read the *Mahesha Vyakarna* will be able to understand. In time, I myself will explain it. Learn it by heart, and read it without interruption. By reading it, you will lose all sin and will become as white as snow." The *Mahesha Vyakarna* is the 14 sutras of Sanskrit sounds said to have been revealed by Shiva to Panini, in a very archaic form of the language, from the same era as the earliest *Upanishads*. In this myth of divine revelation, Shiva is said to have shown the very sounds of nature itself hidden in the phonemes of ancient Sanskrit, and this is the basis of the magical practice of *mantra*. In the earliest days of the Sanskrit language, it may have been a tonal language like modern Chinese. Remnants of three tones have been preserved in the chanting of the Vedas, but the original tonality was inflective and not musical, the modern intonation being only an echo of the past modulation. When Mother Mary visited Sri Angan, Jagadbandhu appeared to her and told her that the *Harikatha* contained the knowledge of the moon, and that sometime in the future she herself would present a commentary to the world which would explain some of its meanings.

One of Jagadbandhu's disciples was a man later known as Sri Sripad Sishuraj Mahendraji. When a young man, he had a vision that Krishna himself had been born in the world. He went into the forest looking for him, and became a destitute renunciate. Jagadbandhu appeared to him and told him how to find him at Sri Angan. It was a journey of 200 miles, and Mahendraji arrived at the ashram filthy and exhausted. The gatekeepers pushed him away from the gate, and he fell face first into the gutter, which was an open sewer. Inside the ashram, Jagadbandhu knew what had happened, and asked several small children who were playing near his hut to go outside and find Mahendraji, and to tell him that he would be admitted in the evening when the ashram fed all the local beggars. Jagadbandhu told the children that they must speak with Mahendraji because he was in such poor condition that he might not last until evening unless he knew he would be admitted. After he became part of the ashram, Mahendraji practiced traveling kirtan. He would walk the streets with his kirtan group, and used money which was given to them to support orphans and neglected children. Mahanam was a child who was given to Mahendraji by his parents who could not afford to keep him. Mahendraji became the head of the ashram after Jagadbandhu's death, and Mahanam succeeded him.

In 1901, while in Calcutta, Jagadbandhu took a vow of silence which he was to keep for more than seventeen years. He returned to Goalchamat and took up residence in a thatched hut with no windows at Sri Angan. Until 1911, he remained in the hut unseen, with a series of his disciples taking care of his needs, such as providing food by leaving it at the door, which he would take only after they were gone. In 1911, there was a period of 12 days in which he took no food, and the disciples broke the lock on the door and entered the room to check on him. The disciples prayed for him to eat again, and he began taking food once more. The disciples changed the lock on his door at this time, so that they could enter the room if needed. In 1913, he became very ill, and doctors were brought to help him. He refused treatment, but recovered 3 days later. In that year, his disciple Sishuraj Mahendraji took charge of caring for the avatar, and in 1918 he reappeared to the public. During the 17 years he remained in the hut, he emerged only twice, once in 1913 and once in 1916, during his birthday celebration in the ashram at the request of Mahendraji. During the years in seclusion, he would communicate with his disciples by notes, left at the door. Despite not leaving the hut, he seemed to know everything that was going on with his disciples' lives, and would give instructions or chastisements to them in his notes. His way of being was evidenced in little experiences, as when he would sometimes leave food untouched which was prepared in the ritual way for him by a proud brahmin, but would accept the simplest food offered in true devotion from a *dalit* or a Muslim. During these many years, he appeared to his disciples and others in dreams and visions.

In 1918, his disciples discovered him in very poor health, lying on the floor of his thatched cottage. Some of his followers organized a Kirtan party to pray for him, and he began to recover. He emerged from his hut naked, and mute. The disciples were overjoyed by his reappearance, and carried him in a chair to the home of one of his disciples, later returning to the ashram. In the following months, he began to speak again, just whispers at first. He seemed to be like a five-year old child, and his eyes did not seemed fixed on anything physical. Within a few weeks, as many as 500 people each day were coming to take *darshan* from him. He gave little direction to his followers verbally, but continued to appear to them in visions and dreams.

In 1920, he was given a rickshaw and his disciples used it to carry him outside the ashram. In September of 1921, while he was being carried to the rickshaw, the avatar fell to the floor of his hut, and his thigh suffered a compound fracture. Doctors set the bone, and he seemed otherwise undamaged. An herbalist came on the 13th of September and changed the bandage to an herbal dressing. In so doing, he twisted Jagadbandhu's leg and the compound fracture was greatly aggravated. The avatar cried out, but in the next three days, his mood became very serene. He died in a fever on the 17th of September, 1921.

SAYINGS OF JAGADBANDHU

Here are some of his teachings, published by his disciple, Ramesh Sharma -

In this dark iron age, sin is ripe and man wanders about under the influence of his destiny without turning his mind to truth and purity. When a man is possessed with the dark spirit of sin, he does not listen to good advice, and mistakes evil for good.

Live in peace. Be devoted to your own kin and have simplicity. Follow the ways of the world without recourse to sin. Man's life is not for sin. It is meant for devotion and culture. Walk in the path of purity. Your simple life means the success of my Mission of Liberation.

Always speak the truth, and never tell a lie, even if you are confronted with death.

Avoid adversely criticizing others like poison.

Animal sacrifice never promotes the prosperity of anyone. The end of the sacrificer is painful. Follow the path of harmlessness with the vigor of a lion. Do not hurt anybody.

Private conscience is a great virtue.

Man is apt to be carried away by sensational things. He loves commotion. Do not be carried away like this. Do not despair, but follow the path of universal love steadily, honestly and sincerely.

In this dark age of delusion, lust overtakes you all. This is the great "go" of this dirty world. Self-deception and betrayal prevail. You are to be very careful here.

Always take into consideration the elements of time, place and person.

Wine ruins a man.

Do not waste time.

Do not look upon women with alluring eyes. Delusion makes you forgetful of everything. Look upon everyone on earth as your kin. Be polite to all.

Self-preservation consists of self-control. The body can be preserved only by constant purity, discipline, and freedom from contact with anything evil.

Always entertain your brethren, friend, neighbors and kin, with truth, sympathy and purity, and never cherish quarrel or envy in your mind. Feed the hungry to the best of your power. Keep to the path of duty.

72

Go where the saints abide and avoid fickleness and excitability.

Do not go to evil places, do not see evil sights. No not touch evil things and take no evil food. Avoid bad society, bad taste, anger, the requests of evil persons, bad gifts and bad books, by all means. Do not indulge in envy and malice in churches and societies. Blaming others leads you astray. Honor all. Envy and malice are great sins.

Cultivate the habits of reading scriptures, kindness to animals, devotion to truth, and take light food. Maintain your dignity and never crave worldly pleasures.

Walk without fear. Think yourself alone in the world.

JAGADBANDHU AND MOTHER MARY

Mother Mary said on several occasions that Jagadbandhu witnessed the creation of this planet. That creation was flawed, like a miscarriage, and this flaw is the source of the terrible suffering which characterizes human civilization. Jagadbandhu saw this, and committed himself to the salvation of our world, those long eons ago.

No one can accurately describe the relationship between Mother Mary and Jagadbandhu. The devotees of Jagadbandhu, members of his ashram, refer to her as "a great devotee of Jagadbandhu" but this is due to their own devotional nature. Those of Jagadbandhu's ashram, being devotees themselves, see her also as a devotee. In America, is has been falsely reported that she started a "Shree Shree Provo" sect, based on a corruption of the name Sri Sri Prabhu Jagadbandhu, and that people who worked for her at The Inn were members of this sect. This is completely false. She rarely spoke of him, but when she did it was generally to share some teaching she had received from him telepathically or to tell a story from her life of some incident in which he had played a part.

For instance, she always wore an amulet or locket with a picture of Jagadbandhu around her neck on a mala, or necklace, made of dark wooden beads, and there is a story about how she came to have it. When she was speaking with Jagadbandhu's devotee Mahanam in Calcutta after her arrival in India in 1950, her eyes went to the mala around his neck with a small picture of the avatar on it. She knew that these necklaces were given for life, as blessings are given along with the mala, and carry special meaning to the one who wears it. She asked Jagadbandhu in her heart to give her one, and to give it to her without having to ask for it, as she also knew that it was not proper for her to ask anyone in the ashram for one. She kept this prayer silent.

At Sri Angan in Faridpur, Jagadbandhu's ashram, there was a young monk named Utpal Bandhu Bramachari who wore a unique necklace, and knew its origin. More than 50 years earlier, another young monk had been sitting with Jagadbandhu on a riverbank while the avatar meditated. Suddenly, the avatar got up, and making a comment as if he were renouncing the world, he ripped off his mala, his last possession, and threw it on the ground. The young monk picked up off the ground every bead, and had the beads re-strung along with a picture of Jagadbandhu in a locket. This necklace was passed down to Utpal.

When Mother Mary visited the ashram at Faridpur, Jagadbandhu appeared to her and gave her much confidential information about the ashram, as well as giving her the prophecy about the forest glen in the Himalayas which she would eventually find some months later.   On the same night Jagadbandhu appeared to Lady Mae, a young man in the ashram named Uttaran had a dream that someone should give Mother Mary a mala, and that it should be put around her neck. However, the only monk in the ashram with a mala was Mahanam, who refused to give his up and said, "I'm too selfish to do without mine." An eight-year-old boy who was in the room said that there was another monk in the town who had such a mala, Utpal, and Uttaran ran off to find him. Uttaran soon came back with Utpal and wished to be the one to put the locket on Mother Mary's neck. Utpal said, "No, it's my locket. I'll do it myself." When Utpal put the locket around Mother Mary's neck, he began to cry, because he knew what he was giving up. She began to cry as well, because Jagadbandhu had given her the locket in his own way, based on sacrifice, without her asking for it.

From at least 1944 on, she was in telepathic contact with him every day of her life. He called her "Mediki." As an example, she remarked that when she had been deeply troubled by the problem of knowing how to recognize those people who she could truly help, in contrast to those who would simply use her energy for their own selfish or egotistical ends, Jagadbandhu said to her telepathically, "Don't talk to the masses, they would not accept. Mediki, look for the bitter cup, overflowing, to the soul that needs help. Listen carefully, such a soul may have something to teach you. Allow those who have drunk from the bitter cup to come, ready to serve. Those who are ready will have drunk from the bitter cup of suffering and they will be the only ones who are trustworthy when the day of service comes."

He also told her that in her future work, she would suffer greatly, because wherever she saw evil, she would have to speak the truth and expose it, no matter what teacher or group was involved. He said to her, "You have demanded from the Creator that there should be no martyrdom on this planet for speaking the truth, and now you must live that." She remarked, "How I suffer, because I must speak the truth." She gave much thought to her third trip to India, which never happened, in this life at least. She planned to build a spiritual community in India which would be a prototype for the future work, based on her vision of spiritual people and the scientific community working in co-operation with one another, similar to the ideas presented in her essay *Before Our First Club Was Formed.* She spoke many times of how difficult it would be to again deal in India with those false swamis and priests who are motivated by egotism and selfishness, and she predicted that the third trip would require her to give up everything physical. But she could still make a joke of it all, and said, "I'll have to give up everything, and if I lose my robes, I'll just have to become a naked sadhu."

She said that sometimes Jagadbandhu spoke through her. This is not in the sense of trance or channeling, but refers to a process called "overshadowing." This process takes place when an enlightened soul voluntarily relinquishes control of the physical vehicle, but still observing with full consciousness from the inner planes, to a higher Being, so that some service may take place. Some esotericists maintain that Jesus had such a relationship with the Christ, a Divine Being who worked through the initiate Jesus. Anyone interested in researching that idea will find it scattered throughout the works of Alice A. Bailey and others of some Theosophical traditions. Similarly, Satya Sai Baba said three avatars worked through him to further the Divine Plan. Very much like Mother Mary, Satya Sai Baba told his disciples that they should not convert to Hinduism if they were born to another religion, that if they wish to follow his teachings they can do so by being good Christians, good Muslims, good Buddhists, or any other faith. All the real ones sound this universal message, and stress it is how you live, not what your beliefs are, that is the measure of a man. Jagadbandhu was a contemporary of the Bengali saint Sri Ramakrishna, who was the embodiment of religious unity. Since the time of Sri Ramakrishna, more and more people have understood that at the heart of every religion are the same fundamental teachings and ethical principals, yet in their dogmas, these same religions dissipate into disputation and enmity.

5. MOTHER MARY'S FIRST TRIP TO INDIA, 1950-1

The Sufi Hazrat Inayat Khan had two American disciples who were classically trained pianists named the Cleveland sisters. In the early 1950's, they lived in the Los Angeles area home of a Dr. George Ferguson, who was an old friend of Mother Mary and a member of the Hobby Clubs. One day the doctor called Mother Mary to tell her of a dream which he had, in which Jagadbandhu had appeared to him. He invited her to visit his home and to meet the sisters. She happily accepted the offer and stayed with them for ten days, regarding it as a chance to get away from it all.

The doctor told her that in the dream, Jagadbandhu planted a fruit tree, and watered it for 30 years. He stood over the tree and said, "Where are you? Where are you? Come out! I planted this tree for you." During these years, Jagadbandhu would say to devotees, "Come. Sit under her tree. If your answer is to be, a fruit will drop off and hit your head." The doctor dreamed that after many years, Mother Mary would come to sit under this tree upon the same rug Jagadbandhu had used for his own meditations. Monks and priests would bring her ancient manuscripts and lay them on low tables in front of her. One monk would read from the Sanskrit manuscripts to her. Later, when she visited the Jagadbandhu ashram in East Pakistan, she said that this scene from Dr. Ferguson's dream came to pass, sitting on the rug under the fruit tree with the manuscripts and low tables, and she became very reflective at that moment. She thought to herself, "I must plant a tree for Jagadbandhu," and at this very instant a fruit dropped off the tree and hit her on the head.

On the first night she stayed at the doctor's home, Inayat Khan, who was no longer alive, appeared to Lady Mae and made a prediction to her about her upcoming trip to India. In the middle of the night, she woke up and saw him standing over her. He told her that she would meet Jagadbandhu, as he had done, and that she would be transformed, as he himself had been when he had been called to Jagadbandhu. Inayat Khan told her that in India she would learn of the ancient and modern Sufis who have been with humanity since its most ancient beginnings, and that this knowledge was for the future work. He further gave her certain information to be relayed to his son Pir Vilayat about the disposition of teachings which had been buried in a garden in France in the 1920's and left behind when the family fled the Nazis at the outbreak of World War Two. He also gave her some information for the Cleveland sisters.

A few weeks later when she was preparing for the trip to India, she went to the passport office in Los Angeles, and while waiting for her visa appointment, Paramahansa Yogananda and several disciples including Daniel Boone came through the door. The author of *Autobiography of a Yogi* glanced at her and in that moment they each understood who the other was. Yogananda took the seat next to her and told her that he was going to die soon. He said to her that he had some disciples who would need spiritual guidance after his death, and asked her to take these as her own disciples. To his surprise, she told him that she did not believe in taking disciples, and considered it an untoward interference with another soul's evolution. He replied that they truly needed special help on the path because of the unique development of their character, and he asked her to simply help them. She said, "I will not take them as disciples, but I will walk with them." He was happy with this answer, and told her that he had the knowledge to send them to her after his death, much as his own guru Yukteshwar had appeared to him after his death as recounted in his book.

Of Yogananda's followers, it was Daniel Boone who would eventually become the closest to Mother Mary, and who would play a role in events at The Inn a decade later. As an example of the unique character of each of these disciples, Daniel said that he was born with *siddhis,* or latent spiritual powers, from another life. He left his home in Texas at an early age to become Yogananda's disciple, and finished high school while living as a monk in his ashram. When a swami from India was visiting Yogananda, the Paramahansa called Daniel before them and asked, "Did you come to me for *siddhis,* or did you come to me for God?" He replied, "Guruji, I came only for God." The second swami said, "You are a wise man." Sometime later, Yogananda took Daniel aside, stood in front of him, and while looking him directly in the eyes, took Daniel's *siddhis* away.

Mother Mary had a nick-name for Daniel, "Boom" instead of "Boone." Henry Fuller worked with explosives, drilling wells through bedrock, taking on jobs which no other contractor would touch. His nick-name was then, "Boom-Boom." Both of them gave considerable time and effort to help her in a number of endeavors.

When Mother Mary arrived in India on Sept. 20th, 1950 she knew no one and had great difficulty making contact in Calcutta with the Jagadbandhu ashram. She had a grand total of $243 in her pocket when she got off the plane. She took a room in a hotel, then hired a taxi driver, and every day they would go out and look for the ashram. After some days of this, a Muslim houseboy told her that she was being conned. The taxi driver had no intention of finding the ashram, because if he found it, she would no longer need him. The houseboy told her that he would find it for her himself if she would hire another taxi for him, and he was able to find it in one day. When she arrived at the ashram, she asked for Mahanam, the man who when a student in the U.S. in 1933 had given a lecture in Los Angeles about the avatar, from whose lips she had first heard Jagadbandhu's name, and who was now the head of the ashram. However, he was away on a lecture tour, and there was no one there to receive her.

She was bewildered by the strange culture of the ashram, but finally met one man named Novogour, of whom she said, "When I looked in his eyes, I knew he was someone who could help me." She could not pronounce his Bengali name, and always called him by a nick-name, "Nova Grudge." Novogour had many contacts, and introduced her to many people in the Calcutta ashrams and temples. She eventually was hosted by Benu Ghosh, a friend of Novogour, who gave her the third floor of his family's home to live in. He built the third floor of his home as an addition to house a 120 year old yogini. While the work was being done, the elderly yogini told him that she would never live there, but another spiritual woman would. This yogini died two months before Mother Mary came to India, just before the addition was finished. Benu Ghosh had been miraculously healed, brought back from near death, by his guru when he was a teenager. His guru told him that he could repay the debt he owed for this by being Mother Mary's guide, and he led her all over India and Tibet.

One of her goals in visiting India was to go to the Faridpur ashram called Sri Angan where Jagadbandhu had lived in seclusion for so many years. She could not understand Bengali pronunciation very well, and always pronounced "Faridpur" as if it were something like "Fairy Pool." Since this district was now in East Pakistan, it was difficult to get a visa to cross the border as both the Indian and Pakistani governments were trying to restrict travel, especially by foreigners. She bought a ticket anyway, not really appreciating the difficulty that might present itself. Mother Mary then went by train to Sri Angan, accompanied by Mahanam, who had returned from his tour. As they were approaching the border, he asked her if she had a visa. She said no. He told her it probably wouldn't matter, as they don't always check everyone on the train, and she was able to get through. When she spent the first night in the ashram, Jagadbandhu appeared to her at daybreak. He gave her a description of her work ahead, telling her of her future trip to the hidden city of initiates in Tibet, and a forest glen in the Himalayas in which she would have one of the most exalted experiences of her life. He also gave her much confidential information about the inner workings and history of his ashram, including some secret details which she could use in the future to confront people in the ashram who might try to block her way, as would soon take place. He gave her the inner meanings of the small book called the *Harikatha* he had written in Bengali and Sanskrit with unknown words from some older tongue which has never been fully deciphered by his devotees. He warned her that her knowledge of this text would cause great enmity toward her by some members of the ashram. She stayed at Sri Angan for several weeks. Dr. Ferguson's dream of Jagadbandhu's tree, and monks and ancient manuscripts beneath it, came to pass.

When she returned to Calcutta, she met a Bengali businessman from Dhaka who begged her to come back to East Pakistan with him to speak at his temple. She didn't really want to do it, but eventually agreed to go, and applied for a visa to visit East Pakistan. An official of the Jagadbandhu ashram became very jealous of the attention she was receiving from this businessman and others, and sought to block her trip by floating a rumor that she was a Russian spy, in order to deny her the visa. This rumor caused her tremendous heartache, as once such a rumor gets started, it is almost impossible to dispel.

There was a lawyer in Calcutta named Jnan Kumar Chatterjee who, along with his wife, had decided to commit suicide after taking out a large insurance policy naming his 20-year old son as beneficiary. On the day before he planned to die, they were riding on the bus when the lawyer heard two men in an adjacent seat talking about an unusual American woman, Mother Mary, who they were on their way to visit. He asked if he and his wife could come along and were told, yes. When they reached Mother Mary's third floor quarters where she daily met with many people, the lawyer immediately realized that the people sitting on the floor were all mixed up in caste, not separated as would normally be the case in India at the time. This made an impression on him, and he observantly sat waiting, watching how Mother Mary interacted with the people before him. When his turn to speak with Mother Mary came, he put his head in her lap and suddenly blurted out the whole plan to commit suicide, leaving the money to his son. Mother Mary told him, "You did not give life and you have no right to take it. Your son will quickly squander the money, there will be none left, and he will curse you for it." The lawyer soon realized the folly of his plan and abandoned it. He was deeply grateful to her, and soon was often coming for *darshan,* bringing his son as well.

Chatterjee found out about the spy rumor, and went to the chief-of-police of Calcutta to try to end it. The policeman told the lawyer that the Pakistani and American consulates were already aware of it, and it was now out of his hands. Chatterjee was not satisfied with this answer and soon began to harass the policeman regularly to do something about the problem.

This being India, even the chief-of-police of Calcutta had a guru. Chatterjee had the idea that if they could make a connection with this swami, then he would be able to help them procure the visa for East Pakistan, but didn't know how to get in to see him. As it turned out, the guru was giving a public talk in an auditorium soon after, and Mother Mary was ushered into the hall, accompanied by Benu Ghosh and the chief-of-police. The talk had already begun when Mother Mary entered the hall, but in mid-sentence the swami, Sri Viswajit Maharaj, stopped speaking, and went into *samadhi* for an hour and 45 minutes. When he came out of *samadhi*, he asked for a purple rug to be brought for Mother Mary to sit on, and when she was seated next to him he turned to her and said, "You have come to India unknown and will leave unknown, but I know. I know who you are and why you came. Come with me." He soon left the stage, took her alone to another room on the second floor of the building, and spoke with her for several hours. The audience was left sitting in the hall, waiting for him to return.

After a couple of hours, the two did return to the hall, and the swami spoke to the crowd about Mother Mary and why she came to India. Mother Mary later said that indeed, this was the only person who understood her mission to India, and that in the future the two of them would work together to fulfill that mission. They spoke again the next morning. In addition, he privately asked his disciple who was the chief-of-police to help resolve her problem with the rumor. The policeman took care of this by having the official of the Jagadbandhu ashram who had spread the spy rumor brought in and questioned in the presence of Benu Ghosh. After the interrogation, this official was made to write and sign a confession that he had made up the story himself, and that it was completely false. The visa came through soon thereafter, again with the police chief's help, and she was off to Dhaka. She said her welcome in the city was very festive, with lights strung all around a temple in the warm tropical evening.

Back in India, she made many complaints to the visa office about the slow processing of her visas, but they came to no avail. Eventually, Benu Ghosh asked her the details of her troubles and realized that there was another office to whom she could complain, so he took her there. While waiting in this office she met a woman sitting in the next chair named Shakuntala. She told Mother Mary that she was married to an Australian man, and that they planned to emigrate to America. When Mother Mary told her that she was American, Shakuntala said, "I thought so," and asked if she could come for a visit as she had something important to say to her. She came to Mother Mary's third floor rooms the following day, but did not feel comfortable talking with her in the presence of others, so she invited Mother Mary to visit her in her own home the next day. The story she told was quite remarkable. Twenty-four years before, an elderly man had approached her father in a park. He said to her, "There is a hidden city in the Himalayas of saints and yogis. Jesus Christ visited this city. Every 12 years, a man is sent out to meet someone. I am that man, sent to meet you. You have a six-year-old daughter at home. When you get home, take her on your knee and tell her about meeting me, and that when she is 30, she will meet an American woman who will know of this city and will tell her of it." The father did as he was asked to do.

Shakuntala told Mother Mary that she had never thought of this again until she met her in the visa office. She was now 30 years old, and asked Mother Mary if she knew of this city. Mother Mary said yes, and told her of it. Mother Mary usually referred to this city as "Uttakesh," but this actually means something more like "Up in the High Mountains," and is not its true name, which she almost never uttered. Sometime later when Shakuntala found out that Mother Mary was actually planning to go to this city, she caused a commotion, and demanded that Mother Mary take her along. Mother Mary explained to her that one must be invited to go there, and that she must not try to follow her. When Shakuntala returned to her home that very day, the elderly man from years ago had come to her house looking for her, with the intent of taking her to the hidden city. He had been very agitated when she was not there, but he gave instructions to her brother regarding what she must do in preparation for his return. For some time after this, Shakuntala spent as much time as possible with Mother Mary, even sleeping on the floor at the end of her bed. She also accompanied her on a second trip to Faridpur. Mother Mary said that she never saw Shakuntala again after leaving Calcutta and was concerned to find out if she had made it to the city.

While staying with Benu in Calcutta, Mother Mary was asked if she would like to travel to a museum of the Great Ones, first established around 1750, in which artifacts of the lives of the Great Ones are housed. Along with a few monks of the Jagadbandhu ashram, she and Novogour piled into a jeep, and spent several days traveling to a place near a river where there is a walled compound in which the museum is located. As they drove off, Mother Mary asked all aboard to contribute to the gas money, but the driver refused to accept any help for the costs, simply offering his car and time as a service to her. After some hours, they stopped for gas, but the gas station attendant told them that the tank was full. None of them could understand how this could be.

After more than two days of travelling, they reached the museum. When she was walking on the grounds, she realized that she had been here before in visions and dreams, and that in a certain spot she had seen a great tree, and that upon a bench beneath that tree she and Jagadbandhu had spent many hours talking. She asked the director of the museum about the tree and bench, and he said yes, there was such a tree with a bench in the exact spot she remembered, but it had been cut down 80 years before to make room for the roof of one of the buildings. The director told her that each display of the Great Ones takes many hours to unwrap, so that in the one afternoon she would be there, she would have the opportunity to examine only one. He asked her which one she would like to see, and she replied, "Jagadbandhu." They carefully unwrapped many artifacts of his life, including the sandals he was wearing at the time of his death. While she was examining these artifacts, one of her party wandered around the museum, and made a discovery. He came shouting back to her, "Mother, Mother, you are here!" He showed her the display from one of her previous lives.

After many hours on the return trip to Calcutta, they arrived at Benu Ghosh's home and the jeep promptly ran out of gas. It had gone all they way there and back on one tank, a five-day journey. They all considered it a minor miracle.

In the late fall of 1950, she left Calcutta for Hardhwar, and the ashram of Benu Ghosh's guru, who was no longer alive. When they reached this ashram there were 72 swamis from different places gathered there, and a great banquet was held. Mother Mary performed an ancient dance before these swamis, who were perhaps among the very few who could understand it.

With Benu and his mother, who cooked for the three of them, she traveled to nearby Rishikesh, where she was hosted by Swami Sivananda and his ashram The Divine Life Society at Laxmanjula. She was given the robes of a swami by the yogis of Rishikesh.

80

Later in her life, she would wear these robes "only in service," as she put it. When she performed some deliberate service, such as to meet with a spiritual group or give a lecture, she would don these robes, and the necklaces she called "my credentials," each of which had a special meaning. In her daily routine, she usually wore the most ordinary garments, and would go completely unnoticed by the casual onlooker. During her stay at this ashram, Jagadbandhu again appeared to her and gave her a technique by which she could reach *nirbkalpa samadhi*, the contemplative state of Union with the Divine which is the goal of yogic practice. She was not always well-received in Rishikesh, as when she told some local yogis that their tantric practices amounted to a form of psychic vampirism, and that they should instead get married and learn how to live with a woman.

From Rishikesh, she traveled to the Tibetan border, but could not obtain her visa to enter Tibet. Mother Mary, Benu Ghosh, and his mother, took rooms at the Government Rest House, and while waiting for the visa to come through, she practiced the yogic technique given to her by Jagadbandhu in Rishikesh for 14 days at the end of December and beginning of January of the next year. She did enter the state of *nirbkalpa samadhi*, but her body turned black, and Benu was afraid that she was dying. He stood over her and said repeatedly, "You must come back. Your work is not finished." She returned to her body and it healed after some days. In several weeks, she was stronger than before. News of this got around from the employees of the Rest House, and her visa came through. The local people treated her with great respect after her *samadhi*.

She and Benu were taken into Tibet and led to the hidden city of 5,000 initiates. She walked without shoes on the holy ground. One man she met in this city was a great hatha yogi, and she explained to him that since the time of Lemuria or Mu, hatha yoga was no longer the path for people of earth. She told him of a planet on which hatha yoga is still practiced as a path, and she said that he soon left this body consciously to take incarnation on the other planet.

She was given a room with a veranda, and hundreds of initiates assembled below while she lectured them on "Service to Humanity." She called upon them to share their knowledge with one another, and sought to lay the groundwork for a world-wide meeting of the Great Ones in order to further the Divine Plan. She also suggested to some renunciates that they would be better off spiritually if they learned to live in the world, living a married life and handling the problems of worldly existence. She said it would be very difficult for them, but they and the world would be better off for it. She predicted that some of them would accomplish this course of action by being reborn in the West. She suggested to others that they should come and go into the world and back into their retreats, learning to deal with the world's jarring vibrations bit by bit.

The theme of saints and sadhus living openly in the world, cooperating with one another and setting an example for humanity, is found throughout Mother Mary's writings and public pronouncements, and was an important part of her message for these initiates as well. The saints and sadhus are custodians of ancient spiritual science, such as the spiritual science of longevity, and she implored them to use this knowledge for the welfare of mankind. In India and Tibet, it is customary for gurus to share their spiritual knowledge only with their own initiated disciples, and Mother Mary asked the saints and sadhus of the holy city to share their knowledge with one another, and to not simply reserve it for their own lineage. She suggested that the ancient spiritual sciences be disseminated to those who would not misuse it, whether or not they were initiated in the guru-disciple tradition.

She explained to the inhabitants of the hidden city why she did not take disciples, which seemed very strange to those sages and saints who had been born in the Hindu culture of India or the Buddhist society of Tibet. She said, "Of all living human beings born into a body, no two are created exactly alike. A guru or a teacher can take that individual as far as they can, but he cannot take that individual to his own light, because he does not have that individual's light, he has only his own, regardless of how great that teacher is." This statement by Mother Mary is not metaphorical, it is absolutely literal. Every human being is a unique light before the Creator, emanating from the Creator. Of the many who heard her speak, she said only a few understood her. However, those few presented to her a plan by which they could cooperate with her in the work. They instructed her that after her return to America, she should open some kind of center at Mt. Shasta, and promised her that they would use their spiritual knowledge to send people to her. This took place from 1961 on, after she bought The Inn. She said, "10,000 came."

After leaving the hidden city, Mother Mary and Benu traveled gradually across the mountains. They reached the forest glen which Jagadbandhu told her about in Sri Angan. In this glen she had her Divine Empowerment, in which the Energy that created the universe flowed through her. She danced barefoot, and Creation danced with her. Jagadbandhu again appeared to her, and told her that this Energy must never be misused. These times in Tibet were what Jagadbandhu had referred to when he told her in 1944 that her purpose in coming to India was "to walk barefoot on the ground." They eventually reached Lhasa, and she visited the Dalai Lama in the Potala when he was still a boy. When she stayed at the Potala, she was shown several rooms in a lower level of the palace which she said were guarded by the two tallest men she ever met. In these rooms were housed artifacts of human history going back more than 60,000 years, including writings in an ancient pictographic script. When the Chinese took over Tibet, Buddhists tried to save as many of these artifacts as they could, but many were lost.

She said that the three and a half months she spent in Tibet were the most important months of her life. Among the most cherished mementos of this trip were two leaves presented to her in Tibet. Swami Vivekananda wrote of a monastery in the Himalayas which Jesus visited after leaving the Holy Land. The monks of this monastery have carefully preserved a scroll which chronicles the life of Jesus at this monastery, known as "Issa" to them, and that scroll still exists today. Several Westerners have seen this scroll and written of it, including a disciple of Yogananda. On the long journey to this monastery, which is accessed from Kashmir, there is a tree next to the path which gives pilgrims shade, growing where no other tree grows. It is said to have been planted by Jesus himself, and the leaves were from this tree.

When she returned to Calcutta, she had no money. Her husband was barely making ends meet in Los Angeles, so she got in contact with Henry Fuller and asked him to send her $20 every week or two by post in care of the ashram. Henry did so, but when the letters arrived for her, there was only $10 inside. She wrote him several letters asking him why he was sending her only $10, and Henry would write back with a $20 bill enclosed each time. But still she would receive only $10. This bothered Lady Mae to no end, and when she was back in Los Angeles, the two of them discussed it at length and came to the conclusion that someone, probably in the ashram, had intercepted the letters,

82

removing the $20 bill and replacing it with a $10, knowing that if he took all of it, the flow would stop.

On the eve of her departure from India, on October 7th, 1951 the Jagadbandhu ashram of Calcutta gave a farewell ceremony for Mother Mary, for which invitations and mailings were prepared and sent. The American Vice-Consul in Calcutta, Miss Mary Fischer, was in attendance. The complete name of this ashram is "Sri Sri Prabhu Jagadbandhu Mahanama Prancharan Samity" and the notices were sent out under that name. When she left India at the end of her second trip in June of 1966, a similar festive ceremony was held for her, and more notices were printed up and sent out at that time as well. Soon after the death of Mother Mary, copies of these notices were given to the Mt. Shasta Herald newspaper, which published one verbatim on Feb. 12, 1970 under the headline *"Mother Mary Honored by Hindu Religious Cult."* This notice has now become the "evidence" cited by various frivolous historians in the assertion that Mother Mary founded a cult, called by them the "Shree Shree Provos," and that the people who worked at The Inn were members of this cult. Nothing could be further from the truth. She was actually fond of giving the advice, "Don't join anything" and encouraged one and all, including her own employees, to follow their own light. Indeed, she considered this the purpose of every human soul.

She arrived back in America from her first trip to India on Nov. 15th, 1951.

In December of 1969, just two weeks before she died, a hippie wandered into The Inn with a message for Mother Mary from the Great Ones of the holy city in Tibet. He had been trekking in the Himalayas and was taken to the city, given the message and sent on his way. Mother Mary laughed out loud at this, and said, "Imagine that, a hippie found his way into the holy city! You have to be invited to find it. They're teaching me a lesson by using him as their messenger - Don't Judge." The message he bore was that the Chinese had not yet reached that part of Tibet and the city was at that time still safe, although some inhabitants were moving out.

In India, there was historically a spiritual lineage called the "Shramanic" tradition, or the forest-dwelling ascetics. Do not confuse this word for "shamanic" as they have completely different roots. The Shramanic tradition is the origin of the modern Hindu surname, "Sharma" which today refers to a certain class of brahmins, but the Shramanic tradition is older than classical Sanskrit culture, and some elements of it have been discovered in the Indus valley civilization now being studied by archeologists. There are, for instance, images in the Indus valley temples of a naked forest-dwelling ascetic sitting cross-legged under the trees, from whose matted top-knot emerges a river, but he is not Shiva, and the inscriptions for this image are in an unknown language. It is believed that some of the oldest Upanishads actually belong to this tradition, and were adopted into ancient Sanskrit philosophy. They have no reference to, or mention of, any Hindu deity. This is also true of the Yoga Sutras of Patanjali, which make no mention of any Hindu god. Some of the ascetics of the forest were the very same ancient Sufis to whom Inayat Khan made reference, and they would sit under trees as they imparted teachings to their students. In these ancient times, one of the most basic forms of yogic meditation was the practice of counting numbers in series. The image of sitting under a tree, studying spiritual teaching, evokes this ancient era, and appears several times in Mother Mary's accounts of her travels in India. She sometimes called meditation, "Sitting under your life tree," and one can imagine just how old this metaphor might be.

6. THE GREAT WHITE CHIEF

In the mid 1950's Mother Mary made her first visit to see the Great White Chief, Eachita Eachina, in southern Mexico. She was given the address of a café in Mitla, and the name of a man who would meet her there to take her to the city of the White Indians not too far away. She went to this café, and asked for the man. Everyone ignored her. She asked several more times and no one answered. This exasperated her, and she simply sat at her table and waited for something to happen. After a while, some children in the café told her that the very man she was looking for was seated at the next table, and had been the whole time. This man, who Mother Mary referred to as "the runner," did take her to the Eachita Eachina, whose name means "Mighty and Wise One."

From the Great White Chief, she learned that the tribe was descended from a group of people who had come to earth from another planet in ancient times, to deliberately make a contribution to the evolution of humanity. They have kept their knowledge from their original planet alive through the many generations. Eachita Eachina is himself the 32nd leader of their tribe, and he told Mother Mary that he was 123 years old at the time he met her, although he seemed much younger.

According to the Great White Chief, many centuries ago, Jesus visited the White Indians and took a member of the tribe as one of his 12 disciples in the New World, along with a member of the Hopi tribe, and a tribe in Wyoming. In his lifetime working publicly with the people of the Western Hemisphere, Jesus was known as "the White God Who Came from the East." The White Indians have kept alive the teachings they received from Jesus, and Eachita Eachina shared these written teachings with Mother Mary.

In the 1955 book *The Coming of the Great White Chief,* Dorothy Thomas writes -

> "The Indians have a set of records written on books of buckskin, which they have handed down from generation to generation. The records are regarded as highly sacred, for they contain the history of their people for many generations prior to the coming of the Great White God. They are the only Indians as far as I know possessing a set of records originating to B.C. times. They are written in a language no longer spoken by them except for the Mighty and Wise one who learned it from his father as a responsibility handed down from the beginning of their family"

One of the teachings of Jesus given to the White Indians, which made a great impression on Mother Mary, was translated as the following -

> Unto all men I give this great Knowledge - to know that within them, they possess patience and tolerance. Those who seek to cause their patience and tolerance to grow, should also seek Me, for I am patience and tolerance also, and those who by their right of force shall cause their patience and tolerance to grow shall become Masters. They shall attain the highest goals and they shall teach the scholar that which I have willed unto them. But those who seek not my

unbounded limits of patience and tolerance shall go back to the bottomless pit, where naught but ignorance and vice rule. Seek ye the unbounded, which I have willed unto you, and your reward will be a place in my Father's realm. For by attaining greater patience and tolerance, you shall never break my commandments and laws. They are the foundation of all my teachings.

In 1959 Mother Mary asked Eachita Eachina if there was anything she could do to help him in his work. Just a few weeks later she received a letter postmarked Logan, Utah from the wife of a man named Natoni Nez-bah which informed Lady Mae that her late husband had written a book detailing his travels with a man named Paul Dressel to Indian tribes and lost cities in Latin America, including a trip to the White Indians. Natoni, or "Tony," Nez-bah was a man of partly Cherokee ancestry who had been adopted by the Navaho. He was also adopted by Eachita Eachina as his son, as described in the book. He was a member of the Mormon Church of Latter Day Saints. He had written the book some years before, and a woman named Sarah Hawkins had typed it into manuscript form, but it was rejected by several publishers. Unfortunately Tony Nez-bah died before he received word from one publisher who was interested in the book, and by the time his widow tried to follow up on the project, that publisher had gone out of business. The book gives many of the teachings of his adoptive tribe, and other native peoples of the New World. The manuscript has certain elements reminiscent of the tales of Col. Percy Fawcett, a Theosophist who vanished in 1925 searching for a lost city of "White Indians" in the Amazon.

The wife and daughter of Tony Nez-bah found Mother Mary by way of an introduction from a UFO channel of Native American descent named Bessie Arthur, and Lady Mae remained in contact with them for some years. The second production of a manuscript was a difficult and time-consuming process, but eventually Mother Mary received a copy and she printed it on Henry Fuller's printing press.

Among Mother Mary's personal effects at the time of her death was a 6-page single-spaced typewritten account of the White Indians which includes about one-half of the Dorothy Thomas text, as well as more information about the White Indians not found in the Thomas book. It gives details of Nez-bah's 1935 visit to the White Indians. The authorship of these pages is unclear although it was probably written by Nez-Bah himself. During the 1940's, Natoni Nez-bah was invited to give lectures at many local Mormon churches, and his text was circulated among Mormons at these events. It was widely copied and discussed. Certain elements of the story especially resonated with Mormons, such as the description of the garments which the White Indians were said to wear, which resemble garments used by Mormons in some ceremonies. Two themes of the book *The Great White Chief* refer to the fulfillment of Mormon prophecies. The first is that native peoples have ancient metallic plates which contain the history of pre-Colombian New World civilization, and the second is that Native Americans and Mormons will cooperate in the future to build a Temple for the re-appearance of the Christ. In 1953 Spencer W. Kimball, who was at that time a member of the Quorum of the Twelve, wrote an article to refute the typewritten pages, which were now well-known among Mormons. Although Kimball took issue with some of the information in Nez-bah's account, what seems to have disturbed the Mormon leadership was Nez-bah's refusal to take anyone from the Church to visit the White Indians. Several Mormon authors who were acquainted with Tony Nez-bah, including Norman C. Pierce, drew from these pages in their own writings, and this type-written account was probably the source of Thomas' information.

Here is an excerpt from this typewritten document, a version of which is also found in Thomas' text -

The White Indians are a nation of very light skinned Indians living in the Southern part of Old Mexico. Their walled city lies in an almost inaccessible section of the high mountainous region deep in the South of Mexico almost to Guatemala.

To reach this Shangri-La of the New World, where the white man's civilization has not penetrated due to his complete exclusion, one must first go to the capital city of Oaxaca, then to the ancient ruined city of Mitla. From Mitla one must resume the journey on horseback or on foot, as there are no traveled roads or highways that lead to this fantastic city. After five days of almost continuous climbing, one comes across some high table land that opens into a magnificent valley of transcending beauty. It lies at an elevation of about 10,000 feet. Within this valley is secluded the beautiful walled city of the White Indians, where it has remained untouched and unspoiled by the evils of civilization since it was built long before the time of Christ. The habitations cover an area about nine and one half miles long by about eleven miles wide, or about a hundred square miles. At the northern end of the valley steep rock cliffs two or three hundred feet high form an effective barrier, while on the east, west, and south sides is a wall built of stone that varies from five to twenty feet in height. This completes their protective encirclement with guarded gates the only means of entrance and exit.

The laws of the land of the White Indians decree that only those who speak the Indian languages and in whose veins flow the Indian blood shall enter their dominion, and the white man has thus far been effectively barred as well as warlike tribes of Indians. All the buildings, homes and temples are very light or white in color on the outside as well as on the inside and present a very attractive appearance, forming a city which approaches perfection in its layout and architectural design.

The people are all stately and tall, being from five feet-eight to six feet-two inches in height. Their skin is very light; their hair is brown to very black. The color of their eyes varies from hazel to deep blue or black. Their clothes are all woven by hand and differ considerably from all other tribes. Instead of wearing the customary shirt and trousers, they wear long white robes that reach almost to the ground and which they fasten down the front with three sets of strings. A girdle is wrapped about the waist, and the long sleeves are sometimes tied at the elbow with a drawstring. A cowl-like hood is worn over the head and white-tanned moccasins cover the feet. Certain symbolic marks are placed upon the robes over the breast, navel, and on the hood over the forehead. The people regard these symbols as very sacred.

Men, women, and children dress alike in these hand woven white woolen robes and all of them live a life of simplicity that is very near perfection in its order and arrangement. One does not say, "This is mine or that is yours," but all possess everything together and use it according to their needs. The farmers, for instance, put whatever they raise into the great storehouse. The wool weavers, pottery makers and leather workers do likewise with their products, and then all is made available for the common use of all the people as needed. They have no money and need none for themselves. All commerce with other Indian Tribes is carried on by the barter or exchange system. There are no rich, nor poor, and every one shares the abundance they have. Once when I was presented with a beautiful pair of moccasins, I offered a handful of pesos in return for them, only to be rebuked by the Great White Chief with soft spoken words, 'My son, our hills are full of that metal and we find it useful only for tools and ornaments.'

They are a very clean people having no vices nor bad habits, such as the use of tobacco and liquors. They live principally upon a vegetarian diet of fruit, melons, and raw vegetables, and are all very healthy and beautiful in their appearance, walking erect with excellent posture that gives an impression of almost effortless motion or gliding movement. They are very devout, and pray several times during the day and night, each prayer being very sincere.

They follow the belief, "I am my brother's keeper." Should any sickness or sorrow fall upon one of them, everyone else is ready to do all possible for the unfortunate one, as each person feels that he or she should be responsible for each other's welfare and happiness. No ill feelings nor misunderstandings exist among them; because the usual basis or motives for such conditions do not exist among them. All are very happy and they know not of greed, hatred, malice or scorn, and because their substance, their welfare, and their happiness are shared. Theirs is the perfect life. Their mode of living has been with them for many generations just as the firm traditions and beliefs have been handed down from generation to generation that they should live this way.

The Great White Chief has on many occasions called convocations of Indians from across the Americas, and Tony Nez-Bah became a representative of the Navajo nation to these gatherings. One of these took place in the region of Lake Patzcuaro and another at Lake Michoacan. One such gathering was described in the Magazine section of the Salt Lake City Tribune on March 31, 1940.
From Dorothy Thomas' book -

"During the great conference in 1940 in Lake Michoacan the Mighty and Wise One informed all the Indian delegates that the time had come according to the Voice of the Great Spirit for them to build a magnificent Temple, to His name in fulfillment of the promise and tradition that has been handed down by them and that the Indians should carry out this work. He showed them the plan for this great and beautiful structure, which when completed would cover as much land as a Salt Lake City block."

The theme of the White Indians coming to the United States and building a sacred temple in cooperation with Mormons was a favorite subject of Mother Mary's informal talks. She said Beloved John and Eachita Eachina would lead them, and they would not be welcomed at first. Mexican immigrants rarely are, as in the Woody Guthrie song, *Deportee*. Long ago, Jesus gave the leader of the White Indians a rod which he will carry with him to the United States. Mother Mary said that all people will know when this time has come by a sign in the sky, seen and understood by all. On a few occasions, Mother Mary made comments to the effect that she knew the inner meanings of Mormon doctrines. One of these teachings was the identity of "the Three Nephites" who are in fact the three biblical personages, John the Baptist, Beloved John, and John the Revelator, who have remained with the master Jesus on the earth plane until the fulfillment of the Divine Plan.

Eachita Eachina wrote a letter to George Albert Smith, the eighth President of the Mormon Church, regarding the time when the Temple would be built. Following is the text of this letter written on buckskin, shown by Chi Chi Suma of the Quiche Indians to Eachita Eachina's adopted son, who translated it and provided a copy to Mother Mary.

To My Brother, the Great White Leader,

Salutations.

When he, the mighty and wise one, comes among you, he shall speak and all shall listen and harken unto him. All things shall be given unto him as properties and possessions, etc. He shall have everything at his disposal too, as the Great Spirit directs.

All things that the Indian people have shall be shared equally with you. There will be no high and no poor. Those who are at the bottom shall be placed at the top, and those who are on the top shall be placed at the bottom for you have rejected and left behind the things which the Great Spirit has given you in times past. He, the mighty and wise one, will select men who are the best fitted for each office and position.

All wealth and possessions will be used by both sides under his direction. All wealth of the Indian people will be combined with your own wealth, and all food supplies shall be used by both sides as needed. Neither side shall hoard or keep anything hidden from the other side, but all shall have and share equally of the total.

Great farms will be worked by both the white and Indian people. Flocks and herds will be raised by them both. Great and large buildings shall be built by both sides together, and all shall worship the same God together at the great place, or the site where the mighty Temple shall be built. White people and Indian people shall both work together and also build the beautiful city.

Many shall remain here, and many shall go from here. Seven years work and all things on the temple shall be completed. Many will refuse, but many will accept, and those whom I shall take will be as a handful of sand from the shore. Some will fall away, but I will hold all that are in my hand. Some will deny or refuse me. Many will not understand, many will not care. Nevertheless, all things shall be done and all laws of the Great Spirit shall be obeyed in good faith.

The righteous shall do great things, and the wicked among you shall be destroyed. All things shall be done in a quiet way.

88

We shall come peacefully if we are accepted peacefully, but if we are not accepted peacefully, we will come to destroy, for those who hold these things in scorn and derision shall be destroyed.

It is the Voice which speaks, even the Voice of the Great Spirit. We come in large groups and great numbers. We seek not to destroy but this is the command of the mighty and wise one, for the Voice of the Great Spirit has spoken to him. He asks that he be received with his people in the Great Amalgamation, for you and they shall be as one.

He has spoken. It is finished.

Eachita Eachina

Mother Mary told an unusual story about the fate of one of the seven copies of *The Great White Chief* which she gave to the medicine man who she met in the theater with Henry Fuller. When Eachita Eachina asked her to print the book, he specifically asked that it be given to the council members of the Six Nations. The medicine man from the theater accomplished this task at a meeting of the tribes in Canada. In Idaho, a young man was sent to Federal Prison as a conscientious objector. While in prison, he met one of these very council members, who acted as a spiritual advisor to Native American inmates and anyone else who might be interested. The conscientious objector was shown the book, and became fascinated by it. The council member gave it to him. After he was released from prison, he wanted to get out of the United States for a while and took a trip to Europe. In Germany, he was holding the book in his hands in a café when someone nearby noticed its title and told him that she was a member of a German spiritual group who were in touch with the Great White Chief. This group had bought an island for the purpose of building a community which was to be based on spiritual values, and had received some teachings from Eachita Eachina. They had never seen the book published by Mother Mary before, and it was a treasure to them. When the conscientious objector returned to the U.S., he spent some time tracking down Mother Mary, who no longer lived at the address printed in the book. He finally got her address at The Inn and wrote her of his experiences. One of her friends went to Germany to track down the spiritual group.

Mother Mary made a curious statement that the area around Mitla "floated in the aethers." One of the White Indians has elaborated on this, saying, "Mitla, including the mystical mountains there-with, is not a country, it is not a sub-continent. Mitla is much more. The edges of the hills fold up into the aether, where one looks sideways at the moon, where one can glimpse that blue crystal pool of water by the Mitla San Pablo Church."

Mother Mary set aside the first copy printed of *The Great White Chief* and in early 1962, just after buying The Inn, she made another trip to Mitla to present it to Eachita Eachina. Sometime after her first visit, Lady Mae read the Dorothy Thomas book and noticed the story in it about Charles Lindbergh. According to Thomas, the aviator flew over the city and saw it below, but when he mounted an expedition to find it a second time, he never caught sight of it again. When Mother Mary returned to Mitla, she asked the runner who came to escort her to Eachita Eachina about Lindbergh, and why he was not able to find their city a second time. The runner replied, "You're coming from Mt.

Shasta this time. Have you ever noticed the unusual clouds up there that obscure the mountain from time to time? We've got the same technology here."

This is the forward to *The Great White Chief* written by Mother Mary in 1960 –

The time has come when the knowledge of our material world will give way to an ushering in of the Spiritual World that will bring enlightenment to all those who desire sincerely to know the truth about all things in order for truth to grow and become manifested within each and every soul upon this earth.

I, Mother Mary, believing that man was created by the Great Spirit out of love and nature, was placed by the Creator in man's pathway to chastise man when he becomes disobedient or to reward him with abundance when he learns to be a true Son of God.

The problems of food, shelter, and longevity are more conscientiously felt by those persons who have tasted the bitter cup of life than by those residing in more mechanized surroundings. This, however, I believe, is a blessing in disguise, for those who live simple, thoughtful lives do not have to unlearn so many things in order to reap the Creator's abundance in nature's storehouse.

I, Mother Mary, feel that many dangerous misconceptions, such as in the misguided use of true knowledge for purposes of aggression, are hampering man's current efforts to master space. Unless a definite change is made before it is too late, nature will carry out its God-given mission and destroy mankind. If, on the other hand, man realizes that he is the receiver of knowledge, nature will provide sufficient for all the needs of mankind, with a wealth of leisure and abundance beyond the concept of mortal man. Therefore, to accomplish this most desirable state of affairs, it will be necessary to combine actively the relearning of ancient laws under the guidance of the truly Holy and Wise Ones.

The Bridge of Brotherhood can be built only with stones of true faith, love and patience of selfless individuals with the Holy Wise Ones whom the Great Spirit chooses.

When Man has learned from bitter experiences that moderation in all things is desirable and he tempers his own desires in the oil of compassion for his fellowman, then truly has the seed fallen upon fertile soil.

The seed of the Father's love was planted in the mind of man when he was created. It needed only tears of compassion for his fellowman to fertilize, cause germination, and bear the fruit of understanding of the source of all wherein man becomes in truth one with all and all with one.

As it is quoted in all of the Sacred Teachings throughout the world, our Heavenly Father asks that all those who seek him must be honest with themselves, setting aside worldly experiences, humbly asking within themselves for the Father's guidance and becoming, thereby, as a little child.

Many nations have achieved a measure of greatness and then declined because they have forgotten the importance of true spiritual wisdom and the showing of

90

proper respect for those rare individuals who were and are blessed by out Creator to act as the receivers of it.

That is the reason why the truly Holy Men have been hesitant in showing themselves, for they cannot force knowledge upon individuals or governments. They can offer it only under circumstances that would tend to guarantee its perfect use for the true betterment of mankind.

For they will not be party to special favors for the individual or nation wherein advantage is sought or implied. Mankind should function as one family with duties assigned and responsibilities equally shared before true spiritual progress is possible. Only then will man have the opportunity of learning the true history of civilization and also what is necessary to manifest the Father's abundance in effectually solving the problems facing each nation and individual today.

I, Mother Mary, have the following special message for the mothers of the world:

"Are you not the Temples consecrated for the ultimate perfection of all humanity? Dedicate yourselves truly with love and understanding that the Rays of All-abiding Love may be emanated. Pray, listening carefully for guidance and the way will be made as clear as crystal ---"

Brothers, it is my wish to serve, if only in a small way, realizing that the Creator of all is bringing his lost children together so that He can improve them in order to make one true, harmonious family upon this earth; and to accomplish that objective He will cause all of his worlds to serve each other. Did he not create them from one substance?

Through an Indian this manuscript reached my possession. I feel it is truth and in my way of believing serving unattached waiting for guidance from the Great Spirit of all good.

Amen   Amen   Amen

To change any of the wording of this manuscript would lose its true mission therefore it is left just as it was written and if Echa Tah Echa Nah, The Great White Chief, deems it necessary in the near future where I can serve in this way I am ready.

In publishing this book the author's purpose is to tell of his experiences, wording the text just as it is found in the manuscript, leaving some things out as intuitive guidance directs through a feeling that comes over my entire being.

Mother Mary

7. THE MEETING AT SAND FLAT IN JULY, 1962

The mother of Maxine McMullen could not drive past a sign advertising "Psychic Reading" without stopping. As a child, Maxine met many psychics, most of them frauds, and became quite perceptive at spotting their tricks. She learned important lessons in spiritual discernment very early in life, and was well aware of the need for such discernment. She was a keen observer of certain patterns, as when years later during the time she owned "The Golden Mean Bookstore" in Ashland, Oregon, she noticed most of the books shoplifted from the store were from the astrology section. Shoplifters were apparently not interested in books on the power of prayer.

The first of her three husbands was an engineer in the early rocket programs at White Sands, New Mexico. She met there a life-long friend, Daniel Fry, also an engineer in the programs, who claimed to have been taken up in a spacecraft, and who further claimed that he had helped a man from a spacecraft obtain a false birth certificate so that he could establish an identity and enter human society. During the 1950's a gathering of UFO enthusiasts and people interested in all kinds of off-beat spiritual and psychic subjects was held yearly at a place called Giant Rock in the desert outside Joshua Tree, California and was hosted by George Van Tassel, the father-in-law of both Daniel Boone and Norm Paulsen, disciples of Yogananda. Maxine attended some of these gatherings and made many contacts there. Mother Mary attended these gatherings as well, though they did not meet there.

In the late 1950's Maxine was reading the Bible when she saw a passage which indicated to her that the disciple Beloved John had made a commitment to remain in the physical body until the reappearance of the Christ. She was absolutely certain of this interpretation, and asked everyone she met in the next few years who was interested in spiritual subjects if they had any contact with Beloved John. All said no. Her friend Cindy Luddington told Maxine of a spiritual woman staying in Mt. Shasta and Maxine drove up to meet her. When Maxine arrived at the Black Butte Inn, where Lady Mae was staying as a guest, she was not there. She had gone up to Sand Flat for the day, and Maxine drove up the mountain to find her. Maxine drove into the meadow, and saw an older woman sitting on a log. She parked her car, and walked over to the woman. The first thing she said to her was, "Do you have contact with Beloved John?" Mother Mary said, "Yes," but would not speak further on the subject at that time. Maxine became closely involved with Mother Mary and the spiritual work until her death in 1979.

Just after Christmas in 1961, when Maxine was staying at The Inn, helping to clean the hotel after a large holiday banquet, both she and Mother Mary were impressed with the thought that they should call a gathering of seekers and servers to be held at Mt. Shasta during the first week of July, 1962. Lady Mae later said if they had known how much work this would eventually entail, they might have never done it. She said the most arduous task of all was confronting the selfishness of her own personal mind in order to free it for the service ahead, and spent many long hours in this endeavor. They sent invitations to everyone who they knew to be interested in the spiritual work, which must have been a very great number of people indeed. Many did respond, including Nola Van Valer and her circle of students including Eltra Gentry.

The many who came, assembled at The Inn during the first days of July. In the lobby of The Inn, next to a large stone hearth, many talks were given by various people including Nola, Sister Thedra, Elaine Pratt Bragg, and Mother Mary. Some tape-recordings of those talks still exist and a few were transcribed and published by Cindy Luddington and are reprinted here. Mother Mary specifically asked that no financial donations be given to her, but encouraged each person in attendance to use their own money for whatever purpose they themselves believed to be important. One last member of The Order of Directive Biblical Philosophy, Grace Martin, was present for the gathering.

Mother Mary spoke to the group and told them a little about how she had come to Mt. Shasta. She said, "I have been coming here for many years, even before I met Mrs. Bense's group. At first I was like a lot of others, and I thought that I should be qualified to go inside the mountain. Through a wonderful man by the name of Mack Olberman I learned something else. To look at, he didn't look like much. He would jar me by kidding me in a rough diamond style. When I got serious he'd say, 'You damn dreamer, you.' He used coarse language, and at that time I was easily shocked as I thought I was so pious. I hadn't learned then to go in the highways and the byways of life and I thought I was coming up here to be a good student. I have not been inside the mountain and if it isn't divine will, I don't care if I ever go inside. I want my temple to be in doing. It doesn't have to have a place, and it doesn't have to be a creation of man or the saints. I want to be in the mixing bowl of the world. I'm not a teacher - I have too much to learn. I will not take students. I will not take disciples. I have learned the lesson of that in other lives and I have the memory of it. I want to be the temple not made by man. I want to be the temple that dwells within the temple of Creation. I want to be, not to teach, but to be. Do make this Fourth of July fruitful, if it's possible within your being. Go by yourself. Ask your inner self. Can you be a do-er, a server? A thinker is one thing, but a do-er is marvelous."

A large banquet was held on the Fourth in the restaurant of The Inn, and the next day the group went up the mountain to Sand Flat and spent several days camping in fellowship and contemplation. The stones from the large fire-circle at their gathering spot in the meadow remained in place for the next 40 years, until 2002.

Among the group were several people who claimed to be "channels," and according to Maxine one of these channeled a message from the Masters, "Relax. Enjoy nature. Be natural. Many of you are so high-strung in expectation that if one of us came out from the mountain, we'd scare you right out of your bodies." Maxine herself went for a walk away from the group, and to her surprise met one of the adepts of the mountain who had emerged from a retreat dressed in his spiritual robes, then led him back to the main group. While speaking with the group, this adept mentioned the book *The Lost Language of Symbolism* by Harold Bayley. One of the group, Trudy Allen, had a bookstore at 430 Walnut Street in Mt. Shasta, and in the months that followed she ordered many copies of Bayley's work which were bought by those who attended the meeting. Maxine kept in contact with this Brother for the rest of her life. In 1972, Maxine called again a similar gathering at Sand Flat. About 75 people were present for a large prayer circle on July 4th. On July 5th, one of the adepts of the mountain, not dressed in his robes but in ordinary clothes, visited those who remained from the larger group.

Over the years, many, many people have come to Mt. Shasta searching for the adepts of the mountain. Some have managed to accomplish this, more often in thought than in the physical body. The gathering in 1962 was truly unique, as it was the only gathering in the 20th Century where an adept from one of the retreats mixed with a public group, openly representing the Brotherhood.

According to Cindy Luddington, some of the events which happened during these few days were -

"An emissary from the Brotherhood appeared in public."

"A teacher from Atlantis was given an initiation in a public place, something never done before in such a manner." This refers to an experience which Elaine Bragg had in the lobby of The Inn on the evening of July 4th.

"A contact from the Andes made a permanent trip north."

"A representative of the Great White Chief came to Mt. Shasta."

"A stranger, walking through the group, left an iron tablet."

On July 8th, when most of the participants had gone their own way or returned to The Inn, Elaine Bragg found a poem left for her in The Inn's office. Several days before, Mother Mary mentioned in a talk to listeners in the lobby of The Inn that a special message would be given to Elaine, and that poem, *TO TEACH*, is reprinted below.

In the piece below, the transcript of a talk given in the lobby of The Inn and reprinted here from the Inspiration Center Newsletter, *the reader should note that several of the numbered list, such as the numbers 13 and 20, are expressions of the philosophy of The Order of Directive Biblical Philosophy, and are examples of the importance Mother Mary placed on these teachings. Even in the midst of what seems to be an extemporaneous discourse, the ideas of "Summary" and "Past Experiences" appear in the 13th and 20th places.*

THE VOICE IN THE WILDERNESS

from a tape-recording of MMM speaking on July 4th, 1962 and edited by her - published in Cindy Luddington's Inspiration Center Newsletter

Persons from many places have answered an inner call to Mt. Shasta. A Master Teacher is speaking. We can only bring you fragments of this speech for that which was revealed on that day and in the days following was of such tremendous import that it cannot be given in its entirety.

A voice from Mt. Shasta, the Heart of The Mountain; it has many names and is known by many all over the world, and many have heard and recognized. It is the voice of the Creator in action.

On the inner planes, this Mother voice is the Mother to all thought for those who walk the earth in disguise. Many turn to this guidance and tenderness when they have no one else to reveal their identity to. The prophets have been guided by this voice for many ages. It is not strange to them, as it is to many who feel loneliness in being cut off from their people.

94

The American Indians also know this voice. They have a name for it, "The Great Spirit." The East Indians have their name for this voice. The American races, white and black, have at some time or another heard this Mother voice.

Yes, Yes, Yes. Wise Ones are among you, walking the earth and working side by side with you. Seek and ye shall find. Knock and it shall be opened unto you. It is not permissible to give the following talk by this Wise One in its entirety, but we may bring you these fragments. Within this condensed report, in single sentences keynote, the Key to the door in your own Secret Chamber, you may find your own

1. It isn't just one retreat. The whole planet is being called at this time. The Retreats are training counselors for the work, so it can be brought out. We are waiting for this day to come.
2. Women are going to serve more marvelously than in any other cycle. That is why we see so many women going to lectures. Man is the do-er. Women are the vehicles.
3. You must not sleep any more. Awake. Awake. Awake.
4. Some Sacred Keys are being given at this time everywhere by this Great Silent Voice.
5. The highest Angels known to Creation are dropping down closer to Earth, as it is possible.
6. Creators are all in action, because they are responsible.
7. There are Angels of Being, in the body and out of the body. Some never take a body because they don't want to be crystallized into form. That is a step down in Creation.
8. The sound of the wave is JOY, JOY, JOY, and that sound is the one word of power in Creation. Nothing can be created without sound.
9. The Brothers of Solitude never give anything sacred while man is warring. The Retreats close when man has war. This call that has been sent forth was never done and will never be done again. It was created good. It cannot be void. It must be fulfilled. How great is our Creator! How patient is Creation!
10. Every word we speak comes back to us in some form. Directing sound with right feeling makes good karma.
11. The Truth is the Sword Jesus talked about. "I come with a Sword." You will be made over by using the word of Truth. Even the Great Prophets, even the Great Wise Ones have to be born over again. That is the Sword of Truth. It must happen to all.
12. The Saints come together through their purity of thought for a certain purpose for the future.
13. All mysteries must be unveiled for the summary is taken into action with thirteen. No more darkness. It is the way. No more Truth hidden to the one that knocks. Knock! It shall be answered.
14. To the Babblers, give no proof, but to the True in Heart, give proof.
15. Phylos, the author of *A Dweller on Two Planets*, often repeats these words, "So much to do and so few to do it."
16. The gathering of wisdom of the Great Plan. When we are together, who knows who will be the one to light the Flame again?

17. Nothing is too small. Sometimes the smallest things are the great things.
18. Anyone can be used. It doesn't have to be a Wise One. It doesn't have to be a sacred order.
19. Yea, be your own teacher. Live that which you are learning.
20. In the ancient time of the Brothers of Solitude, twenty was the building of the past, the gathering of all wisdom together. On the day of teaching, the great day of gathering will be over. But we must try together, living more than teaching. Speaking of twenty, it is the mathematics of the Ancients, the Brothers of Solitude, which today seems to be lost and is promised to be revealed again.
21. To be tolerant. The Great White Chief of the White Indians has said, "Jesus said Tolerance is one of the greatest virtues of the Path." To think, Jesus told his white tribe that Tolerance is one of the greatest virtues, and he tried to teach this to his disciples. They couldn't attain, so he went to the mountain to weep. To me, that was something beyond the world. As a rule, the people of the world are not tolerant.

We cannot bring out more of what was said that day, and the following days. It is our hope that you can find the hidden meanings in the keys we have given, by the Mother Voice. We will end her talk, which in actuality was of many hours, and was several days of steady teachings, not formal, but spontaneously, coming as gentle showers of rain, the Rain of Spiritual Knowledge, a baptism of the spirit. A closing statement of Mother Mary's talk, at one time, we leave with you. She said, "They thank me for the privilege of giving this to you. The Great Ones are thanking me! That they had they privilege of bringing this to you."

And I thank my Jesus, the Christ, for opening my mouth, and obeying what They want me to say. Not my will be done, and all that is in Heaven, Thy Will only be Done. Bring it down to earth, the fulfillment of the Kingdom of our Lord, Jesus Christ, the Way-Shower, that all Beings and Wise Ones bow to, for He shall lift this planet up unto where he promised.

"I lift all men up," He said. Including the Wise Ones, the Saints, the Sages, Sadhus, Prophets, and humble souls, the meek that shall fulfill the Kingdom of God.

Amen - Amen - Amen - So be it

July 4th, 1962, *comments by Elaine Pratt Bragg in the same informal gathering as the previous talk by Mother Mary, in the lobby of The Inn, transcribed and printed in The Inspiration Center Newsletter, with an introduction written by Cindy Luddington*

Another speaker is rising, not formally, but casually, speaking quietly as all in this group do. There is a hint of tears in her eyes. It is Elaine Bragg, the one who carries the wisdom of the Future as a balancing torch within her. A torch she cannot lay down, nor speak of, nor give out, or use, for that time is not yet. This knowledge, so precious, which she has been entrusted with, would serve to confuse man more than help him. Knowledge such as she carries is dangerous and a heavy load, for it will build for mankind, when man is ready, and it would destroy too, if falling into the wrong hands.

They chose the carrier of this knowledge well. She is a perfect chameleon, blending in with all peoples, a woman of many talents and abilities. A woman of beauty in bearing and face and form, and with humor as a shield. Yes, yes, in this age, woman is indeed the vehicle. The chalices of knowledge walk among you.

Elaine Bragg Speaking

I don't think I can say anything that could be as great as what Mother Mary has said. My cup is full and running over. How many of you feel that way?

Mother Mary has asked us over a period of years not to recognize her greatness, that the great are small, but many times she has brought tears to my eyes because of her greatness.

I have a few items in my files that I would like to bring to your attention. Sometime ago, the Order of the Brotherhood of Light gave me teachings about "the Network." I believe the Network is present tonight. First there is the Elohim, the Lords of Light, Chancellors, Mediators, Scribes, Message Bearers, Teachers, Organizers, and Students.

They told me this, also, on August 22, 1961 -

> "Our purpose is to bring the Light of God through the Wise One, Jesus the Christ, to the Universal Consciousness of all inhabitants of this Sphere. We stand United in this cause. Names are but stations in the Network of our Organization. A Network of Key Units, spread over the entire earth, will be able to project Power, God Power, at a Time of Crisis. The veil will be rent. All will know the Word of Power and the Power of the Word. The key to the door of light will be given when all may walk through.

> "Memories will be restored. The Spirit knows All, IS ALL, and motivates all things when the Soul allows it to be done. A nucleus will be established which will give us a real civilization for the future, the New Age that is to exemplify the Spiritual values, and the unfolding development of the Seven Senses. There will be motivation of thought through spiritual channels, the basis of receiving thought. The keynote of vibration in Universal Harmonies will be established upon this planet, or plane. All in the Radiant Light of the Christ, Jesus."

Recently, I was working in an office assignment in Long Beach, California, and I was doing some calculating at my desk, when as I reached over for some additional paper, I received the following message. I haven't changed any words, but part of it was personal instructions, which I shall not read. Here is a little of that message -

"Heed every signpost along your way, for they are marked. Your major procedure will be indicated. Watch and wait. I take up the cross for you to follow. I carry the burden, for now the weight is LIGHT. Yes, LIGHT. Forever and ever, the Rainbow will give the Light. Watch for the ARC of the COVENANT. The Covenant will be the reward. Take up the Cross and Follow Me. I am your Brother, Jesus."

In February of 1960, I received this message from Phylos. It seemed to pertain to this evening, and all of these days. I'd like to give it here -

"I greet you in the name of the Brotherhood of the Shasta Temple. I am Phylos. My wish for you will be expressed in three words, Love, Unity, and Attunement. We attest to the Unity of Our Plan to be manifested through the Love of the Wise Ones, reciprocated by your thought and attunement with Us, all of You.

"We ask that you realize the scope of all assignments. We do not state that each has his own assignment in the work ahead, but rather, that we wish you all to know that there must be a balance reached by the blending of all, Unifying the process of development and understanding. We urge that all understand this point.

"Personal opinions, whims, desires, do not have a place in the overall pattern we are placing before each one. A blending of Minds. A Unification of Souls, and Attuning with the Great Pattern is stressed at this time. We lend our assistance to help make this realization possible. We desire that you realize the plan must be fulfilled through your unity with us, and the Love and attunement, unconfined by personalities.

We do this all in the name of our Great Master, Savior. You are the Beloved Disciples, the Servers of the Great Plan."

This day was promised to us by Phylos over three years ago and it is most impressive to realize that we are here for a Great Purpose and a purpose that will bring forth the New Plan, under our Beloved Jesus, the one whom we are all working under, including Phylos and the other Wise Ones. Two years ago, I had the pleasure of being one of the seven points on a mission to this mountain, and many wonderful and unusual circumstances have taken place since that time.

*July 6*th*, 1962 - from a talk by MMM, transcribed in the Inspiration Center Newsletter*

As sunlight filters through the trees in the mountain splendor of Mt. Shasta, as also do the inspirational teachings sent out to each and all by the Teachers.

1. To our messenger: Empty your mind. Vibration for spiritual work. You are in this group for benevolent reasons. Principle for your group, "feed my sheep."

2. Accept help now on the physical plane wherever it comes from. Polarization is coming.

3. Would all recognize us or look through the outer that we may present? There are those among you in your group who are our teachers, those from the Angelic realm who have incarnated for this age. They are the most insignificant and the most inconspicuous and the most quiet as to what they are.

4. Each go into the forest unto himself and forget all previous forms of communication with us. Just enjoy the natural beauty that is here. All who are of the Christ Ray will be led. So each must be unto themselves, for this is the ultimate - God and man in direct communion.

5. We have watched each who answered the call and know and understand the difficulties each has had to release to find the way. This is an initiation and testing time for all and it is not over yet. Each will find release and understanding unto themselves.

6. Tomorrow, look for the strangers!

7. We must gain servers who are loyal to humanity. Father, God, faith, purity. Love is the entrance to serve in the Universal cause.

8. You have been given knowledge of many types and must discern what is safe to give to the world now. Mysteries are being given again and it is up to each one to develop discernment. Only Laws are kept secret for now. Word power and tone vibration cannot be given for a while yet.

9. Have child-like faith, coupled with humility. Once again, take a look at motive for service. Be unaffected in thought, as is your Beloved Jesus, the Christ.

10. Only in Divine Tolerance will you prevail through testing and re-adjustment. Bonafide is the meaning.

July 8th, 1962 - *from Cindy Luddington's Inspiration Center Newsletter*

On this date many of the pilgrims, travelers or what name you may give them, had dispersed. Some had stayed on at the Inn to enjoy the beauty of Nature and the congenial surroundings. Elaine Bragg was one of those who had stayed. It was a pleasant day, and she was in conversation with several persons in the lobby of the Inn. It was the same lobby in which on the 2nd of July a very remarkable and wondrous circumstance had occurred involving her. She had been promoted to a higher sphere of service and awareness, for work well done.

The one precipitating that event was with her now - the Contact from the Andes. There were several others with them in their conversation, and they did not notice the stranger who silently walked beside the desk, and then vanished down the hallway.

The telephone rang. Elaine rose, and went to the office to answer. Upon the desk was a sealed envelope addressed to her. Within the envelope was an unsigned message. A recognition of her station as a Teacher of Ancient Knowledge. Written on scratch paper -

TO TEACH - is to listen at all times to the voice of God
It is to sing and impart that song to every hungry heart.
It is to nourish each tender seedling with the moisture of your own tears.
It is to search tirelessly and ceaselessly for the answers for others.
It is to grow gently and steadily like an oak with outspreading, protecting arms.
It is to stand like a rock so all can reach out and steady themselves.
It is to bend like a reed against all winds.
It is to listen to the wisdom of each student no matter how low or high.
It is to give with all that is within you and strive for all that can come through -
As an expanding vessel to each as they ask or seek, making no difference in manner,
Be it a stumbling one or a master of wisdom.
It is to teach with heart and soul as if speaking to your Beloved Wise One.
It is to love, greatly, and shine on all alike and to release each, keeping no ties that bind.
So each individual can come your way and drink and eat, and pass on his way with no weight of gratitude or ties, leaving as an individual.
It is to hunger as each hungers and thirst as each thirsts, to be fulfilled as each is fulfilled.

July 10, 1962 - *from a talk by MMM, transcribed in the Inspiration Center Newsletter*

1. To all students of light who received the vibration of the Love Ray, know this, you are taught direct.

2. Awaken your identities and your individuality, for this is the order of the coming age.

3. Long have you slept, unaware of your birthright. It is now time to answer the call within your own soul.

4. We of the Brotherhood are once again coming to you to talk with you each, so that all can fulfill their mission. Who have come through this phase of testing and initiation taking place, that all are not aware of.

5. Seek within your own self and you will know where you are and if you have passed the refining of the past months.

6. There are no complete failures as many have believed, for has not the Christ said, and before Him, the ancient wisdom taught, "It is not the Father's wish that any be lost." Let the stumbling blocks be your stepping stones and if you have fallen and your heart be sincere, then rise again and walk with pride, ever upward and onward.

7. Each time you have stumbled and fallen and risen again has kept you close to your beloved Earth, which in the final analysis, keeps your feet on the ground and provides balance and teaches tolerance.

Given by spiritual telepathy to the seeker and server, Lady Mae.

A New Dispensation - *by Mother Mary and Cindy Luddington, The Inspiration Center Newsletter, Nov. 1966, describing the material found above*

These fragments have been gathered by the order of the teachers of mankind. They are presented now to mankind to awaken man to his own Divinity, to his own deep, hidden Godhood, and to make man realize that Sacred things, Sacred happenings, Sacred teachings and Initiations, are not mystic happenings of legend and fiction, but are happenings all the time, here and around you, in your own America and all countries everywhere.

Many Americans today will agree that perhaps there are such happenings, but feel that those happenings cannot possibly take place in their own land, in their own country, or in their own time. They might dream of a faraway place in the mystic Himalayas, or in Tibet, India, Asia, China, but not here, now, in our modern times, in America.

We present these fragments expressly to convey and convince each and all that Sacred happenings ARE taking place in England, Poland, Russia, India, China, and ALL countries on Earth. You need not search the four corners of the World, for that which you seek shall manifest to you, anywhere, at any time. As has been said for ages, "When the student is ready, the Master comes." Never has anything said been more true. Remember it, believe it, work for it.

You speak to Angels unaware. The Masters walk among you and watch you. The Brotherhoods are here in your lives. If you but look, if you but hear, and if you but search, believing, you WILL find them. They are physical beings and they walk among you in all stations of life. There is no station too low for them to manifest in, no life so downtrodden or despicable, that they will not hear, if that soul calls for help, no matter how silently he calls in his own darkened closet. God hears, and God sends his workers; they will come. Though one's sins be as scarlet, the Lord sees not thy sin, when you call upon him. Love makes all things white as the driven snow. The teachers point the way to the White Land.

Often the psychic abilities are a hindrance rather than an asset to the real workers, for in the glamour of the super-mundane gifts, one often loses sight of the clear goal, and finds oneself branching off into diverse paths, unknowingly.

You need not have second sight nor the ability to receive by mental telepathy or be a psychic or clairaudient or clairvoyant, and yet you can be and ARE important in the service of bestowing help and guidance to man. All anyone really needs is SINCERITY and the LOVE OF GOD, and the DESIRE TO SERVE. Guidance and teaching will come to all for the Lord moves in multitudes of ways, his wonders to perform.

8. MOTHER MARY'S SECOND TRIP TO INDIA, 1966

CALCUTTA
From The Inspiration Newsletter, May 1966, by Cindy Luddington

Mother Mary went to India as a Mendicant of Old, not having money or any means of getting any, but she went with Faith in the Great purpose of her work, and knowledge that God would provide, as he does indeed supply for all his creatures.

Those who helped were poor people, having no money for their own uses, as all true students are. Henry Fuller, who is a resident of Long Beach, and who makes his living by working 16 hours a day, supplying carrot juice and other vegetable juices through his one man operation, did somehow manage to scrape up enough money to buy a ticket for her to go to India. Al Jennings, a night clerk at The Inn at Shasta, managed to scrape up $20 for a bus ticket for Mother Mary to go to San Francisco, and to stay overnight at a hotel.

She did not land in India with much money, and that was spent for stamps, writing to those who awaited information from India. When the stamps ran out she had to stop writing letters, but one person sent $5 so that she could have a few stamps again. To write from across the sea, one really needs to send Airmail, for by boat the mail never seems to arrive in the States, it seems. It costs around one dollar to send one letter, or perhaps more in India.

Mother Mary gave us permission to print any news that we are inspired to use, as she explained - "You can put anything in your monthly magazine, as you are sending to the American Indians and you know how I feel about them. They are my true friends, plus, of course, your many other readers of all races and beliefs."

We know Mother Mary is anxiously awaiting the arrival of Henry Fuller and Grace Fuller, with the trailer and the documents, without which the true work cannot be done, and the land cannot be utilized. She is awaiting the time when she can again cook her own food, as the food is different there and it is affecting her health unfavorably.

Some of our readers have asked for her address, so that they may write to her, so we will include it now.   Mother Mary Maier
             c/o Benu Ghosh
             Hindustan Park
             Calcutta, India

Although he bought the trailer, Henry never made it to India. Mother Mary returned to the U.S. a few weeks after this piece was published

THE NAKED SADHU

In July of 1966, shortly after her return to the US, a tape of Mother Mary speaking to a group of people in California was recorded. It records the details of the first three weeks of her visit to Calcutta. The following are excerpts from that tape regarding the events in Allahabad, which took place at the Kumba Mela.

I had told different ones that they could not go to India with me, that I wanted to go alone. I told everybody that wanted to go, but I did not tell Andy Anderson for some reason. On January 15th, Henry Fuller was arranging the ticket with Pan Am and asked Andy to go to San Francisco and pick up the ticket. Andy said. "Yes, I'll go and bring the ticket back." Henry made arrangements with his credit card over the phone and Andy went to San Francisco and picked up my ticket, and he bought a ticket for himself. When he came back, I could not tell him no, because I had not told him, and I had no right to tell him he couldn't go.

Four months before, Andy had a vision. He'd seen the crowd that met me at the airport, all the people, and the full procedure that took place. He didn't tell me about it until we came back from Allahabad. I asked him why he didn't tell me and he said, "It was too fantastic, but everything happened just as in my vision." It was 3:35 early in the morning when I arrived in Calcutta and there were these blessed ones with their flower wreaths looking through the gate with their faces to the gate and the customs men left all their stations. Andy stepped aside and went back to the wall. He told me later, "The reason I stepped back was because I was so excited that I was seeing everything as it was in my vision. I wanted to see from a distance the whole thing."

On the plane, I heard a man's voice. I was in a seat by the window and nearby was Andy. Up here, in the air, was an aged man to the chest, with long white hair and a long beard and he said, "I've found you, now you find me on January 25th at Allahabad."

When we reached Calcutta the 22nd of January at 3:35 AM I said to Benu Ghosh, who gives me the third floor of his house to live in when I'm there, I said, "Benu, I've got to be in Allahabad on the 25th and today's the 22nd. You must get me there." I knew that in India now you have to have 20 days to get your ticket to travel, and then you have to be in line with a number. This 25th was just a couple of days away and I was anxious to get there. He laughed. He thought I was just anxious to get there and he laughed. He and his wife had been led to buy tickets eight months before to go to Allahabad. He didn't know about the meeting at Allahabad, but he had bought tickets for all of us. He said, "Mother, yes, I know. I have the tickets ready. Eight months ago." So we were on the train on the 23rd of January. We arrived the 24th.

The 25th I was looking all over the place for this man. Andy and B. Ghosh would laugh because I was looking for his face everywhere. So the 25th we were walking down the midway. Way off in the distance was a man dancing, singing, saying unbecoming words, breaking every rule for that Holy Ground where those thousands of Great Ones were. We were looking at him way off in the distance and everybody was excited because he was breaking every rule. There is a strict rule on this Holy Ground where they meet. When He came up to us he was dancing, slobbering and he was going on.

I had asked Andy when we were in Calcutta, "Andy, make arrangements with Benu for all the expenses, and we will pay when we get back. We don't want to handle physical money, not because it's money, but as the use of it is a rule. We will not handle any money. Will you give me a promise not to handle any money and make arrangements?" He said yes.

Here comes this man dancing, kicking his legs, unbecoming to his surroundings. He comes up to Andy and said, "Give me rupees, give me rupees." Andy gave me a knowing look. Pretty soon the man danced over to me and bumped me. He hurt me because he was very rough. Then he went over to Benu and did the same with him. Benu and I were becoming angry because of his roughness. He went back to Andy and he went right up close to his face. Benu and I were looking at Andy. Andy's face took a shock as if he had the greatest spiritual shock he ever had. We looked at him. Pretty soon, Andy went to his back pocket and pulled out his wallet and was going to give the man some money. He shook his hand and said, "Nay, nay, nay." Andy looked at me again. All of these priests, high priests, and monks saw this wallet full of money and all rushed up begging for money. This wonderful great man kept moving them away just with his hands, just with his hands, and would not let them get near Andy.

Then he came and started dancing around me. He would come close and I almost fell over. Then he got right up to my ear and in beautiful Oxford English he said, "Mother, I've been waiting a long time for you. Now that you've found me and I have found you, I must leave immediately. Mother, way off in the distance, when the real is separated from the unreal, in Bombay there is a large fortune for your mission. It has been there a long, long time, Mother. When you return to America, you must prepare for the dividing of the way. You will have to be strict with people, but it should be done with love. Adieu, Adieu, Mother, I must go."

Then he went over to Benu. He danced around Benu and Benu was angry. Benu grabbed him by the shoulders and was just ready to shake him when he disappeared right in his hands. "Oh Mother, a Great One!" We all saw him disappear.

A week or so later when we were in Calcutta, Benu came up to the third floor and he said, "Mother, I am to give you a piece of ground. Will you, I, Andy and Novogour go to this piece of ground tomorrow?" I said yes. A taxi came and we went on this ground. He said, "Mother, take off your shoes, walk on this ground and see if this is the ground." I took off my shoes and he said, "I'm going to show you the markers for this ground." So he took me around and showed me the boundary stones.

I walked according to how I felt and was impressed to stand on one of those markers. I stood on this marker and all of a sudden on the next marker right in front of me, stood this man from Allahabad. He was naked and he had a saint's topknot up on his head and his hair was dark. He faced me. He said, "Mother, turn to your right" and I turned right. He said, "What do you see?" I said, "I see a lot of ground and buildings way off in the distance." He said, "Now turn facing me." I turned. "Now what do you see?"

"I see a lot of ground and way off in the distance I see some trees." He said, "Turn to your left. What do you see?" I turned to my left and said, "I see a lot of ground and also trees ion the distance." He said, "Mother, these sections that you see, will be specific circumsections when the need is come. They will each be for certain types of future service work, and each section has its own purpose. This ground is for separating the real and the unreal. It will be done silently, the wonders to be performed. Everyone who walks on this ground will be changed. You will have a part in it. When you return to America, you must be more of a disciplinarian in order to separate the real from the unreal, and it must be done with love."

In the retreats in India, and otherwise like at the gathering each twelve years, they have a section for each type of Great One. Here were women naked ones, here were men naked ones, here were different types and they all had their sections. Benu had said to me, "Mother, do you want me to make arrangements for you to go with the naked women?" I had said to Benu, "Truly, they are wonderful, but if I took initiation with the naked women, I would have to live their way of living. I cannot do that, Benu, because I am coming back initiated to help the Great Ones gather. I would lose my spiritual freedom wings. I would be tied. I can not do it."

I knew this Great One when he was naked on this marker. I knew he was wearing these other things for some reason so I asked him. I said to him, "Why did you come to me on the plane with white hair and a white beard and aged? In Allahabad you had a red, dirty rag on you, your hair was dark, unkempt, and you had rough ways. Why did you do that? Here you are, a naked sadhu."

He said, "On the plane I represented age and wisdom. At Allahabad we had to find each other to serve. Here you see me as I am, as I live. I am truly a naked sadhu as your mind has figured. From time to time, I will be with you."

Now this little tape -

Here follows a transcript of the tape recorded in India of a talk given in the evening of the day she stood on the boundary stone. It was played at this point in July, 1966 for her listeners, and the tape recording transcribed above was removed from the recorder in order to play it. The original tape is lost, but this transcript was printed in India.

ADDRESS TO DEVOTEES IN INDIA

My Sons and Daughters of the World,

Please hear me. Now to you here, my sons and daughters, I give my blessings. I have come from America on a very holy mission. And I was ordered by the Creator to visit India in this Holy Mission. The whole human family is sick and decaying. There is still time when we can and should do something. A most important thing to be done is to secure a large tract of land permanently on which to gather the holy saints, the true sadhus and the holy mothers.

For the saints do have wisdom and expect nothing in return for themselves. Having these saints on a permanent ground isn't for their benefit, but for the sake of all of us. It is necessary for all of them to be one permanent ground in order for their powers to build and grow. This is our only hope.

Peace organizations time and again have come together, but nothing has been done for all the human races. Organizations have failed.

What is the cause of war? Each nation has karma and none escapes suffering from its karma. History repeats itself over and over. Has anything been gained by war for any nation? Perhaps for a time, if a national leader gets his way for good but shortly after he dies the human family falls back into its selfish way of living again.

The ancient writings and manuscripts tell us out of the East comes the light. Who has this light? The saints have it.

A man like Mahatma Gandhi, who brought freedom to India, will be hailed more in the future because all nations will taste of the bitter cup of suffering. What power of good has been done by a single man such as Gandhi! Picture in your minds what the power can be when the saints are gathered in one place. Even as we step on that ground, our minds must change.

Predictions have been made that 1966 and 1967 will be trying times. I will stay here in India and help gather the holy saints, the true sadhus and the holy mothers. The mothers will hold this place to keep sons and daughters like a happy, holy family, so the saints can give of their knowledge and teach an understanding of wisdom.

My heart is aching, my soul cries out for all life. The cause of history repeating itself is the separation of race, caste and religion. Each one feels they are right. Then the power that money gives in the material world is the downfall of all races, castes and religions, and takes the place of fear of these powers that money gives.

Religion has also come together, but nothing is being done for all. Men and women, as it is today, will not make things better for all living life. There is always some personal motive somewhere in the plan.

I say again, the holy saints are the only hope. They are builders of light. They must be gathered together.

Let us not just talk about doing, but let us be doers. Each one can do something no matter how small it may be. It adds to the chain reaction of good. Your conscience will tell you just what you can do. For in the real, there is no great and no small. Nothing good is ever lost. Let us from this moment start doing what is needful. And do not come just to visit, but have something you really want to do.

Benu Ghosh has given land to start the gathering. He took me to see the land this afternoon. There are some friends coming from America by the name of Henry Fuller and his wife, and also Al Jennings. Henry Fuller is bringing me a house trailer to live in, and a truck for travelling. Benu Ghosh is putting a tent on the land, so it will be started.

Now, in the meantime, I can be contacted at Benu Ghosh's house, Hindustan Park, Calcutta. And again, I ask that you do not just come to visit, as it will take too much strength, and I wish to use my energy for the gathering of the saints. My blessing to all.

A SECOND ADDRESS GIVEN IN INDIA

Here follows the text of a second address given soon after the first, at the Kali Temple in Calcutta, also taped and transcribed in India -

My sons and daughters, I give you my blessing. My mission is a very holy one coming from America. There are a few saints and mothers left. Some sadhus are real and are trying to live their life the best way they can. These few can save the good that is left. They would not sell what they have become for any nation, caste, race or religion. We need to save the wisdom of the saints, true sadhus and mothers. Religion as it is becoming is enslaving the true seekers of the spiritual life.

What have the young to look forward to? As it is, their minds are turning to the reverse. Look at the youth all over the world. Some young leader gets an idea, and if he is strong in mind, he can lead whoever is around him and the rest follow like a belled goat. I have seen in India the same as in America, only America is so materially minded she is asleep spiritually.

Untrue mothers and sadhus, thinking of prestige, power and rupees, are influenced by politicians for what they can give. So those sadhus use this for their own gain. Even holy days are sick and decaying. There is still time to secure a large tract of ground permanently for the holy ones, so all can come together to build their wisdom. Each is different in his own way. Alone they do not have the strength to heal the world, but together interlacing their wisdom like a rainbow gives strength and power to them, which the world is sadly in need of at this time. When they are together apart from the world yet in the world they can save what good is left.

Rishis, the wise in the Himalayan Mountains, voiced the time would come when they must come down and bring their disciples with them. Krishna spoke of it, Gauranga spoke of it, and Jagadbandhu spoke of the third lila combination of all things. I have said this for many years. When I was here in 1950 and 1951 Benu Ghosh took me to the Holy City of Uttakesh. I said the Holy Ones should come out in the world now and then to get used to the world's vibrations and keep going back and forth, as it is very hard for the pure to stay in the world very long. I have had a taste of this when I would go into seclusion. This has an effect on spiritual thought and body. True ones do not have a place in the world. That is the reason they go into jungles and mountains. But the time is here when they must come into the world or nothing will be left.

There are trying and dark days coming. 1966 and 1967 is the beginning and from then on. All nations have karma, and none can escape karma. History repeats itself over and over, and this time with men and women in their conceit of power that money gives them. But when the law of nature gets angry, then how great are they? The wise do not interfere with the world's way of living. They let experience take its course, so worldly people also suffer karma. This takes time for growth and is the reason why saints as a rule go away. They must also learn that the time is near when they must serve because of their disciples in other lives. They must come into the world to help them because of their connection in other lives. They cannot escape the responsibility of having disciples. There must be love and tolerance for all the human family found regardless of nation, race, caste or religion.

Why have you been created? Different in race, yes, but you breathe the same air, you live in the same world. Now think this over! There is no man or woman of today who can solve the problems of the world. If a superior person came and could heals the ills of the world, would the human family as a whole accept him?

Tolerance and patience are lacking. Animal nature in humans seems to kill for defense and fear. So does the wild animal kill for fear, defense, and food. The wild animal in nature has the smell of a human person when he is near him and when he is in danger. Only in this bitter cup of life does one awaken and think of experiences and teachings. Now at my age - 71 - I am not in India for foolishness, this is very serious.

India is a very ancient nation. She is the starting point of the spiritual light of the world. The ancient manuscript writing speaks, "Out of the East comes the Light." The saints are IT. Now I wish to say, curiosity seekers have no place with me. There is no time and I should not give my strength. Also, personal lives of people should not come to me for blessing. My mission is to bring the saints, the true sadhus and Mothers together. When the time comes that these Holy Ones are on the ground, those that need blessing and do walk on the ground will have it. Because there is still time, but short, if you know of a true sadhu and want to serve, bring them to me, or make arrangements so I can go to them. I have a house-trailer and a truck to pull it. I will live in this trailer and go to streets and mountains. This would help and give you blessings in service. Now this is my own feeling - the good and bad leaders of the material world are back in bodies, a battle of good and evil and having its effect on the world. Also, the real ones want to finish their part in this world and do not want to come back in physical bodies any more.

I will not take invitations to speak, only if it is of a spiritual nature, and I must know the reason I am asked and what is going to take place. I have had two experiences which were not good. The first was being asked by a guru questions he had no right to ask. Being a guru, he should have known better. The second was a large public gathering. Why did they ask me to come and who was responsible? They did not even have the common courtesy to introduce me. People wondered why I was there and who I was. I want to investigate before I leave India who was responsible for such an action. This is the reason for not taking invitations unless I know it is for a spiritual purpose. I do demand respect and should have an apology for this action. I will not visit personal homes unless it is for a specific reason. This I must do because of the real, and time is short. I want all to know that in this entire life I do not take disciples, and don't expect to take disciples now, because I remember in other lives of not taking them, so I am not in this life. I have come to be with the Holy Ones, and not serve for a few, but for all.

Mother Mary said that she never saw the naked sadhu again. She died less than four years after going to the Kumba Mela in Allahabad. However, Andy Anderson did. When Andy bought the tickets for India, he thought that he would be accompanying Mother Mary in her mission to build a spiritual community in India, a mission he had frequently heard her describe. He didn't realize that on this visit, she planned to go alone, and that the community would be built later. Some weeks after returning to Calcutta from the Kumba Mela, Andy was staying at the Ramakrishna Mission when this adept appeared to him and took him out of his body. Andy was taken to a place that can only be described as a museum of human history, kept by the adepts, which had artifacts going back more than 60,000 to 80,000 years. And among the oldest of these artifacts Andy said there was a very small spacecraft. Similarly, when Mother Mary visited the Dalai Lama in Lhasa in 1951, she was taken to some rooms deep in the lower levels of the Potala in which she was shown artifacts which were also of very, very ancient origin, more than 60,000 years - no spacecraft, though. Here follows some of Andy's account of his experiences in India.

CAVERN OF TREASURES
by Andy Anderson

In January of 1966, I made the longest plane ride of my life with Mother Mary. I was surprised how well she handled such a grueling trip. We had a stop in Hawaii, then an unexpected stop at Wake Island, due to some problems with the plane. From the air, Wake Island appeared like a huge doughnut. We also stopped in Tokyo, Hong Kong and Rangoon. While all these cities showed a lot of lights from the air, Calcutta seemed dark and foreboding - very few lights could be seen from the air.

On arriving, I was amazed by the large number of devotees on hand to greet Mother Mary at the airport. I had a strange dream before the trip began of her being surrounded by a crowd of worshipful devotees, but I didn't think so many would be possible.

Mother Mary was taken to reside in the home of Benu Ghosh, while I was taken to the Ramakrishna Mission to get a room. Many students and travelers stayed there to take advantage of the low rents. I was so exhausted from the trip that I collapsed on the bed, forgetting to pull down the mosquito netting over the bed. When I awakened, it looked as though I had a fantastic case of the measles. But I was lucky, as I didn't get ill from anything. The next day I became acquainted with the Benu Ghosh family. He had a pleasant wife, a son, and four daughters. Many times I ate a noon meal with them. Soon I was accompanying Ghosh, who was a publisher, on many business trips in India. We made a trip to the Kumba Mela in Allahabad, with other members of the party including Mother Mary, Benu's daughter, and a servant. The Kumba Mela is regarded as one of the most holy events in India. During a twelve-year cycle, it is held every four years at one of the four holy cities in its turn. I was surprised to see how green and clear the water is in this part of the Ganges, so different from the muddy, dirty water near Calcutta. We took a boat on the beautiful green water of the Ganges, and I was startled to see the body of a priest float in clear view under the boat. It must have been a priest, judging by the top-knot on his head. It was their belief that that those who die in the Ganges during these holy days would never have to reincarnate again.

But an even stranger event was to come. As I was walking past the unending rows of tents near Allahabad with Benu and Mother Mary, a small brown-skinned man, in only a loin cloth, came dancing wildly about us. As I didn't know what to make of it, I finally pulled out my wallet and offered him some rupees. For the first and only time in India, someone turned down the offer of money. In the meantime, I'd been keeping my eye on some suspicious-looking characters who were edging closer to us. They had long knives hanging about their waists, and were dressed in an Arab-like fashion. Suddenly, the little man leapt in front of them and they scattered. I could only wonder what he said to them to make them leave in such a hurry.

A wondrous experience was waiting for me when I returned to the Ramakrishna Mission in Calcutta. A soft laugh awakened me one morning, and I heard a voice say "Master Junior." I was stunned to see the aethereal form of the wild dancer from Allahabad. I had never been called "Junior" since my boyhood days, and had never mentioned it since to anyone. It must have been his way to let me know that he knew all about me. Before I had time to think about it, I had joined him in the only out-of-body experience I've ever had. It was probably best that I didn't have any choice in the matter, as I'm sure I would have refused to make such a trip.

I found myself almost immediately in a high cavern that seemed more like a museum. I was given a whirlwind tour. One area was obviously devoted to religious objects, but being from a more materialistic society, I was more interested in secular objects. These records were not devoted to any particular religion or culture, such as that of the Hindus, but rather the history of mankind through the ages. In what I saw, an emphasis was placed on the art works of man. There was an unending display of painting, sculptures, and other works of art. Another thing I remember is a machine I took to be a spaceship, but may have been only an aircraft of some sort. Also, there were other objects nearby, of which I could make no sense. I wish I'd had more time to examine these strange objects. My guide forcefully pointed out some objects of art as if they should have special meaning to me, but I didn't understand.

In a short time I found myself back in Calcutta. I was in a whirl of confusion, but at the same time I felt strangely energized. No doubt I missed a big opportunity because of my lack of understanding. I wasn't about to mention such a strange experience to anyone, but later I told Mother Mary what had happened. She didn't seem too surprised. Later, Mother Mary became deathly ill during her trip to see the Dalai Lama. When I saw her at the railroad station with Benu, I feared for her life, as she looked so ill. As soon as possible, she was on a plane back to the United States. Complications of this illness probably contributed to her death in 1970. I remained in India for a couple of months more, leaving at the end of August. This experience in India sent me on a spiritual quest that would have never been the case as otherwise.

9. THE LAST YEARS AT THE INN

At the end of "the Summer of Love" in 1967, a great many young people left the San Francisco area for greener pastures. Some of them went to Mt. Shasta. Around this time, Mother Mary's network of helpers and co-workers who had been with her for many years began to break down. Henry Fuller and Elaine Bragg were busy with events in their own lives. Daniel Boone had a difficult time supporting his family in the depressed economy of Siskiyou County, and moved from McCloud back to the Giant Rock area in Landers, where his wife's family lived. Al Jennings, who had followed Mother Mary to India, stopped off on the way back in the Philippines to investigate psychic healing and did not return to Mt. Shasta until 1969. As she had become ill in India, she could not run The Inn without help. She spent much time in seclusion. Some young people stepped forward to the work that needed to be done, but some problems surfaced as well. One couple who supervised the day-to-day operations of the hotel and restaurant were discovered to be cheating their younger workers out of whatever meager financial resources they might have had, and this couple was summarily sacked when the facts came to light. Linden Carlton and Robert Williamson regularly drove Lady Mae to Ashland, Oregon for healing treatments with the therapeutic-touch healer Joe Jessel, and eventually rented an apartment there so she could stay over for more treatments and rest.

Linden, Robert, Bill Varrier, and Saul Barodofsky accompanied Mother Mary on her last trip to the Southwest to visit Native Americans in the summer of 1967. During this trip, the five people were cooped up in a car together for three weeks. On the trip, Mother Mary sometimes dropped a few hints about her work with the Native Americans, and some comments she made during the journey have found their way into this book. As they reached the Hopi reservation while returning from Oklahoma, the group ran out of money. When the Hopi elders realized who she was, remembering her well from her relief missions, they reached in their own pockets and gave her whatever money they had to help her return to Mt. Shasta. This was particularly touching to Saul, as the people who helped them were very, very poor themselves. She met for some time with elderly women from the tribe as part of her spiritual work during this trip, and visited the small adobe dwelling kept for her on the Third Mesa for the last time.

By the fall of 1967, only a small number of young people including Helen Ruth, Jack Darrow, Clark Coffee and a few others comprised the staff of The Inn. Mother Mary said that she "put a call out in the aethers" for those who could hear, and waited to see who would respond to that call.

After a long day's journey from Haight-Ashbury on a very hot day in October of 1967, I met Mother Mary at The Inn around 11 in the evening. The first thing she said to me was, "Don't do drugs. It gets in your cells, and has a negative influence on your consciousness. The younger you are when you do it, the worse it is for you. Drugs will ruin your discernment."

Mother Mary rarely spoke of the *siddhis,* or spiritual powers, conferred on her in the Himalayan forest glen. She believed that showing these powers off was unethical, and called it "using powers for display." Sometimes though, something would leak out. Once she mentioned that she had a method by which she could see the past of a person or object, and in the case of a human being she could go back through their past lives and into the future ones as well. In the summer of 1967 Linden Carlton met a despondent young man in Redding, California named Joe, who believed himself to be a female soul trapped in a male body. Today, he would be politely called "a transgender individual," but no one used this term in Redding in the 1960's. The situation was dire, and Linden thought to himself that if he took Joe to Mother Mary, she would know how to help him. When they reached The Inn, Mother Mary was sitting on a couch in the lobby, and welcomed Joe with open arms and unconditional love. Helen Ruth gave him the nickname "Pepe." Mother Mary told him he was spiritually connected to the Great White Chief. Later, she privately went to Linden and said, "If you never do anything else in this life, bringing Pepe here is the most important thing you have ever done. He is the first person I have ever met in this life who took incarnation on this planet by choice." She evidently could see all of Pepe's previous lives back through his first one on earth. If she ever mentioned someone's past lives, it was never to say, "You were Cleopatra" or some such thing as the psychics do, but it was always a bit of information about the individual's purpose in life, a purpose which may take many lifetimes to fulfill.

Saul Barodofsky, who later became the leader of The Dervish Healing Order, was very close to Mother Mary, but he wanted a teacher. She of course refused to take disciples, but she understood his wish and sought to help him on his own path. Since she really didn't like to give anything more than the most general advice to people, lest she influence their path, she had to find some creative ways to help people without actually telling them what to do. When Saul asked her for her help in finding a teacher she said to him, "Ask anyone you think might be your teacher if he has heard of Jagadbandhu." Saul went off, and asked anyone he thought might be his teacher this question. No one knew of Jagadbandhu. This was somewhat disheartening to him, as he knew Mother Mary would not have idly stipulated this detail. One day he met Samuel Lewis, affectionately known as Sufi Sam to the San Francisco spiritual community, who was the disciple of Hazrat Inayat Khan, and an initiated teacher of the Chisti order whose full name was Sufi Ahmed Murad Chisti. Saul asked Sufi Sam, "Have you ever heard of Jagadbandhu?" He replied, "No, never heard of him." From the sound of his voice in that very moment, Saul knew in his heart, this is my teacher.

Curiously, in his writings about his spiritual travels in India Samuel Lewis mentions meeting Swami Ram Dass, also known as "Papa Ram Dass," and who should not be confused with the LSD guru who adopted a similar name. Swami Ram Dass early in his life visited Jagadbandhu and heard him make the statement, "Initiation by a guru in the modern world is superfluous." Swami Ram Dass recognized Jagadbandhu as a saint, but could not accept Jagadbandhu's pronouncement on guruism and in his writings sought to refute Jagadbandhu's admonition. Like Swami Ram Dass, modern Hindu theorists are still busy defending caste and atavistic beliefs in the name of orthodox Hinduism, some even teaching "The guru is greater than God." These pious theorists demonstrate the truth that orthodoxy is *Avidhya*.

In addition to Saul, a number of other young people who knew Mother Mary later became disciples of Murshid Samuel Lewis. These included Jabbar Williams, Judith Erickson, Gypsy Updike who took the Sufi name Basira, and the couple Mahbud and Sylvia. On September 10th, 1969, Samuel Lewis visited The Inn on his way to Canada, accompanied by Saul and Mansur Johnson. Mother Mary was not there at the time as she was taking healing treatments in Ashland, but Samuel Lewis spoke with Helen Ruth for a time. During the same trip, he also visited several people who had previously lived at The Inn who now lived in Southern Oregon, and together the party visited Crater Lake. Afterwards, the Murshid said to Saul that he would accept "any and all" connected with Mother Mary as his disciples, which to him meant accepting a deep responsibility for the progress of another soul. He was once asked, "What do you want out of life?" His reply was, "To see the Light of Spiritual Realization emanating from even one of my disciples."

In the summer of 1968, someone left a copy of *The Sufi Message* by Hazrat Inayat Khan at The Inn, and Mother Mary was implored to talk about Sufism by her staff. Even though she considered herself in seclusion, and was not usually seeing people, for some reason she decided to give a public talk on Aug. 12, 1968 about Inayat Khan and his tradition. This was the last public talk she ever gave. Many young people who were living in the area came to hear her speak, and the restaurant overflowed with listeners.

Among the information she presented was the statement that Sufism is older than Islam, and has its roots in a group of adepts, 36 men and 9 women, who have been with humanity since the beginning of the world, and who embody the ways of the Creator. She called this group "the Wanderers" said that these Great Ones observe the evolution of the human race, for the benefit of the Creator, and that if you ever happened to meet one, you would not notice him or her, as they have "the true being" and are entirely incognito. She stated that the Wanderers have their counterparts on other planets as well, and that they preserve the essence of human evolution from one cycle to the next. Before Atlantis, before Mu, the most ancient of Sufi saints begot a race of people who lived in spiritual wisdom, and many of them are still in the body. When in the holy city in the Himalayas in 1951, she spoke to the saints of that city of the need for enlightened souls to come together and cooperate in the work. She said on this evening in 1968 that such a meeting had since taken place, and that saints and Sufis from all over the world had met incognito to further the Divine Plan.

Regarding Hazrat Inayat Khan himself, Mother Mary told her listeners of how Inayat Khan appeared to her in the middle of the night in 1950 at Dr. Ferguson's home, telling her that he had met Jagadbandhu and that he was transformed by the avatar in 24 hours. He said to her that she would be transformed in India, as he had been. He spoke to her of the ancient Sufis, and told her that she would have contact with them in India, and the modern Sufis as well. She had great respect for Inayat Khan and considered him as someone through whom Jagadbandhu worked to further world salvation and the development of the consciousness which will emerge in the Seventh Root Race.

Few people today, in the new millennium, realize that Inayat Khan was the first master of North Indian classical music to perform in the West, and that he had Debussy as a student. His vina still resides with the Debussy family. He was instrumental in introducing to the West that harmonic system latent in Rag Malkauns, based in the harmonic structure created by the tonic, fourth, and flatted seventh, which was pioneered in Europe by Cyril Scott, and which Debussy used extensively. In the Indian tradition, this harmonic system is said to be "the music of the Djinns." Cyril Scott regarded it as the system of the nature spirits or devas, and wrote of it in his book *Music, Its Secret Influence Throughout the Ages*. A knowledgeable listener will find compositions from Inayat Khan's family tradition, or gharana, imbedded in Debussy's "Afternoon of a Faun."

After explaining to the group why she did not take disciples, and encouraging them to follow their own light, she said. "The slow way is to be your own teacher, under your own life tree. It's a slow way. You can go to a great teacher, as companionship and fellowship, but no one can take you to where your light is. Every animal, flower, tree, every life visible and invisible, will come to perfection, and sooner than you think, because destruction is forcing the issue. The negative and the positive must balance each other. When these Great Ones give their service, age after age, it quickens us."

During her talk she made the comment, "All the ancient religions were given through fire." This did not seem too far-fetched to those who had shared a campfire with dear friends and family on the slopes of Mt. Shasta, or who had kept a solitary vigil until late at night with the last flames of a campfire becoming embers.

In the second volume of *The Lost Language of Symbolism,* Harold Bayley writes -

> "As *tan* meant *fire,* the name VOTAN resolves into VO-TAN, 'The Giver of Fire.' In Gypsy language, *potan* means *tinder,* and *tinder* does not differ from the adjective *tender.* Fire was originally obtained through the friction of *tinder*-wood or *timber. Timber* may equated with *tambour,* a drum, and the words *wood* and *wooden,* as also *Wednesday,* may be traced to WODAN or HU, 'The Giver of Fire.'"

Mother Mary also said to us, "If the young people here today want advice from me, my advice is to go into the forest and learn the power of the music people call discordant. When you are ready, you will be called." She told those in attendance that the work of The Inn was to be a contact point for all the spiritual brotherhoods, retreats, and traditions of real spiritual knowledge, and not just for a single order or retreat, such as the one within Mt. Shasta. There is some reference to this in the July, 1962 material as well.

In the summer of 1969, a Buddhist group from San Francisco named Kailas Shugendo came to Mt. Shasta to climb the mountain as a kind of walking yogic practice. Some members of the group came to The Inn and asked to see Mother Mary. They presented a copy of *The Way of the White Clouds* by Lama Anagarika Govinda as a kind of calling card, and mentioned that their teacher was the only disciple of the Lama. Mother Mary was in seclusion and did not generally meet with people, but one of her employees spoke with the Buddhists and told them that their message would be passed on to her. When Mother Mary came downstairs for lunch a few hours later, she was told about the visit of the Buddhist group, and of their request to meet with her. Neal Meshon showed Mother Mary his copy of *The Way of the White Clouds* and she took a momentary glance at Lama Govinda's picture on the back of his book. She then said, "He's real. I want to meet with them." A young man who lived on the mountain was dispatched up the slopes to find the group and relay the message that she would meet with the Buddhists and spend the night above Bunny Flat with the group at their campsite. He caught up with them at Lake Helen, at the base of the Heart. Among the members of the Buddhist group was a 17-year-old Arthur Russell, who later became well known as an avant-garde cellist.

Lady Mae considered this meeting a happy occasion, and went across the street with Linden and Robert to Mt. Shasta Market to buy picnic supplies to share with one and all. She walked up and down the aisles filling a shopping cart with hot dogs, hamburgers, and all the rest, including some stuff for those who might not eat meat. When she got to the counter, the clerk totaled up the bill, and it came to something like $32.43. She took out her wallet, and counted all the cash she had. It came to about $8, and as Linden and

Robert watched, she asked the clerk, "How much did you say that was?" He said, "$32.43, Ma'am." She counted the same money out again, and it came to about $20. She asked the clerk, "How much was that again?" He said politely, "$32.43." She counted it out for a third time, and it came to exactly $32.43.

When she returned to The Inn, she donned her spiritual robes and the necklaces she called "my credentials," and went to Bunny Flat. In the evening, the Buddhists returned to their campsite from the top of the mountain in groups of two and three. She spoke with the gathering for many hours before a great roaring fireplace, and some of the Buddhists did a fire-walking practice based on Japanese Shingon meditation. She said in a nostalgic mood that this meeting reminded her fondly of her times in Tibet.

Around this time in the summer of 1969, while I was visiting Lady Mae one afternoon at The Inn, she called her employees into the restaurant and directed three young men, including Jack Darrow, in what to do with her archive of material, including the Phylos material given to her by Maud Falconer, after her death. She told them in front of me that they should take care of it for 20 years, and at that time they would know who to give it to.

While speaking in The Inn's restaurant, she recalled an experience which she had at Panther Meadows in 1960. When Lady Mae saw clearly what had become of the Ballards' organization, the "I Am" movement, she was filled with regret for having suggested to them in Los Angeles years before that they should start the group. She went up to the meadow to be alone, and cried. At that moment, Phylos appeared next to her and said, "Stop your crocodile tears. Some good will come out of it. Who are you to say that the real is not coming forth? You yourself say, 'There is no great and there is no small, and nothing for the good is ever lost.' From 1934 until now you have been doing the same thing, crocodile tears. Those who have come into the I Am movement can never go back to what they were before. All of these people are finding their own life-tree path. They will have to earn their way. You did a service, and now you're crying about it, thinking that you acted wrongly in giving your advice. Why waste those tears? The Great Ones shed no tears. They are solid in their service, not concerned with what takes place. In service, you learn. Do not concern yourself with the religious people. Thieves and prostitutes will help you more in the spiritual work than will the religious, who are selfish in their aspiration."

On this afternoon, Mother Mary also gave out much information about the retreats inside Mt. Shasta. She spoke of the Temple above Mud Creek, where Nola and her family entered the mountain through a large rock which swiveled open like a door, and told of another large rock near Red Butte which is also an entrance to a retreat. She had discussed these things many years before with Mack Olberman, and seemed to remember these places well from her life at Mt. Shasta in Atlantean times. While she was talking about these doors to the mountain, Jack went to his room and brought back his copy of *An Earth Dweller's Return,* and showed Mother Mary the frontispiece, which has a picture of a large rock in the forest with the words inscribed on it, "Be Ye Doers of the Word." He asked Mother Mary if this was the rock near Red Butte, and she said, yes. She then gave this advice, "If you are meant to find an opening, you might see a deer, who will lead you to it. Follow the deer. The Brothers had four deer that they trained, but one was killed by hunters. My husband Max saw one of them. He told me that it seemed to take on a human face, and beckoned to him to follow."

During this discussion, she said, "How perfect everything feels at this moment."

A Dweller on Two Planets contains the following advice to those who seek contact with the adepts of Mt. Shasta - "The one who first conquers self, Shasta will not deny."

Late one evening in the fall of 1969, after everyone else in The Inn was asleep, Mother Mary spoke with another young man and myself about ancient lives gone by and the future work to come. While she was talking, she became very serious and stood up with her arms raised to some other world of being. Looking beyond the material world, she addressed God and said, "Oh Creator, there must be no more martyrdom. It was the Way in the past. It was the Way for Jesus, but it must be the Way no more. I ask You, no, it is my right to demand of You, that martyrdom must no longer be the Way for people of earth." Having never seen anyone speak with the Creator before, this experience made a great impression upon me.

Usually when I visited The Inn, I returned to my cabin up on the mountain in the late afternoon, hitchhiking part of the way if possible, but walking if I couldn't catch a ride. When I left The Inn on this night, it was well past midnight and I didn't feel like walking ten miles in the middle of the night. As I had my sleeping bag with me, I bedded down in a nearby abandoned, overgrown orchard, taking refuge under a bent bough laden with apples, which was like a canopy over my head. I lay in my sleeping bag pondering everything which I had just heard and witnessed and fell asleep after some time. When I woke up early in the morning, I opened my eyes to see that the branch above me was full of ripe apples and I simply reached up to pick one for breakfast, and ate it. I thought to myself, "This is a moment of true perfection." I took several more apples for later, and went back up the mountain.

Ten years later in the spring of 1979, Jack Darrow and I were travelling around Europe on Eurail passes, and on the night of the Wesak Full Moon in May we were in the city of Salzburg, Austria. On this night I had a dream about the orchard, and it seemed that I was back in it. It was a happy dream of a forgotten place, and I was reminded of the entire experience of that night. Since I left Mt. Shasta in 1970, I have every year tried to return to Sand Flat on July 4th, and after coming back to the U.S. a few weeks later in June, I went to Mt. Shasta for my yearly visit. I decided to drive by the orchard for old time's sake and found to my amazement that it had been cut down a few weeks before, with all the wood now stacked as cordwood. I immediately realized that the dream I had experienced on the night of the Wesak Full Moon was the goodbye to me of the Life which had manifested itself to us in this world as these trees. That Life had shared my experience as well on that night in 1969, and remembered me as it left this world, reaching out to me in the dream.

Jack and I kept in touch for many years through many changes in our lives. We had known one another before each of us came to Mt. Shasta and remained friends after the death of Mother Mary on January 4th, 1970 when The Inn was closed and everyone who worked there went their own way. But I lost contact with him in the late 1980's when he moved to the University of California at Santa Cruz to get a B.A. in the field of Asian Studies. I ran into him unexpectedly on the street in Berkeley in January of 1990 and told him of an ethical crisis through which I had recently tholed, when my job was eliminated after confronting my boss with evidence of his unethical and illegal actions. My second son was born five days after losing that position, in September of 1989. Jack and I sat and talked for several hours in a café, as people do in Berkeley, catching up on events in one another's life. Several days later, he called to tell me that he and the one other man still responsible for holding Mother Mary's archive had decided to turn it over to me, if I wanted it. I agreed to this.

When I retrieved the material from the garage of his former wife Jan Darrow, who also lived and worked at The Inn, I was quite surprised to see that so much of this archive dealt with numerology, as I really didn't think of Lady Mae as a numerologist. The Great Ones give each individual the teachings appropriate to that individual's character, and in my case, it wasn't numerology. To me, Mother Mary said several times, "Love will take you places nothing else can." In writing this book, I have tried to present the material which I think best represents her life and teachings, and have included the numerological information because I know it was very significant to her, even though it was not part of my own experience with her.

In *A Dweller on Two Planets* the Temple within Mt. Shasta is described as being illuminated by the un-fed "Maxin Light" which Mother Mary said was actually a human soul which did not take incarnation as a gross material body, but as this spiritual Light. She regarded the loss of this Light in Atlantean times as a great disaster for the evolution of the human race. On that summer day in her restaurant in 1969, Lady Mae predicted to us that early in the New Age one of the adepts of the mountain will live openly on Mt. Shasta as a representative of the Brotherhood, and that sometime later one of the retreats will be opened to humanity, as it was in Atlantean times. She said that she did not intend to go inside the mountain until that time had come again, but instead would remain in society to serve humanity.

APPENDIX 1 - Writings of The Order of Directive Biblical Philosophy

A STATEMENT OF THE ORIGIN OF THE ORDER
Written on May 30, 1943 by Lillian Bense for Mary Mae Maier

RULES AND REGIME OF FLOW OF THOUGHT FOR THE STUDY AND TEACHING OF THE PHILOSOPHY OF INTENSIFICATION

This is taught by the Azariah Temple of Masters, at the Sachem in Mt. Shasta, who were introduced to the World of Affairs through the Master Phylos, author of the book called *A Dweller on Two Planets* and transcribed by his amanuensis, Frederick Spencer Oliver.

Several years after the demise of Frederick S. Oliver the Master Phylos chose one whom he called "B. E. K. Nown," who was known to him in Atlantean times as "Thirtle" to carry on his work. This work includes the Study of the Philosophy of Intensification as used by the Sons of God in the most ancient Civilization and in Lemuria, and in Atlantis by the Sons of Solitude. Since the time of Atlantis this Philosophy has not been known to have been used. In this age, as it is a peculiar necessity for Aquarian culture, the Messenger chosen has given much attention and time to proving the truth of all assertions made as to its cultural value since 1921.

Ten years was allotted to the Messenger for study to prove the assertions made by the Group at Mt. Shasta, who have had no other messenger for this work other than this writer, of whom Frederick. S. Oliver told his mother, preceding his demise, the very words that would be said when his mother would first meet the messenger. "Much of the matter that Frederick S. Oliver received and published in *A Dweller on Two Planets* was perfectly transmitted." A great deal of the manuscript of the book was not published as given, as a friend of the very young Fred Oliver persuaded him that the Philosophy in it should be changed to suit the demands of a public who were looking for Soul-Mates. Thereupon the manuscript was changed even to inserting a poem which the friend said, "Fred Oliver could not take," and removed a poem given to Fred Oliver by Phylos for the book.

When Thirtle was given the book to read in this life the assertion was made that the poem was not the poem or song that Phylos sang on the way to Suern. This was affirmed afterward by the correct form of the manuscript, which was sent to the Messenger by a friend of Frederick S. Oliver, to whom he had given foreign copyright privileges in return for typing the manuscript. She sent not only the poem, but also the second manuscript that had been given to him by Phylos. This fact in itself proved that the work of the manuscript had been tampered with in the lifetime of Fred Oliver by his friend A. E. P., who became the most bitter enemy of Mary Manley-Oliver in trying to wrest the copyright away from her.

There was an Ideograph in the manuscript that none could read. Just before the demise of Frederick S. Oliver, when it was too late to redeem the time, Fred Oliver said that he was "the Mainin of the story." He also said that "the Ideograph had to be known," and that "it was under a system of action," the foundation of a wonderful system of action under which Life could be better and more prosperous. He also indicated that the proper person would be found who could talk with Phylos, and although it would take years to collect all the items, it would be done with all the peoples of the world being better off for knowing about it, as it was authentic. All of the Mysteries of Life and its interests can be ascertained through the Rules and Regime of the Flow of Thought of the system.

So the mother of Fred Oliver went on encouraged and determined to save her son's work from the Graspers who were trying to wrest control of the manuscript from her. Now, after 22 years the work is far enough advanced to tell about it and write of the Flow of Thought, the Ideograph engendered and given to the Messenger that Phylos appointed 1n 1913.

Notwithstanding the many assertions made by Teachers of various systems of Thought and so-called Masters, there has never been any messenger from the Phylos group of Masters, which embrace the Azariah Group of Masters at Mt. Shasta, other than Fred Oliver, his mother, and the writer of this article, each of whom knew Phylos in ancient times, and worked with him then on these subjects of the Philosophy of Intensification that are solved by the methods of the Ideograph. Phylos himself dictated the Rules, principles, by-laws and Constitution of "The Order of Directive Biblical Philosophy" as he said that the Order might publish the Ideograph and his manuscript. These were said to be needed in the work of the Aquarian Age to supply Spirituality of Thought in a time when many would be seeking Spiritual sustenance.

As the Aquarian Age began on Sept. 16, 1936 of the 20th Century, the lack of Spirituality of Thought has been evident in the discord and wars of these early years of the Age.

A number of books are being made ready which are in reference to the Phylos work. Some of them relate to Numbers. One of them is a Bible story, "At the Watergate of Jerusalem." Others are "The Inner Meaning of the Words of Jesus," "What God Said - The Inner Meaning," "The Development of the Senses" and another from the teachings of Phyris, of the Azariah group. However, Phylos says in the meantime all of the manuscripts under the sponsorship of the Order of Directive Biblical Philosophy, which is chartered by the State of California since October, 1929, are not only under the protection of the Heavenly Cosmic Law but are protected by the Common Law of California and the United States of America.

To whom the foregoing is of concern, this copy belongs to May (sic) Maier of Ojai, California, a pupil of the Study of the Philosophy of Intensification given by the Order of Directive Biblical Philosophy. The forgoing statements are true, and written by Lillian V. Bense, President of the Order of Directive Biblical Philosophy.

Although Lillian Bense repeatedly refers to the formula "As twenty six is to seventeen, so is twenty five and eight tenths plus thirty to twenty four" *as* "the Ideograph," *it should be pointed out that if Frederick Spencer Oliver used this term, he might have been referring to Phylos' signature in Atlantean script, which would be a more appropriate use of the term. However, it is impossible to determine if Oliver actually used this term at all, as Bense may be telling the story in her own words. In other writings, she refers to the formula with this term.*

Mother Mary apparently took exception to the statements above "who have had no other messenger for this work other than this writer" *and* "there has never been any messenger from the Phylos group of Masters, which embrace the Azariah Group of Masters at Mt. Shasta, other than Fred Oliver, his mother, and the writer of this article." *She prepared this text for eventual publication with these statements omitted. Lillian Bense may be regarded as simply not knowing of any other people who had similar contact with Phylos, and was completely unaware of Jerry and Nola Van Valer, for instance. Mother Mary was somewhat more well-informed on these matters. A few corrections have been made to this text by comparing it with an almost identical statement written in one of Lillian Bense's notebooks two weeks later on June 15, 1943, and affixed with the Seal of The Order. One of these corrections is the addition of the words "in 1913," which were not found in the version she wrote for Mother Mary. Lillian Bense later in life referred to her 1913 encounter with Phylos and the subsequent meeting with Mary Manley-Oliver as her "appointment as the messenger of Phylos." She relates this meeting in the following story.*

As Twenty Six Is To Seventeen, So Is Twenty Five and Eight Tenths Plus Thirty To Twenty Four

By Beth Nimrah (Lillian Bense)

A busy week. A pupil entering the door ready for his lesson. The Teacher appears apparently from other pressing duties, and after pleasant greetings seats herself at the table opposite the pupil who has the pencil and notebook in readiness. "The lesson this evening," said the Teacher, "is about the Tenth Principle of Thought. How, if applied to certain circumstances on each Plane of Thought, it will create New Conditions. We will take up its practical application upon the Material Plane, noting the financial aspect of same in relation to the continuity of the 'wherewithal,' in replacing 'wear and tear' to speed the ongoing of its endeavors as the Principle of Thought, without drawing what is generally called the 'Profits' of business. When we are through with that phase of the problem, we will take up the Mental and Spiritual phases of it, as each phase is inter-related to the others. This is evidentially true. The source being Spiritual, prepares for the continuity and the ongoing of the Tenth Principle. The base is material or physical. The introducing link or tie is of the Mentality, which, if the Source is considered, lines up all of the factors, and prosperity is assured on the Material Plane."

"In other words," the Teacher meditatively added, "the Tenth Principle of Thought must be a 'prophet,' in order to make 'profits' on the Material Plane. When we are through with that phase of the problem, we will take up the mental and spiritual surveys of the problem."

"I rather like that idea," responded the pupil, "as I wish to put over a patent and would like to become acquainted with that 'Prophet.' "

"In that case," remarked the Teacher, "you must first recognize all the elements that have, or are, assisting you in your Plan of Work, as the Tenth Principle takes care of them, leaving no avenue wherein these elements may come forward unexpectedly for a division of patent profits. Recognizing these elements is an act of reciprocity."

Just then a knock on the inner door. It was opened an inch or two. A voice, saying, "I beg your pardon, Madame. Could you come for a moment or so?"

The Teacher, rising quickly, but with a little frown upon her brow as if she was loath to leave the problem, yet noting the interest of the pupil in the subject, said, "While I am absent, you may write the names of each element or those who have assisted you, the value of such assistance, noting the number of elements and total value of support given, also the value of your own work and your valuation of the patent, giving fair consideration to all elements. I will return soon and we will proceed to become acquainted with our 'Prophet.'"

In the meantime, the pupil, having almost finished his assignment, opened the French doors leading to the western veranda and resumed his seat, again applying pencil to paper at the round table, not noticing the arm chair which was drawn nearly to the table, at his left, he awaited the Teacher's appearance. When she came she observed the outers doors were open. "Oh, I see you have opened the doors for a friend," she remarked, as she bowed to someone in the arm chair, who said, calling her by name, "I want you to go to Mrs. Oliver's."

"I am not acquainted with any one of that name," the Teacher replied.

"Ask your pupil, he knows" the stranger commanded.

As the Teacher took her seat, she questioned her pupil, remarking further, "This stranger tells not his name, but requests me to see Mrs. Oliver, and says you know her address."

The pupil looked up in surprise. "I see no man and hear no voice excepting yours and my own."

The teacher glanced toward the armchair. There was no one sitting there. "It is rather peculiar," said she. I saw a man in unusual apparel, long hair, head covered with a turban-like arrangement of cloth. A pleasant face with beard, clear complexion, perfect hands. I supposed you let him in from the veranda as the doors were open when I returned to the room."

"Yes, I know I opened them from a sort of an inner urge that they be opened, but I did not see nor hear the man speak."

"The man," observed the Teacher, "seemed to be as others in the flesh, yet not dressed as any one I ever met. His countenance was beaming and friendly as if he had found some one for whom he had sought a long time. Not recognizing him, I imagined he caught sight of you coming here, and, not overtaking you, put in a belated appearance."

"There were thoughts," added the Teacher, "he did not express in words aloud to me, but I caught them. There was some thing about Alferion and others who influenced Isschar about a certain subject. There were names given, but I do not know them, nor do I know of them. We will resume our studies for the evening and leave the passing stranger who has left us."

When the time came for the next weekly lesson with the pupil who was interested in Thought Principles, the Teacher was in the terraced garden with her flowers. Calling to her pupil she bade him to make himself at home, saying she would be there presently. She went up the veranda steps and through the French doors. The pupil, seated at the round table awaited her with pencil and paper at hand. To her surprise and wonderment, the same personage who was there a week before was present and seated at the round table, in the arm chair. To her, this was significant. Appearing two times and at a round table, and seated in an arm chair. This surely meant that something, out of the ordinary course of affairs must be considered. What it meant, she knew not. The man appeared to be a personage of high repute. That particular arm chair was always kept in that place of authority, as a dear member of the family used to sit there and was now away in heavenly places. The Teacher bowed to the Stranger, who said, "I want you to see Mrs. Oliver. This is important. A work that only you can do."

"Yes, I forgot about the address," the Teacher remarked. Then, turning toward her pupil, she questioned if he knew the address of a Mrs. Oliver.

"I do. Is that man here again?"

The Teacher glanced toward the armchair. "He has gone. He was here when I entered the room. Do you know who he is? He seemed to look at you so sadly, as if he were trying to make you recognize him, and that you had committed some error which prohibited you from seeing him, that is, that he regretted you were not on his Plane of Thought. He is not present now. He wanted me to go to Mrs. Oliver, stating that it was important. But how does he know me?"

"Please describe the man again."

The Teacher did so, emphasizing the clear, intelligent gaze of the gentle eyes and voice, the firm appearance of the face and hands, the insistence of his voice and the thoughts he sent to her. One of them was, "A wrong had been committed. Statements had been made that were untrue, and all must be rectified." The Teacher, however did not tell the pupil of the thoughts the stranger sent her.

The Pupil then asked if it were possible to ask questions of the Visitor when he came, the Teacher replying that the Stranger's aspect was that of a man one could not argue with nor question. He simply issued commands or made statements.

Whereupon the Pupil exclaimed, "I have an idea who it is! He comes with me because of my associations with Mrs. Oliver's son who was the amanuensis for Phylos, the author of *A Dweller on Two Planets*. Have you ever read that book?"

"I have not. I have a copy, but have had no time to read it. I glanced through it, noting that it could not be read hurriedly, also noting about the 'Crisis' told of in its pages, as it was not along my line of thought. Hence it was put aside for a more convenient time."

"I differ with you, dear Teacher. If you would read the book, you will find the 'Crisis' in it, is the ultimate thing."

"After reading the index over, first, I noted the 'Crisis', and must say - a thorough study of Thought Principles declare that the 'Crisis' as told of in the book, is impossible and untrue. Your vouching for it being 'the ultimate truth' is at variance with the Stranger's sad gaze upon you. You will probably need to do another stunt in discrimination, or fall down on Thought Principles, as he gazed at you in a manner that indicated censure. I will try to read the book before you come again, and see what the trouble is, or whether I am mistaken," said the Teacher. "We will resume our studies."

The pupil had a questioning look on his face and manner, as he fidgeted nervously with his pencil, but soon applied his mind to the many phases of the evening lesson.

At the time of the next lesson, as her pupil appeared, the Teacher, with an armful of morning glories and buds, and sprays of orange blossoms, was picking some double yellow poppies that were billowing each side of the garden path. The Pupil entered the house and was in his accustomed seat when the Teacher came into the room through the side door with her gay flowers and placed the morning glories and orange blossoms on the table. She held the poppies in her right hand, intending to place them in vases of water on the mantel. Being eight, twelve, and sixteen petaled flowers, she deemed them a novelty in California poppies, accounting for it because of the many bees in the neighborhood. As she placed the orange blossoms and morning glories on the table, her attention was arrested by the now well-known voice of the Strange Visitor in the arm chair, who exclaimed, "Never bring poppies in the house again!"

"Why?" Asked the Teacher. "They are our State Flower."

"Yes, opium, sleep. California is asleep! It must awaken! Civilization is asleep! It must awaken! Sad days are coming. War! Disease! Depression! Misery!"

The Stranger then picked up some of the morning glories, saying, "These are some of my favorite flowers. They mean 'A new day is dawning that will be glorious', but oh, the darkness, the long hours before the dawn!".

"And these, said he, as he picked up some orange blossoms, mean 'spiritual success.' "You must know," he added, "when spirituality of thought floods the individual, then the masses with Light - spiritual light, darkness over materiality will disappear." Looking directly into the eyes of the Teacher as if he would pierce her very soul, "Promise me you will see Mrs. Oliver."

"I will go in the morning," was her answer. Turning to her pupil, visibly affected by her promise to the Stranger, not knowing whither it would lead, and yet not fearing, she requested him to write down the address and leave it on the table. He did so.

Never having seen the lady, nor heard a description of her, she formed a conception of her of brown hair and brown eyes and with a spotted dress on. She was not surprised to see her as she opened the door, spotted dress and all. Introducing herself as one who was giving lessons to a friend of hers and of whom the address was obtained, Mrs. Oliver exclaimed, "He is no friend of mine, he borrowed thirty dollars to buy a suit to wear to my boy's funeral and never paid it back. He is no friend of mine nor of my boy's work. He just works rackets on every one who will listen."

She had not yet asked the Teacher into the house. So the Teacher told of the Stranger's visit, and said, "Perhaps he followed my pupil, so I could become acquainted with you. There is something he desired to be accomplished that has been left undone. If you wish I will come in and talk over the matter with you for further elucidation."

Mrs. Oliver then invited her in, but the room did not appear to the Teacher like her conception of it. So she asked if there was another room.

"There is, but I do not like to invite you there, as that is where I sleep, and I am just out of bed."

"Never mind the appearance of the room, if there is a high backed swivel chair in that room, let us go there."

Mrs. Oliver was evidently surprised. "There is such a chair there. My son sat in it, often, when he was writing his book." She led the way into the room. The chair was covered with bed clothing, which Mrs. Oliver hastily removed.

Thereupon the Teacher sat in it, swinging herself about as if she were meditating. "I know now what is wanted. The title page of your manuscript. Let me see it. Something is wrong about the title page of the book as published."

The Manuscript was brought and placed before the Teacher who turned at once to the title page, saying, "This is not like that of the printed book. Why not?"

"That example at the foot of the page could not be solved by any teacher or professor of mathematics, not even by those of the University, so it was thought best to suppress it," said Mrs. Oliver.

"One who is here asks 'If this problem was suppressed, why not the footnote on page 106 also.' None have solved it!"

"Who is the man, inquiring?" questioned Mrs. Oliver.

"I cannot tell you," said the Teacher. "It is the same one who bade me see you. He stands at my elbow, and tells me to copy this problem, take it home, and he will tell me how it is solved. To then seal and give it to you when you place the next edition on the market. He says that example is the keynote that will solve all the mysteries, and they are to be solved by it in the English Language. Hidden or difficult passages may be solved by the method."

"He says the method was used many Great Cycles ago. Many have tried to obtain it, even in this Great Cycle, Pythagoras among them, with his system of numerology, but he could not figure it out. No one could without being taught. Only those of this Aquarian Cycle whose senses are developed to a certain receptiveness are able to comprehend its workings and read it correctly. As he explains it, it is interesting from a 'spirituality of thought' viewpoint and one I would like to study."

He says, "The Sons of Solitude of Atlantis used it, bringing it from a former Grand Cycle. They disappeared from Atlantis before its deluge and subsidence, so the memory of it and the civilization of that time was blotted out. This is done twice in the time the sun is transiting its great circuit, the earth changing its poles every 13,000 years."

"Another reason is, the people, in general, live from day to day, without connecting the past to the present or future, with no system of memory guidance, or conscious development of the senses in order to carry over from life to life, sustaining memories which will aid in their development in future incarnations. They are generally bound hand and foot by creeds, dogmas and isms. Their bonds are tied by militarism and commercialism, two of the worst phases of the Ninth Unseen Power that has dominated the Piscean Age and carried over to the Aquarian Age for it to give them short shrift as priest. A third phase of this degree of the Ninth Unseen Power will be in evidence shortly, to which the first two are but cat's paws. Hints of this devastating power is given in *A Dweller on Two Planets.* The masters allowed the book to be published on account of the hints given which are true, and despite the mistaken 'Crisis' it contains. This was done so that someone could be contacted by Phylos who could receive the Truth, and understand this particular phase called mentalism and who could receive instruction how to overcome its ravages through knowing its secrets."

"Do you see the man who is speaking? I feel his presence as one I have met before, but I cannot see him," queried Mrs. Oliver.

"Mrs. Oliver, I am not looking at him, but I see him. He is standing at my elbow." The Teacher glanced at the wall surprised to see a picture of the man who was standing near and smiling.

"Why, there is a picture of him on the wall as he is dressed here, the one with the wreath of morning glories twined about it---some of his favorite flowers he told me."

"Did he tell you what they meant?" inquired Mrs. Oliver, because he told Fred what they meant. "I place them there fresh each morning." She spoke in an excited manner.

"Yes, I will write it on a piece of paper and see if it is the same," said the Teacher.

"I declare it is," said her now interested hostess.

The Teacher then spoke of the poppies and what the Stranger said of them which saddened Mrs. Oliver. "What he said about the orange blossoms, I will write down and see if it is the same he told you as he said these flowers were of his favorites because of their meaning." She wrote two words. 'Spiritual success.'

"This proves to me, most conclusively the Phylos the author of the book can communicate with you. I have been looking for you. Will you tell me somewhat about your life?" The Teacher gave incidents of her life, which was a busy one in guiding a family, and as a student of the Bible.

"Will you help me with my work, dear Lady? I am becoming weary. I know mistakes were made in the text of the copy. My son intended to correct them, as he outlined to me, he had been led aside of what the real text should have been, by so-called friends, who read the manuscript. But he passed away before that was accomplished, and I was importuned to publish the book, so I went on, blindly, it seems to me. Now that it is on the market, it must go on, so the people who have put their money in it, will not lose out. I see no other way."

"That matter may be adjusted by placing a corrected copy on sale," said the Teacher.

"I would like to do so," observed the troubled one, "and especially to find that hint given in the book of that devastating power that needs to be overcome, and the knowledge of the Method of Numbers that Phylos tells is revealed through that example."

"This man, whom you call Phylos, says he is now known as Yol Gorro, a name meaning 'will power, strong and persevering, overcomes obstacles.' Is that right? It is a name that leads in direction."

"That is true," stated Mrs. Oliver, adding, as she looked at a picture on the wall, "This is of my son, who wrote the book."

"I have met him on the psychic plane," said the Teacher. "His name is Isschar on that plane, meaning that he can go on if he can influence workers on this side to help him. I now understand many things and see why Phylos came to see me. You were once my mother. Together we will learn the lesson of - **26:17 :: 25.8 + 30 : 24**"

Note - In this piece, Lillian Bense tells the story of how she met Phylos and Mary Manley Oliver. However, the piece cannot be regarded as an exactly factual account, because in the story she uses terms which she learned from Phylos, like "the Tenth Principal of Thought" and "it will create new conditions," before she met him. In any case, this story is uniquely valuable, as it presents Mrs. Bense's overview of the numerical system and its origin. This piece was excerpted for Atlantis Speaks Again.

THE INTRODUCTION TO *THE DEVELOPMENT OF THE SENSES*
by L. V. Bense, excerpts reprinted in Atlantis Speaks Again *as "God Source in Nature."*

In compiling these studies in the development of the senses, through the spiritual significance of their keynotes in music, it is done with the realization of the demand for a synthesized Plan of sense development. This method includes a study of symbols, letters, words and statements of the most importance to students which lead them by easy degrees to teachings that through observation and discrimination will bring them to view the Path leading to the unfoldment of their latent senses, as well as the further development of their five senses.

Even a measure of this unfoldment of latent senses brings joy to the life within, and a new world of fact and fancy in which to dwell. Riches unthought of, unseen and unheard will be within their grasp. All things have ethical values which are far greater than financial values and may be seen by the possessor of well developed latent senses. When the senses are fully developed, the next step is to play upon "the Keyboard of Life." This will give one the Power of the Word, which is the secret longing of every denizen of earth.

With this magical word, the pursuit of happiness will become an assurance of its realization. In this New Age we are entering, the elimination of evil will be accomplished through the development of the latent senses. Evils are not present in the spiritual life. When the spiritual significance of all things are known through Music which has its Source in Nature's God and is the Soul of Nature itself, then Abundant life will be prevalent among all people.

We have come to the Time, that is AFTER THOSE DAYS about which God said, "For this is the Covenant I made…I will put my laws into their mind, and write them in their hearts; and I will be to them a God and they shall be to me a people. And they shall not teach every man his neighbor, and every man his brother, saying "Know the Lord" for all shall know me unto the greatest…" See Heb. 8:10-11.

How can this be? It cannot be until Man's five senses are developed, so that he knows which of his seven senses are latent senses, the differentiation between senses, faculties, Unseen Powers and characteristics. Man cannot comprehend the Laws of Nature, the Law of God, nor the laws legislators make to rule Man, until his senses are fully developed.

Hence the demand for a method of development of the senses that will give minds a readiness and alertness to humanize the beasts of prey who are sapping the vitals of Civilization with their worse than barbarian methods of Thought and Action. The hope of Civilization is in the children who study these Musical Pyramids in the development and unfoldment of the latent senses. A bright tomorrow will be the result, if they follow on, until they can play the Keyboard of Life, as taught by the Order of Directive Biblical Philosophy.

SPIRITUAL KEYNOTES
from The Development of the Senses *by L. V. Bense*

Key of E Minor Harmonic - Aries

Key of B Minor Melodic - Taurus

Key of C Minor Harmonic - Gemini

Key of D Minor Melodic - Cancer

Key of D Minor Harmonic - Leo

Key of A Flat Minor Harmonic - Virgo

Key of E Minor Melodic - Libra

Key of G Minor Melodic - 8 - Scorpio

Key of B Minor Melodic - Sagittarius

Key of A Minor Harmonic - Capricorn

Key of B Major - Aquarius

Key of A Minor Melodic - Pisces

SPIRITUAL PROGENITORS - *attributed to Holtah*

Key of F Major - 1 - Aries - Melchideal and Barbiel

Key of D Minor Melodic - 2 - Taurus - Asmodel and Adnachiel

Key of B Minor Harmonic - 3 - Gemini - Ambirel and Haimel

Key of B Minor Harmonic - 4 - Cancer - Muriel and Cambriel

Key of G Major - 5 - Leo - Virchiel and Barchiel

Key of B Minor Harmonic - 6 - Virgo - Hamaliel and Mechidial

Key of D (Joy) - 7 - Libra - Zuriel and Asmodel

Key of C Minor Harmonic - 8 - Scorpio - Barbiel and Ambriel

Key of G Minor Harmonic - 9 - Sagittarius - Aduachiel and Muriel

Key of D Minor Melodic - 10 - Capricorn - Hamiel and Virchiel

Key of C Minor Harmonic - 11 - Aquarius - Cambriel and Hamaliel

Key of D Minor Harmonic 12 - Pisces - Barchiel and Zoriel

128

"LET THERE BE LIGHT"
from lessons by L. V. Bense

(1) It is said by the great Masters of Thought that at the creation of the heavens and the earth when the first recorded words were uttered that brought the Light, they also ushered in a system of thought for mankind for whom the Light was produced.

(2) This system of Thought was the "Language of Numbers" through which "all things" would be known. The knowledge would be conveyed through a regime of Thought-flow, from one to 9, as all numbers from 1 to undecillions and beyond are resolved into 9. This regime of Thought as a Light would be of mental caliber, and as a Light it would reveal all things, because it came through Spirit-Substance so each one could gain Spiritual perception.

(3) When the Light first came to earth, it was sent from the Multiverse, where all purposes that are to be objectified are formed and ready for promulgation. The Multiverse is the great storehouse and work shop where multitudinous gradations of the One Substance are stored and made ready at the behest of the Creator of "all things" to be furthered into certain Uses somewhere in the Great Creator's Universes. This One Substance does not originate in the Multiverse as it is a place for the culmination of purposes. It originates "beyond" the Multiverse but permeates "all things" and all space, which is boundless.

(4) The light flooded all Space from the Multiverse to the Interverse, thence to the Universe which includes all the planets, stars and galaxies that are known to those on the earth plane. From this Universe of Creations it came to Earth to give light with a brilliancy that would create an "aniverse" for each individual: but to this day there are few people on earth who have learned this fact.

An individual said recently, "There is nothing so precious to me as my Aniverse." Another one said, "I thank God every day for the satisfaction I have in my Aniverse." To recognize one's Aniverse is to defend it and come into the Light of a Consciousness that can comprehend all things. Then one can do as God did when he saw that "the Light was good."

God divided the Light from the Darkness. Light means wisdom; wisdom means the Father, the progenitor. Darkness means the Coordinator. A great purpose is in Darkness as it means the growth of that which is useful and which will balance and harmonize all that is useful through growth. It was intended that this growth of all useful things would be profitable to mankind who would inherit the earth.

(5) It was intended that through the First Line of Endeavor of Darkness on earth it would lead man to observe that which was not only profitable for him, but also that which was useful, good, and beautiful, to give man the idea of what would now be called "a heaven on earth." Because the Light was so divided that there was Darkness, Light

became a positive and negative force - of a Duality. Light would not be Light without Darkness and Darkness would not be Darkness without Light.

(6) The sentence "Let there be Light" is of a flow of Thought numbered 8, which means that through the business tendencies of man he was expected to make a business of observing the relation of all things to each other and to himself, especially in the interrelationships of all uses to himself and others.

(7) Because the Flow of Thought was numbered 7, it came through 25, a business number, and was set up as a Standard Bearer for business dealings of all kinds, for through its manipulations constructive work would come from spiritual motivation which would give great final successes under a Word of Power that was a finality in goodness and Truth. Under this power there would be great activities which would charm with Beauty and Truth. As 7 through 25 controls all business dealing, it is well to know that it means, "Reciprocal dealings are to be made into new conditions by each individual from universal sources on the material and physical plane," as spiritual motivation only can make such conditions. And such conditions will be ongoing through the right direction of balanced uses under the direction of Cosmic Law, or as the Masters of Thought say, "1 - 0."

This is another example of Lillian Bense's writings based on a number chart, which was probably in front of her as she wrote. Her lessons often had numbered paragraphs, which Dr. Zitko also used in An Earth Dweller's Return. *The reader should notice that the section above contains several references to base-10 numerology, and presents something of a problem, as it jumps between base-12 and base-10 references. This problem is found over and over again in the numerological material. Also, in (6) above, it is the word "light" which adds up to 44 and is reduced to 8, not the sentence "Let there be Light," which adds up to 108, and would be reduced to 9. Mother Mary reprinted these paragraphs in* Atlantis Speaks Again, *but omitted the "7" in the first sentence of (7).*

THE STUDY OF THE SCRIPTURES THROUGH FINDING THEIR VIBRATIONAL RANGE - *from* Promises and Stepping Stones *by L. V. Bense, used as lessons by the Order*

The study of the Scriptures through finding their Vibrational Range is not only interesting, but it opens a method wherein a spiritual view may be obtained that can be found in no other way. There is an inner depth of meaning that satisfies the longing soul. "Covet thee earnestly the best gifts and I will yet shew thee a more excellent way." A spiritual feast is necessary to satisfy the soul. The Bible is the most hidden of all the treasures. Within its covers are the richest jewels of the world. These can be learned by reading it over and over, by studying it from a topical point of view, by studying it from a literary point of view, but not least, by studying it from the view point of the Vibrational Range. This latter method proves THE WORD.

Among many interesting passages of Scripture that are readily understood if interpreted by their Vibrational Range, are the following -

Genesis 2:7-17, about the Garden of Eden, its rivers and tree of Life.

Jeremiah 31:22 - the Lord hath created a new thing in the earth, a woman shall compass a man.

Revelation 14:1-6 - the song no one can sing but the 144,000, no one can learn this song, the 3rd verse tells us; easily learned is the secret through the Vibrational Range of the words.

Revelation 21:17 - According to the Measure of a Man. Other parts of the chapter tell us of the city four-square, but do not tell us how God lights the city. This knowledge is within out grasp. Let us follow on to know the lord.

See Romans 8:38-39

MEMORY *by Maud Falconer*

In Ancient times those thousands of years beyond this great cycle, the Memory was not of transient loitering in the minds of people of that time. They were cognizant of the present and of the past at one and the same time: that is, all they had been told was visualized by them in word pictures, if it was a narration of past events.

If statements were made of ethical subjects, but in a figurative language, it was distinctly understood by those the speaker intended to have understand, and flowery language was in common use as both Speaker and Listener loved figures of speech. When both Speaker and listener had the Intent of reciprocity at one and the same time their delight was boundless at Truths given and received for they knew all could understand if the Speaker had the intent that they should understand when he spoke, yet none comprehended unless the Speaker had such Intent.

None, not even children of the family, were debarred from the company gatherings at the table or fireside where one or two would hold forth on various subjects. Doubtless the children and young folks learned a great deal from the manner of speech, the hearing of the Speakers, for when they were addressed by a Speaker, they understood straightway and their answers to a direct question or their talents in expressing themselves in conversation were admirable and not to be excelled by children and young people of today who have been trained by highly paid teachers, yet in their games they were enthusiastic and bubbling over with glee.

Yet, when with their elders they understood nothing that the elders did not intend them to understand, and strange to say, the children had not this power until they came to forty years of age. It was then deemed they were ready to go on in learning and the power of Intent was gradually acquired by them through persistent training.

It is because of the wonderful memory of the people in that past age that we have no records of the aeons of time since "the Beginning." So many fondly imagine there are no records, only what are found in the Bible and through archeological excavations. But there are Akashic records opened to those who may decipher them, and there is the method of ascertaining Truths through contact with Teachers of Higher Planes of thought, who give out these Truths through channels of thought, or face to face, and presence to presence, not in any way obsessing the recipient or using the recipient's vocal chords or body, but by simply talking as do those who are in the body, or by making the Truths known by a series of pictures before the mind of the recipient, or by giving impression to the senses, and of course there were more than five senses used, for those of that age were trained in senses beyond the ordinary five in current use at present.

If we could remember all that was ever told to us and the date of occurrence and the date we read the message or heard the narrative, there would be no need to make a memoranda of the same. What a lot of paper and pencils saved. Little need of books, for we could learn through hearing all statements.

Then again in that far distant time, statements were not made unless they were true, and all knowledge was stored in the memory, on call day or night, and it was the product of Wisdom and Understanding.

It was said in that far away time that the people would fall away from the Pleasant Paths; that is, from the manner of Life where Spiritual Energy was inherent, and memory would fade away. In time to come a method would have to be invented to take the place of Memory. This was to them what we would call a fairy-tale and an impossibility. Today, our methods that we exemplify in universities and schools, such as books and maps throughout the earth, in order to retain a little of what we have been taught or what we have read, are to those people of a far away time just so much silly twaddle and does not amount to the dry shucks of an ear of corn, for strange as it may seem, they know all of us and our shortcomings. "After the age of puberty," they say, "Knowledge should be imparted from teacher to pupil in an unforgettable manner, and most of the time devoted to studies of nature and sports." By this method, the pupil has on tap, at will, knowledge of any subject, from a live teacher, and not through a dead one, "as they call a book."

At that time, nevertheless it was deemed certain by them that the principal event of the aeons would come off in the time of the invention of this method and this event was no more or less than the coming of the only begotten Son of God the Father-Mother-Creator into the flesh to teach man the way to his own home. When this knowledge came to them they taught their children certain truths of the laws of life to teach their children in turn and so on in order to prepare many descendants to observe the laws of life in bearing and rearing children. Peradventure, some particular family would have the honor to be the ancestors in the flesh of the tabernacle of clay which the only Begotten Son would inhabit.

In that far distant time "verities" only were spoken so there was no need of our clumsy method of books and papers to impart knowledge. Besides their method of speaking they used spiritual telepathy with such effect that they could convey their thoughts and portray them if necessary to any distance without wires.

In the time of Atlantis, civilization was a pall upon itself, in comparison to the free delivery of thought of past cycles, so when a man who appeared who spoke "verities" he was attentively received. The time was approaching for a new invention that was to help Memory preserve its legends, its traditions, its knowledge, and its science. A new invention of memory will be made.

Would it help us today to speak only "verities?" Are there a few dozen even who know what "verities" are? Can the average person tell why he believes what he believes or make a statement as to what he knows of the things of Life and why he knows it? Is there any difference between what one knows and what one believes? Is there any difference between a plain statement and one that is preceded by I guess, or I suppose, or I wonder, or I think? If there is a difference, what is it and why?

SPACE *by Lillian V. Bense*

Beyond the Universe is the Infiniverse and beyond that is blankness, a Dark which presses in and through the Infiniverse and the Universe. The Universe is what is known in place-space beyond our earth. The Infiniverse is yet to be charted, and all things have emerged from the Unknown. The Darkness, of which the silence of the Dark Night is but a manifestation, fills all Space and is the true medium that conveys heat, light, and emotive waves of any degree of Speed to their ultimate uses.

Out of the Darkness, the Bolt came that was the nucleus of Alcyone, our Infiniverse, and out of this Space came the forces that formed other planets. This Space is immeasurable by man. As a pin-dot is to the earth, and the earth is to the Universe, so is the Universe to the Infiniverse. There are many discoveries to be made in our Universe before we can claim to know the size of it, and this will take aeons of time, but all that we wish to know is ready for us to know when we are ready to assimilate the knowledge. There are two things which we should have in our mental make-up, Receptivity and Intensity. The first is an individual's mental capacity of being receptive, and the latter is gathered from outside mental forces, as the Bolt in forming Alcyone, and it joins forces with our own mentality and becomes a working force, when our Receptivity gathers it in.

Space in the Philosophy of Intensification means the place where one can eliminate all evils and charm with the true, the good and the beautiful. It also means where man can exercise his powers through communication to make new conditions that will be reciprocal and properly motivated. "Space" is a material-physical term of a Resource of a Spiritual nature that implies it is needed to extend one's horizon in his own universe. The more one has of Space, the more one wants to own of material and physical space. There are some people on earth, who if they had spiritual eyes, could scarcely believe how they appear when they grab space and its contents from other people. If they could see themselves with spiritual eyes, they would wish to jump into space from so high a height they would seem as atoms upon earth. One can feel so sorry for the grabbers of space!

If even a few of the multitude ever came to realize that each individual must have his own universe wherein he is and must be protected to solve his own problems of Life, and do all he can to have thought for the other fellow, and not multiply through lust, then "Space" would be understood. No one on earth really owns any space, only that which he extends by his own efforts without infringing on the rights of others, as with physical space.

As to Spiritual Space each one can own as much as he can comprehend. When he leaves the physical plane, as it really is, he can take it with him as his only possession, and return to earth if his Spiritual progenitors see a need of his return. Each one must come to the realization that Spiritual Sources must first be tapped here on earth before his rounds on earth-space are finished and then go elsewhere to obtain more knowledge of Spiritual Space and learning. However "Space" gives freely and all can learn to communicate through Space by observing certain laws. Just wait until our grandchildren grow up. They will be ready to teach us a few tricks, as we expect them to do great things. They will not be ready to teach compound proportion perhaps, and of course we will insist on that study, and it can be learned through Relativity. Can it? Certainly.

Relativity has much to do with the study of Space and it will help to comprehend Space. The comprehension of all things is the chief knowledge of Space and its interrelationships.

As for its characteristic way in overcoming obstacles, no matter how obstinate they are, Space calls Time into the question and obstacles are eliminated, if not overcome. It knows how to treat offenders. So cheer up, you might learn how from Space! Its ongoings have the right word of Power, so forget your sorrows too, in the knowledge that only the good and true survive.

As to business of any kind in Space, that is of spiritual characteristics. Run by any other characteristic, it begins to decay. That is the reason this civilization is decaying and at continual war, as it is run on characteristics that are not spiritual.

Why not be happy in opportunities in Space for obtaining knowledge, using efforts to eliminate evils through directing uses constructively in Space, balancing them, directing them aright according to Cosmic Law. That would express good motives which in turn would lead to realization. It is through the realization of Space itself that the word of Power comes, a creative word of Power by which one can remove mountains of evil, as all things in Space are ongoing.

THE TERM SON OF GOD

The term Son of God is used by great Masters of thought to designate those of the first great Civilization who were created as "Knowing Beings" as they were conscious of impressions, sensations, emotions, and attuned to close observation without training.

In this civilization which is of the Abrahamic Civilization, Abraham was the first of this Civilization to enter the search for the lost word of power. He found it through his faith in God which was engendered by his obedience to God. It is at this time (of the 40's of the 20th century A. D.) that the right word of power is lost to this civilization as it is so evidenced by the warring world of affairs. It cannot be found unless attention is paid to A Major, the Ruler of the sound which first voiced "Let There Be Light" so there must be some light on the subject. A Major is the keynote. It commands attention, order, obedience, liberty, and right direction of all things, especially uses, which must be balanced and ever in harmony.

GOD'S PROMISES
Sent Out By Him Through The Universal Vibrations
L. V. Bense in Promises and Stepping Stones

When God's promises are sent out through the Universal vibrations there is nothing in the way of their being used, universally, in God's Highway for the good of material conditions, for they are sent out by the Maker of the promises, who is all Powerful, through the vibrations of love and intelligence for the benefit of those who receive them, and have requested His beneficence.

This indicates that when God's blessings are universally needed there must be a universal request for them, that is, more than one person, at least two or three must work in harmony, so that a vibration will be generated that is in consonance with the universal vibration which is always ongoing in its general application. Two is a receptive number but three is an ongoing number, with an ongoing vibration; so it is better to work in harmony where there are at least three. When there are only two working together, then the vibrations must be so harmonious that Christ is in the midst, that is, each of the two must feel the effects of the Christ Spirit. Then the vibration sent out to the Universal Creator and Father of all is received and returned in a glorified manner for those for whom beneficence has been requested, either for the individual or universal good.

When this application of universality of thought is made, the defense is perfect, for God is the defense, and each of the two or three or more in attendance will receive assurance of the answer to the petitions made. If no assurance is received then the petitioner has either a further work to do for himself, or the one or those for whom the petitions are made have a further work to do for themselves. In general, each petition made should be of a spiritual quality, as all material and physical conditions are actuated by spiritual characteristics whether they belong to an individual or a nation. There are differences also in the grades of spiritual characteristics that actuate motives. One must learn to differentiate as to what is spiritual and that which is mental or material.

It may be better for one to suffer physical pain or loss of wealth or position from God's viewpoint than to have all of the wealth of the Indies. It is to ask for our loved ones what is best for them to have, that will improve and enlarge their spiritual characteristics, seeking at the same time to help in all ways that we can to ameliorate their condition, and assisting them to help themselves in a material way. Ask God for His beneficence according to His will, He being the Judge.

1. Each one should be accountable to the Creator.

2. Each should come to an understanding within himself what Heaven is.

3. Each should settle in his own mind the points of his religion in which he is in perfect attunement with the Creator.

When these points are settled then the petitioner is ready to work with and for God, and, it is on the basis of these points he should make his petitions for each name, individual, country or race, in which he is interested for good for them, and follow up his petition and see that it is answered, and if not answered, why not!

When an individual feels his accountability to his Creator, he learns to trust Him more implicitly, more fully, and his faith is increased; he finds the promises of God are sure!

Thus we see, that when the promises are sent out through a universal vibration, they are ongoing. Sent out according to Universal Law, if received they result in a working attitude of mind. The individual will be poised in beauty, love, and work, going on to a new balanced condition that will overflow with the Ongoing Force in all matters of life where discrimination is needed to know the outcome.

The defense will be perfect because it will be of God. New conditions will be spiritually energized. Righteousness will rule in public life, beauty and beneficence in material conditions. New ideals of life will be perceived, and wonder of wonders, because of the application of Universal thought, the individual, or those receiving the benefit, space and distance being no hindrance, will be strengthened spiritually, mentally and physically. They will have a complete understanding, point by point, so that their spiritual growth will be like trees by the river of waters, and the waters are of life everlasting. God's promises from the time first made and given are ON-GOING and are always in effect.

NOTES

The Pomoseltia is the Symbol of the Order of Azariah. It is also the symbol of King David's Key. The Morning Glory is the symbol of a New Coming Day. The Rose symbolizes discrimination.

Trees are relative to birds, they sing before leaves come out in spring, otherwise trees do not bud.

Cell Salts. Kali Phos is the greatest healing agent known to man. It is the chemical base of material expression and understanding. Peppermint tea - one quart a day rejuvenates the body Power.

For sleep put the thumbs in center of hand then close hand and go to sleep.

The Aquarian Age began on Sept. 16, 1936. Since that day, we have all been self-responsible.

After a death, recite Romans 38-39.

The English are ruled by Aries, Americans by Gemini.

We make a new condition when we count in series.

Reincarnation is not a belief, but a law of nature.

Mother Mary did not accept David Davidson's calculation of the beginning of the Aquarian Age, and did not include it in Atlantis Speaks Again. *She did, however, believe that self-responsibility was the hallmark of New Age consciousness, and often stressed this point.*

THE RIGHT WORD
- *L. V. Bense in* Promises and Stepping Stones

Seek to give the right word at the right time for it will be a defense of the giver and the recipient. The right word is a word of power if spoken at the right time. Let your words be clearly enunciated, spoken directly to the person, and carrying intent. Use a rising inflection and call the recipient or hearer by his or her name when you begin to speak, thus calling his attention to what you are saying. Gain his attention and then speak distinctly and with the intent that he will understand.

Remember the WORD is a defense and must be used as a defense. The time is short for the erection of defense, we must use all our resources, and our present resource is the Word of God, and it is our word when used properly.

The forgoing is the first step in using the Word. The next step is to see that it is a Word of Life, of helpfulness, and the succeeding step is to place it with those by whom it will still be Ongoing, as there are those who are hungry and thirsting for the Word of Life, who if shown but a little, would in turn help others. There are also those who are merely curious, and are not ready for the truth. Time must be given to those who will, if shown the way, be Messengers of the Truth. The next step will be to defend the word in unexpected ways, and it is for the individual to use his intelligence in all matters, to give out of his own experience with the Word of God. The Word is the beauty of Truth in the Highways of the Lord, and when one hears this beauty of the Word, his mind is soon opened to the spiritual telepathy, and then spiritual thought as a directive influence in the Path of Life. This leads to Righteousness, and we might go on with this vibration and find that it leads to the man who speaks the Right Word at the right time, being in a state of readiness to send the good onward.

"A word fitly spoken is like apples of gold. A good word maketh glad. Every man's words shall be his burden. The Lord God hath given us the tongue of the learned, that I should know how to speak a word in season to him that is weary. He wakeneth morning by morning, he maketh my ear to hear as the learned. For to one is given the Spirit, the word of wisdom, and to another the word of knowledge by the same Spirit. It is better to speak five words with understanding than ten thousand words in an unknown tongue. Let the Word of Christ dwell in you richly in all wisdom."

Note -An unusual use of the term "a defense" is repeatedly found in the passages above. This term actually refers to the 9th Place in the columns called "Enoch's Throne Block." For example, in the numerological analysis of the word "Heaven" found in Chapter 2, the letter E occupies the 9th Place in the Throne Block, so members of The Order would say this word "is defended by" the letter E or the number 5.

THE UNSEEN POWERS
from scattered entries in Mother Mary's notebooks, and unpublished lessons of The Order
Another version of this text is found in Atlantis Speaks Again
A related passage is found in An Earth Dweller's Return, *"The Ruling Unseen Powers"*

We must know and understand the good and the evil of all the unseen powers of life.

We must differentiate as to Unseen Powers that are over us.

The powers of evil are of a mental caliber and can be made to vanish through Spiritual power.

The First Unseen Power is God.

Heaven is the Second Unseen Power. The vibrational range of the word "Heaven" means that by wishing for a thing or condition, it is possible to create it. This unseen power may also be regarded as one's own inner thought life.

The Third Unseen Power is religion. It is to the "Measure of a Man" what hands are to the body. It dominates the individual, the nation, and the race to a certain extent, owing to the place it occupies in a Vibration. Some people are very pious without real piety, holding to certain rituals or formalities. This is not practical. There are many queer forms of religious belief. A belief that is based upon beliefs, and not upon real knowledge, is impractical and full of fallacies. The progress of the race is determined by the degree attained in eliminating fallacy, those apparent truths that are but seeming and have no true foundation of thought. Religion is the highest ethical instinct of which one is capable that helps the individual to attain a state of mind that is at one with his development.

The Fourth Unseen Power is humanity itself.

The Fifth Unseen Power is Genius.

The Seventh Unseen Power is Spiritual Telepathy of Thought.

Instinct is the Eighth Unseen Power and is of Good or God.

The Ninth Unseen Power is magnetism. Three of the negative aspects of this power are Militarism, Commercialism, and Mentalism. The great number of defense is 9. It is Love and its opposite is Hate. Thought originates in 6 and enters the world through 9.

Intuition is the Tenth Unseen Power, and always makes a new condition. Intuition is not a faculty but a Power of God which contacts the Soul in a scientific manner suddenly, at the needed time. It is common sense to act upon it. Only through sacrifice can a new condition be brought about.

The first evil influence, or negative aspect of the First Unseen Power, is false gods.

The second is spirits who slander.

The negative aspect of the Third Unseen Power is the influence of Belial, who creates anger and invents mischief.

The Fourth Unseen Power has as its negative influence malice and revenge.

The fifth evil influence is Satan, who blinds men to the truth. It sits upon the highest planes of earth. It takes away the benefit of opportunities, and places one in a spiritual net as well as a physical one. This influence cannot be exorcised by tuition, books, rules or regulations. It can only be exorcised by the Christ power.

The sixth great evil influence comes in many forms, attacking the health of the body and mind. The most terrible visitation is when it attacks childhood or old age, and the Watcher may for the loved one accept the Christ power and banish the influence.

The eighth evil influence drives men to despair and discouragement, and sometimes suicide. One should note the phase of the moon when attacked by despair or discouragement, and look out for the same thing at the next recurring phase. "Blues" often return with the exact regularity of the moon's phases. This influence deceives and tortures the soul by pretending to be conscience.

The three negative phases of the Ninth Unseen Power are Militarism, Commercialism, and Mentalism. Mentalism is the most dangerous, and will become more so in the future.

The tenth evil influence comes to us in misfortune and disappointments. Cast out this influence as it is impending and misfortune vanishes.

BIBLICAL CORRESPONDANCES

1. ARIES - Symbol Head - Faith - Hebrews 11, new name Revelations 2:17

2. TAURUS - Throat - stands for the word, voice - Heb. 4:12 & 13:5, Psalms 119:105

3. GEMINI - Arms - Generosity - Matthew 11:27, Psalms 40:11 and 41:1 to 3

4. CANCER - Stomach, solar plexus - Inspiration - Nehemiah 8:10-12

5. LEO - Heart - love - James 5:18, Romans 8:38, 39, Psalms 119:2

6. VIRGO - Intestines - Thought, Labor, Compassion - Romans 8:1-28, Psalms 119:59, Exodus 2:9, Proverbs 23:4, Matthew 11:28-30

7. LIBRA - Loins, Back, Spine - Balance, Justice - James 1:17, Matthew 5:7

8. SCORPIO - Generative Organs - Mercy - Matthew 5:7 & 7:12

9. SAGITTARIUS - Thighs - Defense, Charity - 1st Corinthians 13:1-13

10. CAPRICORN - Knees - New Condition - Matthew 5:16, Hebrews 6th Chapter

11. AQUARIUS - Ankles - Universal Law, Brotherly Love - 1st Thessalonians 49, John 15:12-17 and 5:42 and 13:30, Jeremiah 31:3

12. PISCES - Feet - Understanding, Peace, the material world and conditions - Hebrews 13:2, 1st Thessalonians 4:23

WHEN TO PRAY AND FOR WHOM TO PRAY
Attributed to Holtah

It is not generally known that the vibrations which are for the benefit of humanity are always circulating in the Universal Highway and are always descending upon the inhabitants of the earth. All Good descends without favor upon the Just and the Unjust, as rain that falls upon all.

Why, then, do we not obtain more of the good that falls upon us?

It is not generally known that the Vibrations ascending from the earth do not pulse in unison with those descending from Above. The reason why is that they are controlled by the magnetic influences of the moon. Strange but true. The proof is in the testing. But be sure you test according to the Law of Vibration.

Another reason why many do not have their prayers answered is because they pray only for the self, my son John and his wife, us four and no more. Follow the Universal Rule, find the Universal Path, then pray for others too, as well as for the Self. Know this, that in praying for others you come in touch with the Universal Cosmos. The Universal Aethers enfold you while you are praying, and the Heavenly Father's arm is about you and you are sustained yourself as well as bringing sustenance to others.

Know this - You are entitled by your citizenship under the Creator for food, raiment and shelter, and whatever else you need for your sustenance, be it of Spiritual, Mental, or Material need. Use the promissory note that Paul tells us about in Philippians 4:19. Never pray for what you want. God never supplies wants, so do not waste time. He supplies needs. God is your banker. His riches in Glory are the bank on which the promissory note is drawn. Present that note at any time and any place and it is honored. Try it out and see. If it is not honored, something is wrong with you. Probably you are asking for what you do not need. Then get in line.

When you understand the foregoing and really want answers to your prayers, obtain an ephemeris that will tell you just when the Moon is in certain signs of the Zodiac for the meridian of your locality, for each day together with the time in hours and minutes. For, instance, at the time of the copying of this lesson, it is the Universal Hour of the day, when influences are good for Humanity and the Moon is in Cancer, having come into it yesterday, April 22, 1931, at 4:42 PM for this meridian, Los Angeles. So, we know, for we have tested it out many times, that the Word of the Law of the Lord is true, The Law that is written in the heavens. See Ecclesiastes 3:1,2,6,8, Genesis 1:14, then read Ecclesiastes 3:17, Amos 5:13, and James 1:17, then you will know from where all gifts come. Everything you possess beyond daily bread, shelter, and necessary raiment is a gift, and from whom? James tells you a verity.

Then, in praying, pray for others as well as yourself. Train the mind in two things, to be in Sympathy with those for whom you are praying, and be sure to have the Intent when you pray that the word you are sending to God will reach Him, and it will if you pray in the Spirit. To come into communion with Him, you must be in the Spirit, so be Intent and voice your prayers, silently or audibly, but clearly, taking as much time to utter them inaudibly as to speak them.

Note day by day the time the Moon is in the following signs of the Zodiac -

When in Aries, pray for Direction, for advice, for mental energy, for strong will power that will energize for Good, for persistence, for determination in resenting impositions upon the People. A good time to pray for all people, all races, all countries, as well as for local and friendly conditions among families and friends, for the whole earth is at this time rising to meet the Energy that is being showered upon it, and which when directed into the proper channels, gives forth many blessings.

When the moon is in Taurus, pray for self-reliance, for Self and for all others to have the strength to stand as a tree well-rooted and grounded in high principles. Pray for courage to give voice to one's principles for the edification of all, for this is the sign of the Zodiac that is given to the Word of Power. Here is where you may hear the Voice of God. Here is where you may send out the vibrations of your voice for the benefit of others. Pray that all may have patience for plans to mature for the benefit of the people, for latent energy and mental power to be aroused in the people for their benefit, for practical and constructive character-building, and for training executive workers.

When the Moon is in Gemini, pray for the people to be gently affectioned toward each other, to be ready for emergencies, to keep their minds active, to have a certain sensitivity but not to be quick to take offense. Also to be idealistic, scientific, to cultivate their imaginations, ambitions, and aspirations and to be ready and able to experiment and investigate as those methods of inquiry will keep them young in body and mind. To have a vocation and an avocation at the same time, to be joyful without being frivolous, to aspire to versatility, dexterity and skillfulness in all that they do, trying to excel themselves and not others. To keep pressing forward, having for a mark the prize of your high calling, Jesus Christ.

When the Moon is in Cancer, pray for the homes of your country as well as your own, and read over and over Psalm 127, for the Crown of the Nation is its homes where Love rules the inhabitants. Pray that beautiful environments may be the portion for each individual and that each may be receptive to the highest thoughts, and very conscientious. That each may be frugal, thrifty, economical, prudent and industrious. That each may be sincerely attached to family and be loyal to the interests of each one in the home and in the country, having an abiding love for home and country, and fully understand their duties and responsibilities, being ever accountable, of their own free will, to God.

When the Moon is in Leo pray that the minds of the people may be active and they be good-natured and generous, capable of making and keeping friends. Much depends upon friends, in the Gate, instead of enemies from this time on. Keep friends. Keep up your friendships is an admonition for us from high sources. Exert every quality and characteristic you may have to keep up your friendships. Don't let the sun go down upon wrath. There is no prayer more important for mankind than the prayer for friendship's sake. Pray that each may excel in some particular that will be for the benefit of self and others. Pray that the people may be honest and conscientious, philosophical and philanthropic, industrious and independent, persistent and determined, sincere and ardent in expressing their love and admiration for God, home, friends, sweethearts, wives and children.

When the Moon is in Virgo, pray that the people be receptive to good thoughts. This is the sign more than any other when the people should receive good thoughts that trend toward useful action. Pray that they may be of a contemplative and industrious nature, not fearing useful labor, for Labor is dignified. Pray that they may desire useful knowledge and acquire it, be economical and that all may have a reserve force of strength with endurance, and if ill to recuperate quickly. To be philosophical, to know the principles of cooperation, arbitration, use good language, enunciate clearly, love good literature, beauty, art and sculpture, be idealistic yet practical, be speculative yet frugal, be ingenious and cautious and of all things to be fore-thoughted and understand causes and effects.

When the Moon is in Libra, pray that Harmony, peace, equity, justice, pleasantness, and courteousness will descend in showers upon the people. Pray that refined amusements will be the rule and not the exception, that all will be affectionate, sympathetic and sensitive to surroundings and circumstances for the betterment of each and all. Pray that amiability, justice, kindness, modesty and generosity will be shared in common with each and all, and that each may learn balanced Thought and be ready for the Kingdom of Even.

When the Moon is in Scorpio, pray that each individual may have keen, shrewd judgement, have critical thought and be enterprising. That they may have a reserve fund of that which will make each one independent with true happiness to the end of their days, arriving there with a goodly degree of health, strength of body and in right condition of mind. Pray that each may have longevity with health and mental competence, and mental, spiritual and physical prosperity with such material comforts as will enhance their happiness. Pray that each one will understand that it is not all of life to live, nor all of death to die, for Life is more than meat and raiment, and death of the body does not end all. Pray that all may have a love for Nature, and Nature's Creator, and that each may be natural in manner and in ways of living. May each be scientific, sagacious, daring, creative in mind, and capable of success in all undertakings, and each to learn discrimination and have spiritual success. See 1 John 1:4 and Phil. 2:16

When the Moon is in Sagittarius, pray that the people be generous in thought and material things, hopeful and charitable, frank and outspoken, honest and ambitious, not easily discouraged but persevering, active, self-reliant and ever ready to defend the Truth and those who need defense. To be enterprising, and to love liberty, to be strong-willed and in the fear and love of the Creator, to be scientific and philosophical, to cultivate foresight, fore-knowing, and calculation. To be earnest and sincere, to be aspiring and energetic, and to speak verities and defend them. See Col. 3:14, meaning the bond of perfection in love, tolerance, good-will and kindness.

When the Moon is in the sign Capricorn, pray that the people be studious, quiet, thoughtful channels of a peaceful frame of mind. That they be practical methodical, ambitious and persevering, and to never mind discouragements and disappointments. To make the best of things, the most of opportunities, to make a new condition for spiritual, mental, or moral welfare. These things being right, the material and physical conditions will soon be in line, for the things of the Spirit motivate all else when understood. Pray that they may take care and have caution, persistence and patience, and use concentrated efforts which will bring triumphs, honor, and victory.

When the Moon is in Aquarius, pray for a faithful nature for each one, for unobtrusiveness, patience, determination, attention, studiousness, caution, reasoning powers, generosity, dignity. Pray for the advancement of ideas both practical and theoretical in government, the nation, business and the home and individual. Pray for humanitarian interests, criminal reform, the doing away with obsessions, for the promotion of art and literature, for an appreciation of music, occult research, the recondite sciences and all that will be of benefit to humanity and the individual, for this is the sign where Nature, Science, and Religion vie with each other for the benefit of Man. This is the sign where all that will benefit Man in any way is obtainable with the right effort.

When the Moon is in Pisces, pray for logical methods of living and learning. Pray for people or animals in distress, for those who are afflicted in any way, especially for those who need to toil underground or who need to work at night. That each may understand the blessing of sacrificing for others, for a kind and loving nature, that the only war which should engage the forces of the country is the war against disease and pestilence, and the individual war is the one waged upon one's own character, knowing "that he who overcometh is greater than he who taketh a city." Pray that each one may enjoy beautiful scenery, pleasant environments, completeness, and the happiness of all in general, and that each may be gifted with telepathic faculties and have a desire for psychic investigation, and all studies that reveal the workings, power, and majesty of the Creator.

A dozen people praying even twice a day at certain hours, in the magnetic vibrations of the Moon, are strong enough to overthrow the despotism of evil or adverse conditions. The hour ending at midnight and the one ending at mid-day are especially good as then the forces are at their best. 10 PM or 10 AM are also good, as well as 4, 5 & 6 AM.

Certain evil forces rule certain vibrations at certain times.

THE SPIRITUAL SIGNIFICANCE OF THE ZODIACAL SIGNS UPON THE TEMPERAMENT OF THE PEOPLE - *by Maud Falconer*

That the spirit of the times rules the Temperament of the People, according to the signification of the signs of the Zodiac, may be proven by the one who notes carefully these signs as they occur in order throughout the months in the year. First, one must note the Sign that is passing over the month, as the calendar month does not begin with the zodiacal month. The spirit of the times may be either good or bad, or rather indifferent, according to the "Purpose" and "Determination" of the majority of the people, unless the minority possesses the spiritual power of the word.

In ancient times many had this spiritual power. Much later but few possessed it, until at the present time in this Aquarian Age it has almost disappeared. A Mandate has gone forth since the day of the New Age to arrest its departure, to detain it if possible, until a few more can be embued with it, as from that date on, Mankind must, individually, stand erect, arrayed in garments of Light, and send forth the lost word of Power through the Spiritual Power of the Word.

There are none who do this by saying "I Am," as that is in relation to Man himself but an affirmation of Being, a state of existence, and has no reference to the Word of Power, which is the lost word of the Ancients, and which must be learned in the Aquarian Age. And they must hasten in their studies to acquire it as all, even the highest intellectuals of the time, are sadly in arrears in their evaluation of Thought. This is proven by the state of the civilization of today. If seventeen people had the Word of Power, they could eliminate the evil in the world of affairs.

SONS OF JACOB - *from* Atlantis Speaks Again

Sign	Son	Mother
Aries -	7th - Gad - a troop - overcomers	Bilhah
Taurus -	8th - Asher - happiness	Zilpah
Gemini -	9th - Issachar - he is hired	Leah
Cancer -	10th - Zebulon - habitation	Leah
Leo -	11th - Joseph - he shall add	Rachel
Virgo -	12th - Benjamin - Son of the right hand - Success	Rachel
Libra -	1st - Rueben - Behold a son	Leah
Scorpio -	2nd - Simeon - Listening	Leah
Sagittarius -	3rd - Levi - Crown wreath success	Leah
Capricorn -	4th - Judah - praised	Leah
Aquarius -	5th - Dan - to judge	Bilhah
Pisces -	6th - Naphtali - wrestling	Bilhah

The above table gives the secret of the work for the present great cycle ruled by Aries.

Those of Aries to lead the overcomers.
Those of Taurus to see that happiness is over the earth.
Those of Gemini to defend the interrelationships of the people.
Those of Cancer to see that the people have habitations.
Those of Leo are to see that the resources are used by the people.
Those of Virgo to see that wisdom and success are over the earth.
Those of Libra to teach obedience to the Law.
Those of Scorpio to know the Power of the Word over Life and Death.
Those of Sagittarius to defend the liberties of the people.
Those of Capricorn to see that new conditions for man must be of universal merit and consider the spirit, soul, mind and body.
Those of Aquarius to discriminate as to that which should be ongoing, to be poised in the universal and material states of being, and to judge.
Those of Pisces to teach that opportunity for spiritual or material welfare should be used, and that Spirit is the division of Thought which leads to right action.

Those of the North Gates - Leading Thoughts - to teach that these lessons will have an interpenetrating influence for good upon the people's thoughts and activities, to eliminate evils, to understand the mysteries of life and to use discrimination, and that true Rulership may be established over soul, mind and body.

Those of the East Gates - to teach that Spiritual Energy is to be desired, and Directive ability with wisdom will be added. Analysis and Synthesis.

Those of the South Gates - to teach that New Conditions are symbols of perfected circumstances for a future state of being, and that earth is not the only habitation of man. Resurrection.

Those of the West Gates - to teach that even thought if rightly directed can make a new condition of intelligence, and wisdom plans for it. Elimination of evils.

A Gate is an entrance into a new condition. Those of the Gates are expected to use wisdom to make new conditions for others. Success of Spirit is the ultimate goal.

Sons of Jacob in Relation to the Age of Taurus

Judah - East Gate - Spring - equinox then in sign of Taurus.
Rueben - West Gate or Fall equinox - Libra
Joseph at High Gate - summer solstice - Leo
Asher at South Gate - winter solstice - Aquarius

1 Kings 7:25 refers to the twelve spirits which rule the twelve Zodiacal signs, the twelve brazen oxen on which the laver of brass rests, winged beasts, Lion, Bull, Cherubim. See also 1 Kings 8:7. The twelve columns of the Temple of Solomon at Jerusalem represented the twelve signs of the Zodiac.

The precession of the equinox moves backward at the rate of approximately 1 degree in seventy one and a sixth years. The signs have changed about 30 degrees since then and now we have the following tabulation as the true homologue for the present Age. *(written in the 1920's)*

Judah at the East Gate or spring equinox in Aries
Rueben at the West Gate or all equinox in Libra
Joseph at the High Gate or summer solstice in Cancer
Asher at the South Gate - winter solstice in Capricorn

Fire - Spirit - universal Solvent - Will of God
Air - human mind, mental sphere, reasoning and emotional nature combined
Water - Soul - washing or cleansing power by repentance, relaxation and readjustment of one's whole mental mechanism to the Will of God
Earth - carnal nature, commercial mind, self-interested nature. Body is the temple of God. Never ignore the requirements of the body.

In that Age the vernal equinox occurred in Taurus, and the bright star Aldebaran led the Starry Host and rose in the east with Orion and the three bright stars in the belt of Orion represent three wise men following Him. This occurred about March 9th and was then about the time of the vernal equinox. This is the celestial analogue of the birth of Jesus and refers to the conjunction of the sun and moon in the sign of Taurus, hence the story of Jesus being born in a manger, where the Sun is the Savior and Taurus the bull pen.

APPENDIX 2 - Numerology of The Order of Directive Biblical Philosophy

Enoch's Throne Block

NUMBER CHART

Spirit ♈	Soul ♉	Mind ♊	Body ♋	Spirit ♌	Soul ♍	Mind ♎	Body ♏	Spirit ♐	Soul ♑	Mind ♒	Body ♓	
1	2	3	4	5	6	7	8	9	10	11	12	*1*
13	14	15	16	17	18	19	20	21	22	23	24	*2*
25	26	27	28	29	30	31	32	33	34	35	36	*3*
37	38	39	40	41	42	43	44	45	46	47	48	*4*
49	50	51	52	53	54	55	56	57	58	59	60	*5*
61	62	63	64	65	66	67	68	69	70	71	72	*6*
73	74	75	76	77	78	79	80	81	82	83	84	*7*
85	86	87	88	89	90	91	92	93	94	95	96	*8*
97	98	99	100	101	102	103	104	105	106	107	108	*9*
109	110	111	112	113	114	115	116	117	118	119	120	*10*
121	122	123	124	125	126	127	128	129	130	131	132	*11*
133	134	135	136	137	138	139	140	141	142	143	144	*12*

LETTER CHART

Spirit ♈	Soul ♉	Mind ♊	Body ♋	Spirit ♌	Soul ♍	Mind ♎	Body ♏	Spirit ♐	Soul ♑	Mind ♒	Body ♓
1	2	3	4	5	6	7	8	9	10	11	12
A	B	C	D	E	F	G	H	I	J	K	L
M	N	O	P	Q	R	S	T	U	V	W	X
Y	Z	&									

ENOCH'S THRONE BLOCK
from Atlantis Speaks Again *by Maud Falconer*

A Throne-Block is used as a reference for letters of 3 lines, of spaces containing the English alphabet of 27 letters, 12 letters in the spaces of the first and second lines, and 3 letters in the third line. The most important letter in the alphabet is the letter O, which is the symbol of Cosmic Law. This symbol is used both in letters and numbers. But whenever used, it is a symbol of the Covenant of God to man.

It is well to read in the Bible about that Covenant, using a concordance to do so, as the meaning is little known or observed, for if observed, there would be no war.

The leader of the English alphabet is A, which has the keynote of A major. This keynote demands that attention be paid to Order, the direction and balancing of uses, and obedience to Law.

The letter O also means contact, contract, a promise, as a ring given to a woman by her promised husband.

The letter I is a vowel, and leads to the defense of the English language.

The letter E is the letter of motives, which rule the world.

The letter U is the letter of magnetism in the English language.

The letter Y is the letter of two paths in which the questioner may choose to walk to work out his problem of life.

Remember that vowel letters lead to the unfoldment of the interior senses of man.

The letter W is ruler of scientific workmanship.

COLUMNS OF THE THRONE BLOCK
from L. V. Bense's notebook

The 1st Column gives the direction.
The 2nd Column gives the Word of Power, and relates to material possessions.
The 3rd Column gives the word of interrelationships, and also relates to business.
The 4th Column gives the word of character, personalities, individualities, and is devoted to man's interests, as well as animals.
The 5th Column gives the word of motive, education
The 6th Column gives the word of thought, music, sex, action, beauty, health, labor
The 7th Column gives Law of the Word & the Word of Law, balance, harmony, justice
The 8th Column gives the Word of Life, and of Death. It also relates to real estate.
The 9th Column gives the Word of Defense, construction and destruction.
The 10th Column gives honors, and a new condition.
The 11th Column gives universality, and relates to the public and politics.
The 12th Column gives material and physical things.

MEANINGS OF NUMBERS
from The Development of the Senses *by L.V. Bense*

1 - Always stands for the right, for direction, and beginning

2 - For the word one speaks or writes, and for possessions

3 - Means friendliness, cheerfulness, neighborly

4 - Stands for the self, the home and its interests, and country

5 - Intelligence, poise, education, newspapers and magazines

6 - Work, labor, play, food, and dress

7 - Harmony, justice, peace, music and art

8 - Means life, and learn to choose, make a choice

9 - Defense, journeys, be economical

10 - New things, honor, new conditions

11 - Public interests and government

12 - Everyday life and everyday studies

13 - Summing up things

14 - Be in earnest

15 - Be diligent

16 - Be careful

17 - Do no evil

18 - Do your best

19 - Wisdom

20 - Thankfulness

21 - Wish for the good, true, and beautiful

22 - In communion with God

23 - Opportunity

24 - The best in all things

25 - Perseverance

26 - Rule yourself

27 - Keep busy

28 - New conditions with obstacles to be cleared away

MEANINGS OF LETTERS
from unpublished lessons of the Order of Directive Biblical Philosophy

A - Direction, Leadership

B - Building of Character, Duality, as in Positive and Negative

C - The symbol of an open door which welcomes

D - Humanity, and the self

E - Intelligence, Motive

F - Beauty, Health, Comfort

G - Balance, Harmony

H - The Law and the Word, Discrimination, Mercy

I - Individuality, Spirit and Egoic Spirit

J - The Door to a new condition

K - the Tree of Knowledge

L - Willing Sacrifices

M - M is where every question is answered and every problem solved. Realization.

N - Life and Movement to Thoughts and Activities

O - The Altar where the Sacred Fire burns, Obedience to Law

P - Power from the Highest Sources, Spirit leading Soul into Thought and Activity

Q - Spiritual Success

R - To charm with the Good, the True, and the Beautiful

S - The winding Path, paved with Jewels of Truth

T - The crossroads of life, a reminder of past experiences of human will against Divine Will

U - Uses. Through experience we determine the right paths in which to walk.

V - Virtue, or exemplary behavior

W - Opportunity on every plane of life

X - The Turnstile - which category do you belong to?

Y - The Path of Decision, the Dividing of the Way, Perseverance. Y says "Choose Well."

Z - The Gate of the lesson of discernment and discrimination

& - Ampersand - There are always other things than the one now under discussion.

SOME OF THE HIDDEN MEANINGS OF LETTERS FO THE ALPHABET
AN ALPHABETICAL HABITATION

Edited, from Atlantis Speaks Again, *probably written by Lillian Bense*
from an early draft of The Garden of Delight

A - A seat in a tent. A habitation dominating, denominating, commanding for the good of all.

B - Building a habitation; character as a tree. A and B together can do wonders. Two at least are needed to help build Positive and Negative Forces.

C - A habitation with an open door that all may be welcome.

D - A habitation whose occupant defends it ever to closing the door upon all that is a menace to the weak or innocent.

E - That the habitation has windows and may be used as a watch tower from which one may see afar.

F - That the habitation has a friend, a defender, and has in it its occupant. It has nooks and crannies for beauty, health and comfort for each one who comes in.

G - Tells of perfect balance and harmony that speaks of an open door policy in relation to other inhabitants and that the latch string is outside.

H - The pillars of the habitation that stand for the Law and the Word; discrimination; the God of mercy. *("The Law and the Word" is a numerological term - ed.)* Here one can go in and out with safety, and be at peace with his own soul and the world of affairs.

I - The Individuality of the Inhabitant of the Habitation who must acquire character as a spirit soul possession, and recognize his own Spirit, as a defense.

J - Is the door of the Habitation of the Inhabitant.

K - The tree of Knowledge, which is planted near the corner of the Habitation for the benefit of the Inhabitant. Its roots grow deep in the earth to draw sustenance from the living springs of earth and its soil. It branches forth into Heaven, always pointing to the North, signifying that the Creator of all that is created rules; and to the East toward the sun signifying that the sun is but the reflection of God's love for humanity. The Inhabitant can sit underneath this tree and absorb the knowledge that comes from the leaves of the tree above him.

L - The addition to the Habitation, so that the Inhabitant may prepare a room for the rest and refreshment of the sometime guest who he wishes to come and sup with him. Many times he will make sacrifices to do this, but under the tree of knowledge he has learned to make sacrifices in order to be a friend to every wayfarer, and besides, is not the Inhabitant "his brother's keeper?"

M - The library of books and quaint old manuscripts in the Alphabetical Habitation of the Inhabitant. Here is where all the mysteries of life are secreted in covers of Gold, leather, or linen written on pages of beaten gold and studded with Jewels of truth so the Inhabitant of the Habitation avers. Here he sits and scans the pages o'er and o'er. History, Art, Music Literature, by ancient and modern scholars adorn its shelves. Here is where every question can be answered and every problem solved. Herein is a feast for the soul of the inhabitant and while feasting he is listening to the words that are to him as "Apples of gold in pitchers of silver."

N - The Influence that interpenetrates the atmosphere of the Habitation, where it seemingly gives life and movement to the thoughts and activities of the Inhabitant.

O - The Altar in the Habitation whereon burns the Sacred Fire of the desire of the Inhabitant's Spirit to guide his Soul toward the use and not the abuse of all things.

P - The influx of sudden power from the highest Sources to supplement the Power of the Inhabitant's own Spirit in its endeavors to lead its Soul into the Highways of Thought and Activity. These three (N, O, P) are most instrumental in teaching the Inhabitant of the Habitation that "It profits nothing to gain the whole world" and lose his own Soul.

Q - The 17th letter of the alphabet plants an orange tree at the left of the Inhabitant's Habitation. When it is in blossom and with green and golden fruit, it is the symbol of spiritual success, spiritual power. The tree of knowledge being at the right corner betokens intelligence.

R - The vehicle the Inhabitant uses to convey the fruits of his efforts to other highways, byways, and roadsides. Always it conveys that which will charm away all that is evil, and a menace to the people. By means of its peculiar construction it gathers up the evil and tosses it into the ditches, or it moves it along where it is burned and its ashes are used for fertilizer. Flowers are made to bloom beside the path and sorrows are lessened throughout the world.

S - The winding paths throughout the grounds of the Habitation, winding up and down, paved with scintillating jewels, emblems of the jewels of truth. No one can stray who walks in these winding paths and each one who walks therein may gather all he can carry away of the beautiful jewels at one time. Yet when he returns, he will find jewels and they will be more sparkling and iridescent. These are the Paths of Wisdom leading onward in the ways of Pleasantness, where all the Paths are Peace.

T - The crossroads, way down in front of the Habitation, for by this time it is sensed that the grounds are undulating in Character. One road extends east and west, and one north and south, but stopping at the outer boundary. This is to remind the Inhabitant that his experiences should teach him that the North and South road tells him that "All is well when he allows the Divine Will to control his life." The east and west road tells him that he cuts off the Divine influence by his own will and that he should extend the North and South road further North so others could use the roadway of Divine influence.

U - U is the letter which stands as a warning (upside down) before the door of the Habitation. The Inhabitant must understand each and every word in which there is a U. The U's and the use to which they are put are important as it is an ongoing letter, signifying that through experience the Inhabitant will determine the right paths in which he should walk. Mostly, this experience comes through the letter T, as a reminder of past experiences of the human will against the Divine Will.

V - Tells that the Habitation of its Inhabitant need not be a fixture of or to the Inhabitant, that he may as often as he pleases, but always, whenever he is in whatever Habitation he inhabits, he must use his own directive force in a fixed direction for the purpose of unfolding his own character, developing it along the lines of the highest ideals, and to set an example as his brother's keeper.

W - Stands for the warp in which the Inhabitant of the Alphabetical Habitation weaves his experiences on the great loom of Life. Here he meets the women who come into his life, mother, sister, daughter, wife, and other, to whom he is either a friend or a fiend. Here grow the warts on his Character and here is the sting of the wasp. Here are his wars and here is his weariness. He becomes weather-beaten but by that time he is wise or wears a wet-blanket. He weeps over weights of sorrows or shows the White Feather. Here his words are idle or are words of wisdom. He is a worshiper or a wrangler and wrong-doer. From Here, he can go to work, to his wedding, or to the White House, or to all of them. W is the letter which stands for opportunity on each plane of life. It is for the Inhabitant of the Alphabetical Habitation to open the doors of his heart and mind and let W in and Win through Will. Here is where at last he will stand at the Gate of the Higher Habitation and hear the Great Masters say, "Well done, enter thou in!"

X - Is the gate or post on which four crosspieces or bars work on a pivot at the entrance to the inner passage to the grounds of the Habitation of the Inhabitant. This is so devised that a register is kept of those passing through. The 5th one of a series is a doorkeeper and the 8th one is marked for a life position on the Supreme Bench. The 9th one is marked for a defense in some capacity, the 10th one for a position of honor, the 11th one for a governmental position. Strange to say, all who pass through the gate to the Inhabitant's Habitation are filled with wisdom for the duty assigned by simply walking through the winding path. It meanders over many stretches of the way ere it ends at U before the door J of the Inhabitant's Habitation, and those who walk through pick up some of the Symbol-jewels they see along the winding Path. Those who pass the turnstile of X have a pleasant walk before they reach U. When there, before they ring the bell of T, they sit on a seat under the portico and examine the wondrous stones they have picked up in their walk. There is the Jasper, like that of New Jerusalem, the first stone to garnish its walls. (Revelations, 21st chapter) Another stone was a sapphire, a chalcedony, a tri-color blue, yellow and red stone, symbolizing spirit, soul, and body. There are many of these, and the qualities and characteristics they symbolize are needed by those who want them. He who cares not for jewels has jewels of character and needs no others.

"The emerald means spirituality of thought," said the Inhabitant of the Habitation, as he opened his door to visitors and welcomed them graciously. One asked what the sardonyx meant and the Inhabitant of the Habitation says, "It represents God's justice and is the symbol to remind us that we must each walk over our own self and show no indecision in the crucial moment of existence." A very earnest-looking visitor displayed a chrysolite, asking its meaning. It was explained that its golden brightness should serve to recall in our minds that judgement should balance equally with power. The mystery of life will be given to those who possess this sovereignty of mind. The beryl is another symbol of the value of justice and balance for each and all. It was also the symbol of mercy in its divine in every circumstance of life, and an appeal to wisdom and discretion. The chrysoprasus, colored somewhat like the amethyst, is emblematic of the Key of Power to a new condition and to a new domain of thought and action. While the jacinth is not as bright a color as the amethyst, it is beautiful enough to remind us that some obstacles are more imaginary than real. The amethyst itself is the symbol of forgiveness, as forgiveness is the most precious gift to receive. The Inhabitant of the Habitation told his visitors of the precious stones of the breastplate of which God told Moses and that faith and love were called breastplates to wear by those who do God's will.

After a pleasant visit and refreshments, the Inhabitant led his visitors out a side door to his garden. There they walked in pleasant converse about the jewels which were symbolic of Thought, Action, and Life. There were many resting-places in the garden, in arbors under the tree, beside the shady pools, and many miniature scenes of delight, where trees, pools, flowers and shrubbery were arranged to present a picture-like view. There were little bridges here and there, built of rock over purling brooks, and playing fountains enhanced the view. Some of the visitors were wondering where they would be led in the labyrinth of beauty in the garden of the Inhabitant of the Habitation.

Each of them chose a flower and plucked it, each one choosing that which he had never seen before. The Inhabitant told each of them its symbolic meaning. The he gently led them to the North Gate, saying, "By this North Gate, you leave my Habitation and Garden. Through the North Gate you learn the Great Lesson all earth people must learn, that of discrimination. Peace be unto you." He returned to his habitation to see some visitors picking up jewels in the winding path of S.

Y - In mathematics, Y is an unknown quantity. In electricity, it is the symbol of admittance. Here before the Habitation of the Inhabitant of the Alphabetical House, it pathway leading from the Great Gate down in front of the grounds to the southwest corner, a rather curved and graceful-looking path strewn thickly with seashells, passing to the turnstile X that is half hidden among a cluster of beautiful trees which always seemed to be in flower.

Nearly halfway up this path a side path branches off toward the northwest. This path is not as wide as the main path, and its paving is also small seashells. On the other side of it a border runs of alluring, sweet scented flowers. The Habitation of the Inhabitant is toward the East of the grounds, and the longer curved path reaches to the turnstile of S. There is a path of cactus so arranged that the taller cacti grow along the line of the upper end of the Y path. From there southwest to the the point where the path divides are arranged other forms of cactus with beautiful flowers, until near the point, they are of a low-growing variety , with many dazzling forms of beauty or oddity. Here visitors stop and gaze in admiration at the cactus garden, many going on to the North West end of the Y path. From there they pass to the a wooded part of the country about the place beguiled by the scenery, and from thence on to their own devices, finding it impossible to see over the wall of the grounds of the Habitation, with their view obstructed by the tall cacti of the Y path. They had stayed away from the Path of Decision and their whereabouts at this writing cannot be chronicled.

Z - The next-to-last letter of the Alphabetical Habitation is one of great charm. It stands as a Great Gate on the curved end of the Y path, guarded by "&," the last letter of the alphabet. The letter Z, like X, is used at the beginning of many a scientific term. It is noted in astronomy as the symbol of Zenith. The guardian of the great Z Gate is "&."

& - It is said that the correct name of this letter is "Ampersand." An ampersand has a curious vibrational range in numbers, which means a trending toward a new condition of thought in the cosmos of the Inhabitant, or of his visitors, and also in the Universal

156

cosmos, through opportunity of thought and the Power of the Word. Therefore, "&" is careful who he admits into the grounds of the Inhabitant. Yet, he knows some of them will stray into the wood ere they reach the turnstile. The hidden meaning of "&" is that there are other things under discussion or debate, other opportunities for servers, or like subject, or even those of unlike relevance.

The ampersand was invented by Roman scribes who combined the letters "e" and "t" of the Latin word "et." In colonial America, children finished reciting the alphabet with the phase "X, Y, Z and per se And," which was written, "X, Y, Z, and per se &." This is the origin of the word "ampersand" which in the time of Fred Oliver was still considered the 27th letter of the alphabet.

NUMEROLOGICAL ANALYSIS OF THE WORD "HEAVEN"

Spirit Aries	Soul Taurus	Mind Gemini	Body Cancer	Spirit Leo	Soul Virgo	Mind Libra	Body Scorpio	Spirit Sagitrs.	Soul Capricn.	Mind Aquarius	Body Pisces
1	2	3	4	5	6	7	8	9	10	11	12
-	-	-	-	-	-	-	H	E	A	V	E
N	-	-	-	-	-	-	-	-	-	-	-

Spirit Aries	Soul Taurus	Mind Gemini	Body Cancer	Spirit Leo	Soul Virgo	Mind Libra	Body Scorpio	Spirit Sagitrs.	Soul Capricn.	Mind Aquarius	Body Pisces
1	2	3	4	5	6	7	8	9	10	11	12
-	-	-	-	-	-	-	8	5	1	10	5
2	-	-	-	-	-	-	-	-	-	-	-

The vibrational range of the word "Heaven" means that by wishing for a thing or condition, it is possible to create it. The principal letters of the word vibrate to 31 or 4, and the number 4 always stands for man, or some condition or circumstance related to man. The number of letters in the word is 6, and as 6 is the number of Thought, we have an inkling of the nature of Heaven. That it concerns Life and Death is shown by the word commencing in the 8th Place, the Place of Life and Death. It is defended by Intelligence - E in the 9th Place, the Place of Defense. It has A in the 10th Place, or Righteousness in a new condition, while V in the 11th Place means Beauty and Thought in God's Highways of Life. Intelligence is also found in the Place of Material Things, the 12th Place, showing that Heaven really relates to Life itself, and is a matter-of-fact proposition. N is found in the 1st Place as a Bearer of Light.

Note - The text above appears in "Atlantis Speaks Again" but the chart does not. In this analysis, those readers familiar with an astrological chart will find it helpful to regard the numbered "Place" to be analogous to the Houses, and the letters to be analogous to the signs that may be assigned to the houses. This analogy is not perfect or exact, but gives a sense of the relationship. "Place" is the equivalent of "Column" in Lillian Bense's listing. The first step in the analysis is to ascertain the number of letters in the word or phrase. The second step is to add up the values of the individual letters in the base-12 system. The third step in the analysis is assigning the first letter of the word to its corresponding Place or column of the Throne Block, H = 8, so the word begins at the 8th Place or Column. Refer to the following chart regarding the meanings of numbers in each column for interpretation. Because the number 31 occupies the 7th place in the 3rd row of Enoch's Throne Block, it may also be regarded as a 7 or a 3 in some contexts.

MEANINGS OF NUMBERS IN ORDERED PLACES

The 1st Place

0 IN THE 1ST PLACE - Direction under Cosmic Law

1 IN THE 1ST PLACE - Direction, Attention, Obedience, the Unity of Life

2 IN THE 1ST PLACE - "Let there be Light," a Bearer of Light

3 IN THE 1ST PLACE - Order

4 IN THE 1ST PLACE - Loyalty, Obedience to Cosmic Law

5 IN THE 1ST PLACE - Spiritual Motive

6 IN THE 1ST PLACE - Directed thought and uses

7 IN THE 1ST PLACE - Spiritual Direction

8 IN THE 1ST PLACE - Direction which results in discernment

9 IN THE 1ST PLACE - Spiritual Defense

10 IN THE 1ST PLACE- Overcoming

11 IN THE 1ST PLACE - Universal Flow

12 IN THE 1ST PLACE - Right Direction. Spirit-substance from which all life emerges.

The 2ⁿᵈ Place

1 IN THE 2ᴺᴰ PLACE - Duality, the Soul, the Logos

2 IN THE 2ᴺᴰ PLACE - Archetype. The basis of Spirituality of Thought. Those Thoughts were created in the Universal Mind we must fulfill sometime. We will have a body until those Thoughts become real. If our thoughts are spoken as words, it gives them the power of action. The Word of Power. The power of words is beyond ordinary comprehension. "Man may use the power of the word at anytime with success if he uses it aright."

3 IN THE 2ᴺᴰ PLACE - Differentiation. All things, thoughts, and spiritual aspirations have the Life of God, the Spiritual Sun, and rays come forth as spiritual, mental, and material vibrations.

4 IN THE 2ᴺᴰ PLACE - The Voice of Man. Each of us is a Voice for good or ill.

5 IN THE 2ᴺᴰ PLACE - The Light of the Mind

6 IN THE 2ᴺᴰ PLACE - The soul of a word is the use to which it is put

7 IN THE 2ᴺᴰ PLACE - The Word of Power

8 IN THE 2ᴺᴰ PLACE - Need for a Life Builder

9 IN THE 2ᴺᴰ PLACE - Perseverance

10 IN THE 2ᴺᴰ PLACE - Will, Covenant

11 IN THE 2ᴺᴰ PLACE - All that will benefit Man is obtainable with the right effort.

12 IN THE 2ᴺᴰ PLACE - Possessions

The 3rd Place

1 IN THE 3RD PLACE - Activity, Interrelationships, business, religion, science, the Active Intelligence inherent in Nature.

2 IN THE 3RD PLACE - Form and substance, and the differentiations of form and substance.

3 IN THE 3RD PLACE - An open door which welcomes. "Who could bind the sweet influence of the Pleiades?"

4 IN THE 3RD PLACE - Generosity

5 IN THE 3RD PLACE - The scientific mind, inquiry. This mentality will greatly ameliorate the human condition in the New Age.

6 IN THE 3RD PLACE - Theory and Hypothesis, belief, the sum total of mankind's historical intellectual development. May descend into dogma and disputation.

7 IN THE 3RD PLACE - Intellect must receive its motivating power from Spirit

8 IN THE 3RD PLACE - Choose your friends wisely

9 IN THE 3RD PLACE - Service activities

10 IN THE 3RD PLACE - Recognition in science, religion, business

11 IN THE 3RD PLACE - Public interests and institutions

12 IN THE 3RD PLACE - Activity on the physical plane

The 4th Place

1 IN THE 4TH PLACE - Man, both as an individual and as mankind, his interests, his character, Direction for man

2 IN THE 4TH PLACE - The Light of Character. Character is the storehouse of experience.

3 IN THE 4TH PLACE - Fellowship

4 IN THE 4TH PLACE - Happy the heart where graces reign. Hearth and Home.

5 IN THE 4TH PLACE - Mercurial character

6 IN THE 4TH PLACE - Necessities, uses for the self, home, and environment

7 IN THE 4TH PLACE - Enjoy only that which is good. Feel perfection while enjoying.

8 IN THE 4TH PLACE - Discernment relating to the human condition, and human character, the great lesson of life on earth

9 IN THE 4TH PLACE - The defense of Man, and the weak and innocent. Individual effort to right a wrong.

10 IN THE 4TH PLACE - A new condition for Man

11 IN THE 4TH PLACE - Brotherly love, and the establishment of benevolent institutions in human society

12 IN THE 4TH PLACE - Man's material conditions. Material conditions bind the Ego to matter, temporarily rendering it finite.

The 5th Place

1 IN THE 5TH PLACE - Motives, poise, Spirit motivates all when the soul allows.

2 IN THE 5TH PLACE - Spiritual sources of thought, Motives illumined by the Light of the Mind.

3 IN THE 5TH PLACE - Intelligence. One of the laws of God is that every being, man or animal, is responsible for errors in the degree to which the intelligence reaches.

4 IN THE 5TH PLACE - One's faculties

5 IN THE 5TH PLACE - Mind, mental poise, reason, genius, refinement

6 IN THE 5TH PLACE - The motives behind thought

7 IN THE 5TH PLACE - Ethics. We must learn to transmute physical, material and mental values into spiritual values. Religion is the highest ethical instinct of which man is capable that helps the individual to attain a state of mind that is one with his development.

8 IN THE 5TH PLACE - Discrimination must be used. Seek to differentiate between that which is Mental and that which is Spiritual

9 IN THE 5TH PLACE - Using one's faculties for defense, or to be constructive

10 IN THE 5TH PLACE - A new condition brought about by ethical actions.

11 IN THE 5TH PLACE - Education

12 IN THE 5TH PLACE - Motives on the material plane

The 6th Place

1 IN THE 6TH PLACE - Uses, health, hygiene, food, clothing, labor, all things in regard to use. Right motive or direction for the use of all things. Prosperity

2 IN THE 6TH PLACE - The use of a thing is the Soul of it. Attuned to uses under Cosmic Law.

3 IN THE 6TH PLACE - Imagination

4 IN THE 6TH PLACE - Uses in man's life. Uses show character.

5 IN THE 6TH PLACE - Conscious motives for use

6 IN THE 6TH PLACE - Thought originates in 6, and when directed aright results in works.

7 IN THE 6TH PLACE - Balanced uses. Labor will never reach its completion until Justice and Equity rule.

8 IN THE 6TH PLACE - Discrimination in uses, choose for use or abuse

9 IN THE 6TH PLACE - Use for defense

10 IN THE 6TH PLACE - Uses which lead to a new condition

11 IN THE 6TH PLACE - Uses for the good of all

12 IN THE 6TH PLACE - Material and physical uses. Every thought is a creation of a definite shape or thought-form. All organized thoughts are actions and tend to build up a material counterpart of themselves.

The 7th Place

0 IN THE 7th PLACE - Realization of God's Covenant

1 IN THE 7TH PLACE - Harmony, justice, law, balance, wedding

2 IN THE 7TH PLACE - "In that Light we shall see Light." Naught passes current but that which has a spiritual value. Spiritual sources should be the law of constructive efforts.

3 IN THE 7TH PLACE - Active life under Law, responsibility

4 IN THE 7TH PLACE - A balanced life for the individual

5 IN THE 7TH PLACE - It is from the spirit that there is true motivation

6 IN THE 7TH PLACE - Equanimity of thought

7 IN THE 7TH PLACE - Inner senses leading to spiritual telepathy. Joy moves us forward.

8 IN THE 7TH PLACE - Discernment in spiritual things, the gold of character

9 IN THE 7TH PLACE - Spiritual defense, selfless love

10 IN THE 7TH PLACE - A new condition under Spiritual Law

11 IN THE 7TH PLACE - Regarding institutions of law and justice

12 IN THE 7TH PLACE - Energize material conditions with Spirituality of Thought, also religious ceremony

The 8th Place - the Place of Life and Death

1 IN THE 8TH PLACE - Life & Death, age, the right balancing of all uses which leads to longevity, happiness, and prosperity

2 IN THE 8TH PLACE - Duality of Thought under Unity, Real estate

3 IN THE 8TH PLACE - Cooperation. Also, life always continues in some form.

4 IN THE 8TH PLACE - Loyal to Life on earth

5 IN THE 8TH PLACE - The Questioner of Life

6 IN THE 8TH PLACE - Common Sense

7 IN THE 8TH PLACE - Correct judgement

8 IN THE 8TH PLACE - Discernment

9 IN THE 8TH PLACE - Discrimination

10 IN THE 8TH PLACE - The right choice leads to a new condition

11 IN THE 8TH PLACE - Reciprocity, public honors

12 IN THE 8TH PLACE - A comfortable state of existence

The 9th Place - the Place of Defense

1 IN THE 9TH PLACE - Defense of religion and beliefs

2 IN THE 9TH PLACE - Constructive effort, such as man's struggle to develop true religion. Destructive in its negative aspect.

3 IN THE 9TH PLACE - Ongoing Spirit, or in a material context, travel, transportation

4 IN THE 9TH PLACE - The defense of Man, to defend the weak and innocent

5 IN THE 9TH PLACE - Defended by Intelligence

6 IN THE 9TH PLACE - Defended by Thought

7 IN THE 9TH PLACE - Wisdom, Love, Joy

8 IN THE 9TH PLACE - Defended by discernment

9 IN THE 9TH PLACE - Spiritual defense, to serve and protect, Spiritual Energy

10 IN THE 9TH PLACE - Defense of Righteousness

11 IN THE 9TH PLACE - Civil rights, common law

12 IN THE 9TH PLACE - Defense of material conditions, Spiritual energy vitalizing material conditions

The 10th Place

1 IN THE 10TH PLACE - Righteousness in a New Condition

2 IN THE 10TH PLACE - The Word of Power which leads to a new condition

3 IN THE 10TH PLACE - Evolution, activities which lead to a new condition, overcoming obstacles, leaving the past behind

4 IN THE 10TH PLACE - Individualization, individuation, awakening

5 IN THE 10TH PLACE - Motives and ethics leading to a new condition

6 IN THE 10TH PLACE - Thought leading to a new condition.

7 IN THE 10TH PLACE - A balanced new condition

8 IN THE 10TH PLACE - Honor

9 IN THE 10TH PLACE - Defense of a new condition

10 IN THE 10TH PLACE - Entry into a new condition, the Door, Initiation. "Seek the Ultimate"

11 IN THE 10TH PLACE - A universal word of Power over the physical plane. Spiritual service which leads humanity into a new condition. Human life will be transformed by Spirituality of Thought in the New Age.

12 IN THE 10TH PLACE - A new material condition

The 11th Place - the Highway of Heaven

1 IN THE 11TH PLACE - Direction in the Highway of Heaven, the Path

2 IN THE 11TH PLACE - The Word of Power in the Highway of Heaven, opportunity

3 IN THE 11TH PLACE - Activity which tends toward the evolution of man

4 IN THE 11TH PLACE - Star of Bethlehem, always something very good

5 IN THE 11TH PLACE - Motives for service, ethics

6 IN THE 11TH PLACE - Civilization must be rescued by Spirituality of Thought

7 IN THE 11TH PLACE - Spiritual service under divine Law

8 IN THE 11TH PLACE - Discernment in the Highway of Heaven

9 IN THE 11TH PLACE - Spiritual defense on the Path, rights and responsibilities under Law

10 IN THE 11TH PLACE - Beauty and Thought in God's Highway of Life

11 IN THE 11TH PLACE - The New Age will exemplify spiritual values and the unfolding of the seven senses. Aquarian civilization. The Mentalism and Materialism of the Piscean Age must be transmuted into the Spirituality of Thought of the Aquarian Age.

12 IN THE 11TH PLACE - Spiritual Service for the good of all. Aquarian ritual. Water poured forth for the needy, as in the glyph for the sign Aquarius.

The 12th Place - the Place of Material Things

1 IN THE 12TH PLACE - Direction over the physical plane. Life embraces all things material.

2 IN THE 12TH PLACE - "The Raincloud of Knowable Things," also, one's material possessions

3 IN THE 12TH PLACE - Physical plane activity

4 IN THE 12TH PLACE - Man's interests on the physical plane

5 IN THE 12TH PLACE - Intelligence in the Place of Material Things. The things of the material plane are externalizations of the things of the mental plane, which have in turn counterparts on the Spiritual plane.

6 IN THE 12TH PLACE - the use of material things, for use or abuse

7 IN THE 12TH PLACE - Material conditions energized by Spirit and under divine Law. Also, Spiritual ceremony or ritual

8 IN THE 12TH PLACE - Discrimination and discernment on the material plane, choice

9 IN THE 12TH PLACE - Sacrifice in the defense of others

10 IN THE 12TH PLACE - Entry into a new condition on the physical plane.

11 IN THE 12TH PLACE - Spiritual service on the physical plane.

12 IN THE 12TH PLACE - Material and physical things. The externalization of Life. Willing Sacrifices. In the realm of the highest or spiritual vibration is "Finding the Kingdom of Heaven," which when found gives all lesser things.

Notes and References

Introduction

The source of much of the biographical sketch is a reel-to-reel tape recorded by Cindy Luddington over the space of several days in the summer of 1966, in which Mother Mary speaks of herself in the third person. She clearly intended for this tape to be used as source material for a future biography. Many details were confirmed by comparison with other sources, such as letters.

In addition, many details of her life were recounted to me in 1968 and 1969 by Lady Mae during conversations at The Inn, including comments about Baird T. Spalding, who she knew in Los Angeles in the 1920's. She was of the opinion that Spalding's experiences were genuine, but she also said that the books would have been better if he had ever managed to fulfill his plan to return to India for a second encounter with the adepts described in the books.

Valuable information was also provided by Helen Ruth, Linden Carlton, and Robert Williamson.

Books to which reference is made in this chapter include -

Bryan, Gerald Barbee, *Psychic Dictatorship in America*, Truth Research Publications, Los Angeles, 1940. The 14th Chapter documents the Ballard's plagiarism.

Paramahansa Yogananda, *Autobiography of a Yogi*, Jaico Publishing Co., Bombay, 1963, one of many editions reprinted by the Self-Realization Fellowship.

Spalding, Baird T., *Life and Teachings of the Masters of the Far East, Vol. 1-5,* DeVorss & Co. 1935. These books have been reprinted many times and are still in print. A 6th volume has more recently been released.

Chapter 1, Mary Mae Maier's Years in Los Angeles

Mother Mary discussed her professional career in detail with Linden Carlton, who himself had been a dress designer at one point in his life. He and Robert Williamson preserved many little items of that time of her life, such as her business card in the name of Mae Hamilton, and pictures of her Rose Bowl entries. In researching this book it was discovered that there were at least three people named "Peggy Hamilton" active in Hollywood in the 1920's, one the designer of the famous "Biltmore Gown," and another was a society maven who wrote for Los Angeles newspapers. I believe that "Hamilton" was Mary Mae Hoffman's name from her first marriage, used by her around the time of World War One, and she dropped her nickname "Peggy" when the others came on the scene in the early twenties, but continued to use "Hamilton" until about 1928.

The written piece by Mother Mary is from the Eastern Research Society, Inc., Quarterly Publication, Volume One, Number One, issued May 30, 1958. The first issue of this quarterly was probably intended for distribution from a booth at the Giant Rock UFO convention in the summer of 1958. It contains a gracious acknowledgement of help in its production to George Van Tassel and his family, and Dan Fry. It also contains articles by Wayne Aho and others on the subject of UFO's. Later issues explore other themes.

As stated in the text, Edmund Rucker's piece on Ralph Elmer was first published on Sept. 2nd and 3rd, 1945 in the San Diego Union. It was taken here from the Creative Researcher, Official Bulletin of the Creative Hobby Clubs, Vol. 1, No. 1, April, 1945, Los Angeles. F. N. Parkinson was editor, and Gladyce Berman, associate editor.

Chapter 2, The Order of Directive Biblical Philosophy

The main sources for this chapter are *Atlantis Speaks Again* and the notebooks and manuscripts from which Mother Mary drew the material for that book. In addition, unpublished writings of Lillian Bense, Maud Falconer, and Mother Mary are used as sources, and are identified in the text. The original notebooks of these three people were compared with the published version of *Atlantis Speaks Again,* and some discrepancies were found. Generally, the version from the notebooks was used for this book. Most of these materials have been reprinted in Appendix 1. Information also was taken from letters to Mary Mae Maier from Maud Falconer and Nola Van Valer. Anyone interested in researching base-12 math should visit the web site of the Dozenal Society of America.

I interviewed Dr. Zitko for this book on September 2, 2003. At he age of 91, he was in poor health, but in full control of his mental faculties and was able to easily give me names and dates of events from the 1930's and 40's. I asked him to autograph my copy of *An Earth Dweller's Return,* and he signed it with the inscription "God is love, and love is all. The Lemurian Scribe, Howard John Zitko." After showing Dr. Zitko a rough draft of my text regarding the publishing of the book, he sent me some corrections on Sept. 22 which I have incorporated into the final text. He died on Nov. 11th, two months after our meeting.

Much of the information about Nola comes from many conversations which I had with Daniel Boone in the mid-1990's when he returned to Siskiyou County for about ten years. I met Nola only once. Daniel was among the people who Nola took up on the mountain in 1962, on the weekend before the July 4th meeting described in Chapter 7, in an attempt to find the location of the Temple she and her family had entered in 1930. He and several other people kept going when the rest of the party turned back due to Nola's poor health, and they found the tree near the Temple in which Jerry Van Valer had carved his initials on June 17, 1930.

Anrias, David, nom-de-plume of Brian Ross, *Through the Eyes of the Masters,* Routledge & Kegan Paul, London, Third Edition 1947. Ross and Cyril Scott were close friends.

Bailey, Alice A., *Treatise on the Seven Rays, Vol. 1 - 5,* Lucis Publishing, New York, 1936 - 1949

Blavatsky, Helena P., *Isis Unveiled,* 1877 and *The Secret Doctrine,* 1888, numerous editions published by the Theosophical Society and the United Lodge of Theosophists.

Davidson, David and Aldersmith, H., *The Great Pyramid - Its Divine Message,* reprinted by Kessinger Publishing, Kila, Montana, 2000

Glinsky, Albert, *Theremin, Ether Music and Espionage,* University of Illinois Press, Urbana, 2000. A good biography of Theremin but short on scientific information - apparently much of the science is still classified by the CIA and the successors to the KGB.

Maier, Mary Mae, *Atlantis Speaks Again,* M. M. Maier Publishers C.H.T. Ltd., Hollywood, 1960

Phylos, *A Dweller on Two Planets,* Baumgardt Publishing Co., Los Angeles, 1905, amanuensis Fred Oliver. This was the edition sold by Mary Manley Oliver to support herself in her later years. The money to publish it was given to her by strangers who wished to remain anonymous.

Phylos, *An Earth Dwellers Return,* Lemurian Press, Milwaukee, 1940, from writings by Fred Oliver (Isschar), compiled by Lillian Bense (Beth Nimrai), edited by Howard Zitko (The Lemurian Scribe), in addition, The Order of Directive Biblical Philosophy itself helped to prepare the text for publication, and the Lemurian Fellowship funded its publication.

Van Valer, Nola, *My Meeting with the Masters on Mt. Shasta,* The Radiant School, Mt. Shasta, 1982 and *The Tramp at my Door,* The Radiant School, Mt. Shasta, 1964

Chapter 3, *Atlantis Speaks Again*

All the material in this chapter appeared in *Atlantis Speaks Again,* though not in the same order. Mother Mary did not want this book republished, but the information reprinted here is mostly from The Order of Directive Biblical Philosophy, and was intended for a wider audience than the limited edition of *Atlantis Speaks Again,* which was printed in a run of only 333 copies.

Chapter 4, Jagadbandhu

The biographical information in this chapter is mostly from the following three books, with some details from Mother Mary herself.

Ghosh, Navadip Chandra, *The Life and Teachings of Sri Sri Prabhu Jagadbandhu,* reprinted in 1992 by Henry Fuller, Perris, California

Sarkar, Prafulla Kumar, *A Message of Hope* and *The Life of Prabhu Jagadbandhu* both written about 1920, reprinted in 2002 by Jeff Whittier, Palo Alto, California

Also referred to in this chapter are -

Bailey, Alice A., *Reappearance of the Christ,* Lucis Publishing Co., New York, 1948

Gupta, Mahendra Nath, *The Gospel of Sri Ramakrishna,* published by Sri Ramakrishna Nath, Madras, 1924. In addition to being one of the close disciples of Sri Ramakrishna, Mahendra Nath Gupta, known as Master Mahashi, or "M," was Yogananda's tutor in his youth, and one of the chapters of *Autobiography of a Yogi* tells of his experiences with "M."

Chapter 5, Mother Mary's First Trip to India, 1950-51

Most of the material in this chapter is taken from various tape-recordings of Mother Mary speaking, including the previously mentioned autobiographical tape recorded by Cindy Luddington. In addition, she discussed these experiences with me in 1968 and 1969, many times in fact, in order to make sure I would remember them.

172

Chapter 6, The Great White Chief

This material is also from brief comments found on several reel-to-reel tape recordings made in the late 1960's. The daughter of Tony Nez-bah gave me much information on his experiences with the LDS. Linden Carlton, Robert Williamson and Saul Barodofsky accompanied Mother Mary on her last trip to visit Native Americans in 1967, and provided information about her relationship with Native Americans found throughout the book. Henry Fuller accompanied her on several of the relief missions to the Hopi reservation in the 1940's and also provided valuable information on her work with Native Americans and Eachita Eachina. Note the first page of the 8th chapter, in which Mother Mary writes from India that her true friends are the Native Americans.   She probably felt most at home among them.

Anonymous, edited by Mother Mary, *The Great White Chief, the Valley of the Blue Moon,* M. M. Maier Publications, Los Angeles 1960

Thomas, Dorothy, *The Coming of the Great White Chief,* New Age Publishing Co., Los Angeles, 1955

Chapter 7, The Meeting at Sand Flat, July 1962

The source of the information in this chapter is primarily tape recordings made on July 4th, 1962, and the partial transcripts of these tapes which were published by Cindy Luddington and are reprinted here. More information came from Maxine McMullen, Henry Fuller, Stuart Allistone and Daniel Boone, who all attended the meeting. Helen Ruth gave me a box of material from Elaine Bragg, much of it about July 1962, some of it recordings of Nola Van Valer speaking at Sand Flat on July 5th and 6th, which confirmed details found in Cindy Luddington's writings and compilations.

Bayley, Harold, *The Lost Language of Symbolism: An Inquiry into the Origin of Certain Letters, Words, Names, Fairy-Tales, Folklore and Mythologies* Vol. 1 reprinted 1988 and Vol. 2 reprinted 1990 by Citadel Press. The quote found in Chapter 9 is on pages 78 and 79 in Vol. 2.

Fry, Daniel W., *The White Sands Incident,* Horus House Press, 1992. The original edition of this book is out-of-print, and a second edition with a channeling by Rolf Telano grafted on is the only edition now available.

Luddington, Cindy, *The Inspiration Center Newsletter,* Quartz Hill, California, Nov. 1966. Cindy put the following statement on the masthead of some of her issues - "A Non-Prophet Non-Organization Published and Supported Solely by the Editor, a Staff of One with No Organizational Backing and No Tax Deductions."

Chapter 8, Mother Mary's Second Trip to India, 1966

There are three different reel-to-reel tape recordings of Mother Mary recounting her experiences with the naked sadhu - which she always pronounced with the Bengali pronunciation, chaddhu. The three are virtually identical, except that in one account she gives more detail about his statements to her, such as the advice, "You must be more of a disciplinarian." Andy Anderson, who was present at most of the events described in this chapter, also confirmed many details of the trip, and gave me his type-written account of the experiences.

News of the trip from Mother Mary's letters was published by Cindy Luddington in the March and May, 1966 issues of *The Inspiration Center Newsletter,* including a text of the first address.

Chapter 9, The Last Years at The Inn

The chapter is composed from the recollections of those who were there, particularly Linden, Robert, Saul, and myself. Their still exists a partial recording of the Aug 12, 1968 talk, with further details from the talk, after the recording had stopped, filled in by myself.

Mother Mary was in contact with Cyril Scott, as shown by a letter addressed to him at his home on the letterhead of The Inn, of which she retained a copy, inviting him to accompany her to India.

The quote from *A Dweller on Two Planets* is from the Seventh Shasta Scene, and this section was also included on page 455 of *An Earth Dweller's Return.*

Govinda, Anagarika, *The Way of the White Clouds,* Hutchinson & Co., London, 1966. It might be of interest to the reader to note that Lama Govinda considered himself to be the reincarnation of the German Romantic poet Novalis, Georg Philipp Friedrich Freiherr von Hardenberg.

Khan, Hazrat Inayat, *The Sufi Message Vol. 1 - 12,* Published for The International Headquarters of the Sufi Movement, Geneva, by Barrie and Jenkins, London, 1960

Lewis, Samuel, *Sufi Vision and Initiation,* Sufi Islamia/Prophecy Productions, San Francisco & Novato, 1986

Scott, Cyril, *Music, Its Secret Influence Throughout the Ages,* Second Edition, Samuel Weiser, New York, 1958. The comments on Indian music are laughable, but the information on Western composers is thought-provoking. In his autobiography, Scott says the basic information for the book was given to Nelsa Chaplin telepathically by the adept Koot Humi. The book is dedicated to her. A noted composer himself, Scott also wrote *An Outline of Modern Occultism, The Initiate, The Initiate in the New World, The Initiate in the Dark Cycle, The Greater Awareness, Bone of Contention,* and a number of books and pamphlets on herbal medicine. *An Outline of Modern Occultism* gives a good introduction to modern Western esoteric thought.

Curiously, the man who has often been suggested to be the model for "The Initiate," also called "J. M. H.," is Pierre A. Bernard, the brother-in-law of Inayat Khan. Bernard was the founder of "The Tantrik Order in America" in 1905, the "New York Tantrik

Press" around the same time, and "The Clarkstown Country Club" in 1918. It has been said that events at the Clarkstown Country Club greatly resemble the stories in the three "Initiate" books. He was also the uncle of Theos Bernard, a noted author on Hatha Yoga who was murdered by Hindu nationalists in India in 1947 while trying to reach the Ladakhi lamasery which held the scroll of Jesus ("Issa") that was translated into modern languages by N. Notovitch, Virchand Gandhi, and Swami Abhedananda. Pierre Bernard was the guardian of his half-sister, Ora Ray Baker, who married Inayat Khan. Ora Ray Baker was related to Mary Baker Eddy. Bernard is mentioned by Scott in his autobiography, *"Bone of Contention."* Since Bernard was known to Cyril Scott, this raises the possibility that Scott heard Inayat Khan perform, and he may have picked up the harmonic system for which he is given credit by listening to such rags as Malkauns, Bageshri, or Kaushi Kanada, in which this harmonic system based on the fourth and flatted seventh is found, and which were part of Inayat Khan's repertoire.

Appendix 1 - Writings of The Order of Directive Biblical Philosophy

Many of these pieces are the original text of articles which Mother Mary excerpted for *Atlantis Speaks Again.* They are presented here for their historical value. It is sometimes of interest to compare the original to the version which was published by Mother Mary, and these writings throw much light on the teachings presented in *Atlantis Speaks Again.* The articles by Lillian Bense reveal the mind of the compiler of *An Earth Dweller's Return* and serve to put that work in context. Some details of real significance are scattered throughout these materials, such as the date which Lillian Bense met Phylos and Mary Manley Oliver, 1913, which was described in *Atlantis Speaks Again,* and also the date when the transfer of the archive of Fred Oliver's unpublished manuscripts was made to Mrs. Bense, 1921.

Appendix 2 - Numerology of The Order of Directive Biblical Philosophy

The information on the meanings of numbers presented in this appendix should be compared closely with the parallel section at the end of Chapter 2. The section "Meanings of Numbers in the Ordered Places" was reverse-engineered by compiling the many references to these meanings scattered throughout the writings of The Order. They follow a logical, and astrological, order. I believe that such a list existed and was used by Lillian Bense, Maud Falconer, and Mother Mary, but the original has been lost.